THE
YOM KIPPUR
WAR
THE ARAB-ISRAELI WAR OF 1973

OSPREY PUBLISHING

THE
YOM KIPPUR
WAR
THE ARAB-ISRAELI WAR OF 1973

SIMON DUNSTAN

First published in Great Britain in 2007 by Osprey Publishing,
Midland House, West Way, Botley, Oxford OX2 0PH, United Kingdom.
443 Park Avenue South, New York, NY 10016, USA.
Email: info@ospreypublishing.com

Previously published as Campaign 118: *The Yom Kippur War 1973 (1) The Golan Heights* and Campaign 126: *The Yom Kippur War 1973 (2) The Sinai*, both by Simon Dunstan.

A CIP catalogue record for this book is available from the British Library.

ISBN: 978 1 84603 288 2

Page layout by Ken Vail Graphic Design, Cambridge, UK
Index by Alison Worthington
Typeset in ITC Stone Serif, Sabon, Bembo, Gill Sans and Trajan
Maps by The Map Studio
3D Bird's-eye views by The Black Spot
Originated by United Graphics Pte Ltd, Singapore
Printed and bound in China through World Print Ltd

07 08 09 10 11   10 9 8 7 6 5 4 3 2 1

For a catalogue of all books published by Osprey please contact:

NORTH AMERICA
Osprey Direct c/o Random House Distribution Center
400 Hahn Road, Westminster, MD 21157, USA
E-mail: info@ospreydirect.com

ALL OTHER REGIONS
Osprey Direct UK, P.O. Box 140, Wellingborough, Northants, NN8 2FA, UK
E-mail: info@ospreydirect.co.uk

www.ospreypublishing.com

Author's note
All photographs are courtesy of the Israel Defense Forces Archives unless otherwise stated. Pictures credited to EGIO are supplied courtesy of the Egyptian Government Information Office.

Acknowledgements
The author would like to thank the following for their kind assistance: Mahmoud Bahri, US Department of Defense; Egyptian Press Office; Lieutenant Colonel David Eshel; Commodore Mohamed Gaballa, Egyptian Defence Attaché; Marsh Gelbart; Zaki Ghazi; Sgalit Har-Arie; Jerusalem Post; Samuel M. Katz; Oo'na Matter; Office of the IDF spokesperson; Abraham Rabinovitch; Colonel Yizhar Sahar, Israeli Defence Attaché; Major General Heikki Tilander; The United Nations; Steven J. Zaloga.

Cover photo: 'And the dawn comes up like thunder' – Israeli reinforcements crawl up the escarpment of the Golan Heights at daybreak on the second day of the war. Dawn on 7 October 1973 was literally the darkest hour for Israel, forcing the Minister of Defense General Moshe Dayan to predict 'the fall of the Third Temple' or the destruction of the country due to enemy invasion. With the Israeli population celebrating Yom Kippur when the Eygptians and Syrians struck, the roads of Israel were free of traffic. This aided the rapid mobilization of reservists who were able to reach their units more quickly, but even so the whole process was chaotic and fraught with delays due in part to mislaid equipment and stores. Nevertheless, critical reinforcements reached the Golan Heights in dribs and drabs during the morning to meet the Syrian onslaught. With their leading units within sight of the Sea of Galilee following their overwhelming triumph on the southern Golan, the Syrians inexplicably halted their offensive and the momentum was lost never to be regained. It remains a mystery why the Syrian High Command failed to reinforce success in the south and with it the chance of victory on the Golan Heights. (© David Rubinger/Corbis)
Back cover photo: IDF.
Title page: © Nik Wheeler/Sygma/Corbis.

CONTENTS

INTRODUCTION

At 1830hrs on 10 June 1967 a United Nations ceasefire brought fighting to an end in the Six Day War. In one of the most remarkable campaigns in the history of modern warfare, the state of Israel defeated its Arab enemies and won the priceless prize of defence in depth. By the end of the war the Israeli army had occupied the whole of the Sinai and the Gaza Strip, and gained control of the West Bank of the River Jordan, driving hostile forces away from the coastal strip, Israel's narrow waistline and the areas surrounding the city of Jerusalem. In the north, the Israelis had occupied the strategically important Golan plateau as far as Kuneitra. Before June 1967 Syria had posed a constant threat to northern Galilee. Now Israeli armour and artillery threatened the Syrian capital of Damascus.

The speed and scale of the Israeli victory sent shock waves through the Arab world. Israel's position now seemed secure. She had drawn the teeth of her bitterest enemies, now held defensible frontiers and her demonstration of military prowess had earned respect around the world.

Following the Six Day War, Israel received international criticism for not using her territorial gains to bargain for a lasting peace. Nevertheless, in 1967 Israel had undoubtedly been threatened with outright destruction. In the interests of national security, her military chiefs demanded defensible frontiers and retention of the occupied territories. Domestic opinion in Israel would not have allowed the spoils of this spectacular victory to be cast aside so swiftly.

Moreover, the Israelis drew no comfort from the Khartoum conference of Arab leaders in August 1967, at which the delegates had declared a policy of 'no recognition, no negotiations, no peace'. The Israelis therefore accepted resolutions of the United Nations (UN) Security Council only with strong reservations about Arab sincerity. The key resolution was No. 242 of November 1967, which required Israeli withdrawal from all territories occupied by armed force, Arab recognition of Israel and 'respect for and acknowledgement of the sovereignty, territorial integrity and political independence of every state in the area and their right to live in peace with secure boundaries free from threats or acts of force'.

The translation of these words into action, however, proved an insurmountable task. Israel would only contemplate withdrawal from parts or all of Sinai and the Golan Heights in exchange for full peace with the Arab world. Egypt, by contrast, wanted all the territories, including the Gaza Strip and the West Bank, restored to Arab sovereignty but without guaranteeing Israel unqualified peace in exchange.

President Nasser concluded that only a military initiative could apply sufficient pressure on Israel – and by extension on the superpowers – to force Israeli withdrawal from the Sinai. In the aftermath of the Six Day War, he chose to stay on the defensive while he re-equipped and trained his armed forces before adopting a more aggressive policy.

The Six Day War was barely over when shiploads of Soviet war matériel began to arrive in Egyptian ports to make good the losses suffered in the fighting. To counter Israeli air power the Soviet Union supplied its Egyptian client with an air defence system based on its SA-2, SA-3 and SA-6 surface-to-air guided missiles and associated advanced radars. In addition to thousands of Soviet instructors, Egypt and Syria were to receive some 4,500 tanks, 1,000 aircraft and thousands of artillery pieces, together with light, hand-held missiles for close air defence and infantry anti-tank defence.

The Bar-Lev Line

Nasser now embarked on a form of limited warfare, later dubbed the 'War of Attrition', based on an intermittent, staggered artillery bombardment of Israel Defense Forces (IDF) front-line positions in Sinai and sporadic commando raids across the Suez Canal. By the autumn of 1968 the Egyptians had deployed two armies along the Canal, some 100,000 men supported by hundreds of tanks and guns, all of them well dug-in. For the moment the initiative of where and when to attack lay with the Egyptians.

From a strictly military point of view, it would have suited the Israelis to use a mobile screen to watch the Canal and hold their armour well back in reserve, ready to counterattack any Egyptian incursion. Nevertheless, the political imperative to prevent the Egyptians from establishing a presence in Sinai, however minor, lent an irresistible weight to arguments in favour of defending the water line.

The result was the transformation of the rudimentary canal-side fortifications into the so-called 'Bar-Lev Line', named after the IDF Chief of Staff, General Chaim Bar-Lev. These stretched along the Suez Canal from the Gulf of Suez to the Mediterranean, a distance of some 160km (100 miles).

At the heart of the Bar-Lev Line were some 30 strongpoints on the Canal (Maozim), each screened by a sandbank several metres high and designed to be held by a platoon-strength garrison equipped with small arms, heavy

Israel and the occupied territories, October 1973

The Bar-Lev Line

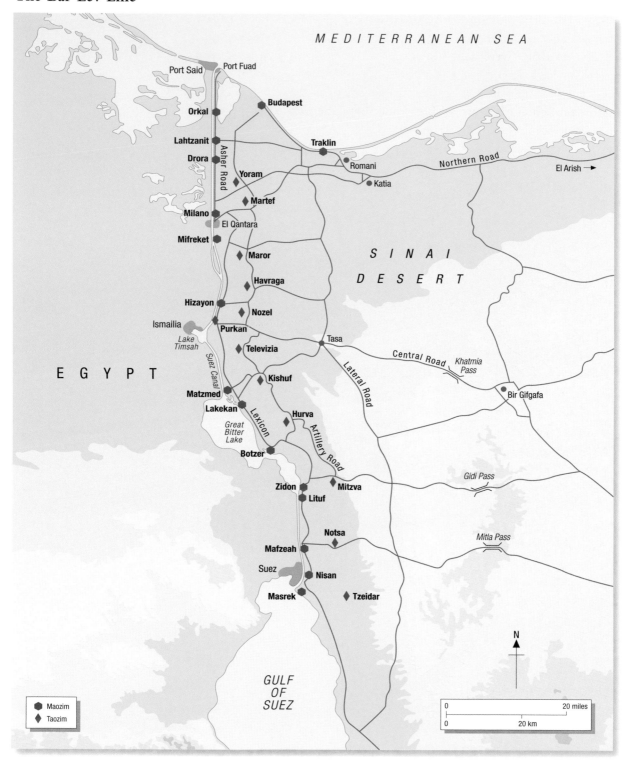

machine-guns and mortars. In quiet times the complement of a strongpoint was customarily half a platoon. Trenches, a sand embankment, barbed wire entanglements and minefields girdled the Maozim.

The Maozim were sited to cover roads and communications junctions stretching back into the Sinai and to control a stretch of the Canal. If the Egyptians launched an attack, the principal role of the Maozim garrisons was to sustain the initial exchange of fire while supplying data on the weight of the enemy incursion and blocking the access roads. On the outbreak of the Yom Kippur War on 6 October 1973, 16 of the Maozim were fully manned, two partially manned and the remainder either closed up or held by small daylight observation teams.

Eventually, the Egyptians raised the sand embankments on their side of the Suez Canal to some 39m (130ft), enabling them to overlook the Israeli rampart, fortifications, tank ramps and second line of defence on the Artillery Road. The Israelis countered with earthworks and planned to build 76m (250ft) high observation towers to look deep into the Egyptian rear areas. However, the outbreak of the Yom Kippur War thwarted this ambition.

When the Bar-Lev Line was built, some of the strongpoints had housed underground oil storage tanks. In the event of an Egyptian crossing, the oil was to be pumped into the Canal and set ablaze in a sea of flame. However, there were problems with the strong current in the canal and the oil installations fell into disrepair, to be replaced by dummies, a fact that was confirmed by Egyptian patrols during the War of Attrition.

Along the first line of sandy hills some 8km (5 miles) behind the Canal, strongholds or Taozim were built, each to hold an infantry company. Behind the ridge, small reserves of tanks were held ready to move forward to firing positions some 500–1,000m (547–1,093yds) behind the Canal to support the Maozim and cover the gaps between them. To the east of the Suez Canal, two roads ran on a north–south axis, the first, known as the 'Artillery Road', some 10km (6 miles) and the second 30km (20 miles) to the rear. The Artillery Road was lined with emplacements for self-propelled artillery and the first echelon of tanks and halftracks in the Sinai were deployed here ready to move up to the defences along the Canal. Armoured reserves were deployed along the second line, the 'Lateral Road', and east–west roads and tracks linked the two principal north–south arteries. Communications to the Bar-Lev Line were secured by radio networks and underground cables, the integrity of which was to prove vital in October 1973.

Initially conceived as an early-warning mechanism, the Bar-Lev Line was completed in 1969, although constant improvements and modifications were subsequently made.

The War of Attrition

The Egyptian response to the construction of the Bar-Lev Line was a sustained campaign of bombardment of the new Israeli positions combined with commando raids across the Canal and a resurgence of guerrilla raids and terrorism within Israel. The bombardment began on the morning of 8 March 1969 when Egyptian artillery opened up along the length of the Canal. Overhead, Egyptian and Israeli jet fighters clashed. On the following day the War of Attrition claimed its first notable casualty when Israeli mortars killed the Egyptian Chief of Staff, General Riad, at a bunker near Ismailia.

The Israelis responded with deep-penetration commando raids into Egypt and an air offensive in which the Israeli Air Force (IAF) struck at the entire Egyptian air defence system from the Bar-Lev Line to deep within Egypt itself. The principal aim of these raids was to pressure Egypt into accepting a cease-fire and simultaneously to force a regime change within Egypt itself.

Thoroughly alarmed, Nasser flew secretly to Moscow in January 1970. He used a threat of resignation to force the Russians to supply the new SA-3 as well as improved SA-2 surface-to-air missiles (SAMs), Soviet technicians and combat

The tank commander and loader of an M48 Magach scan the deserted buildings of El Qantara from the top of a firing ramp on the Bar-Lev Line during the War of Attrition. During the first hours of the Yom Kippur War few Israeli tanks reached the banks of the Canal to support the defenders in the Bar-Lev Line and the Egyptian infantry lavishly equipped with Sagger and RPG anti-tank weapons soon knocked out those that did.

pilots to the embattled Egyptian Air Force. The Soviet air crews were to wear Egyptian uniforms and their aircraft were to carry Egyptian markings. In March, three MiG-21 squadrons were deployed around Cairo, Aswan and Alexandria. There were now some 7,500 Soviet personnel in Egypt, of whom about 4,000 were missile crewmen, a number that had doubled by the end of June and within another three months had increased to 10,000.

It was now clear that the Israeli policy of deep-penetration bombing had failed. In the summer of 1970 the IAF strove to stem the creeping eastward progress of the Egyptians' SAM umbrella. In the 'electronic war' the IAF used US-supplied electronic countermeasures pods to jam the mutually supporting SAM boxes. The results were mixed – the pods were effective only against the SA-2s, and Israeli aircraft losses were now mounting.

By October 1973, the Bar-Lev Line was a highly sophisticated defensive fortification with 30 strongpoints, or Maozim, stretching from the Mediterranean coast to the Gulf of Suez and another line of strongholds, or Taozim, further eastwards, all inter-connected by an extensive network of roads and tracks. The cost of construction is estimated to be in the region of $300 million at 1973 prices.

The protection of soldiers' lives is paramount within the IDF and was one of the primary reasons for the construction of the Bar-Lev Line as a static fortification rather than as a mobile defence screen as advocated by some in the General Staff. It saved many lives in the initial Egyptian assault but the outcome was inevitable against such overwhelming odds. Fewer than 500 men faced 80,000 and, in the first minute of the war, 10,500 shells hit the Bar-Lev Line at a rate of 175 rounds a second.

On 7 August 1970 a six-month ceasefire brokered by the United States came into effect. Both sides were not to alter 'the military status quo within zones extending 50km (31 miles) to the east and west of the ceasefire line'. Nor was either party to 'introduce or construct any new military installations in these zones'. Nasser had no intention of honouring this provision and the SAM sites continued their eastward progress. Israel reacted by refusing to renew talks sponsored by the UN.

The War of Attrition had sapped Israeli morale. Nevertheless, the IDF held the Bar-Lev Line and brought the Egyptians to the negotiating table. This, however, led to a dangerous complacency within the Israeli High Command about the resolve of the Egyptian armed forces and the strength of the Bar-Lev Line. Israel still saw no need to reach a political agreement with Egypt based on withdrawal from the occupied territories.

In contrast, the Egyptians regarded the War of Attrition as a great success, in spite of the thousands of casualties their army and air force had suffered and the mauling their air defence system had received. They had not buckled and from this they drew considerable confidence, not least in their ability to counter the weapon that had destroyed them in 1967 – the IAF.

FIRST STEPS TO WAR

Nasser did not live to launch another war against Israel. His death on 28 September 1970 was followed by a period of uncertainty before Nasser's deputy, the seemingly self-effacing Anwar Sadat, overcame an extreme pro-Soviet faction under Ali Sabri.

Sadat was careful to warn the Soviets in advance that the removal of their chief supporter would in no way affect the Egyptian-Soviet alliance. As collateral, Sadat signed a 15-year treaty of friendship and co-operation. He also bent his efforts towards what he called a 'peace initiative', which he launched in a speech to the Egyptian parliament on 4 February 1971.

Sadat's initiative mirrored a similar proposal presented by the Israeli Defense Minister Moshe Dayan to Prime Minister Golda Meir in September 1970. The key elements in Dayan's plan were the separation of forces on the Canal line, the redeployment of the IDF some 32km (20 miles) to the east of the Suez Canal,

Israeli soldiers are briefed before a raid across the Suez Canal against Egypt in 1970 during the War of Attrition. (© David Rubinger/Corbis)

Egyptian use of the waterway and the rebuilding of the towns along the Canal as a commitment to non-belligerence.

However, Sadat's initiative and Dayan's proposal both foundered on the rock of Israeli stubbornness. Dayan's aide at the time, Colonel Arie Braun, later reflected that in the early months of 1971 Israel had missed an 'historic opportunity'. By May 1971 Sadat had settled on war as the only option and in June announced that he was 'willing to sacrifice a million Egyptian soldiers' to recover the lost lands.

Simultaneously, Sadat pressed the Soviet Union for more arms, including 'Scud' missiles as a counterweight to Israel's nuclear arsenal. The Soviets stepped up arms deliveries while at the same time entertaining the deepest misgivings about the outcome of any all-out war launched against Israel, fearing a repetition of the 1967 debacle. Accordingly, they dragged their feet over the more sophisticated weapons requested by Sadat, which in turn did little to improve the prickly relations between the Egyptian military and their sceptical Soviet advisers.

Sadat, who also sought improved relations with the United States, had always been uneasy with the perception of Egypt as an obedient client state of the Soviets. Trouble with the Soviet Union came to a head in May 1972 when the Soviets and Americans issued a joint communiqué during President Richard Nixon's visit to Moscow calling for Arab restraint in the Middle East. Sadat feared that a superpower détente would place the situation in the Middle East in suspended animation, with all it implied for the regaining of the lost lands.

In July 1972 Sadat announced the expulsion of thousands of Soviet military advisers. He hoped that this dramatic move would shock the Soviet Union into supplying the sophisticated weaponry he needed and also give him a free hand to go to war. The Russians' departure would also earn Sadat kudos in Washington DC. By August some 15,000 Russian personnel had left Egypt. Shortly after the expulsion, several hundred of the Soviet advisers returned and the Russians signalled acquiescence to Sadat's developing war plans. On 24 October 1972 Sadat explained to the Egyptian Supreme War Council of the Armed Forces his aim of securing a lodgement on the Sinai bank of the Suez Canal as a bargaining counter to force Israel to the negotiating table.

Sadat also sought the agreement of his neighbour, Jordan, and his ally, Syria. Egypt and Syria had both lost territory in 1967 but their aims were now different. Egypt had accepted Resolution 242 and was prepared to recognize Israel while Syria was not. Moreover, Sadat's war aims were directed at the recovery of the Arab territory lost in 1967. In contrast Syria, in common with the Palestine Liberation Organization (PLO), which it harboured, was bent on Israel's destruction.

Sadat persuaded Syria's President Hafez al Assad to agree to more limited objectives: the recapture of Arab territory occupied in 1967, a 'just settlement' of

Golda Meir was the Israeli Prime Minister during the October War; a formidable leader given to ruling through a small, select band of advisers known as her 'kitchen cabinet'. Early on 6 October 1973 she took the painful decision not to mount a pre-emptive strike against Arab war preparations. Israel had to be seen by the world to be the victim of aggression or else the United States would not provide military or political support. Without the latter, Israel faced the awful prospect of the 'fall of the Third Temple' and the last resort of initiating nuclear warfare – the cataclysmic 'Samson Option'. (© David Rubinger/Corbis)

the refugee problem and the recognition of a Palestinian entity. The means to achieve these ends were the seizure of the Golan Heights and the eastern bank of the Suez Canal as a demonstration of determination to enlist world sympathy. They would also precipitate an oil embargo sufficiently injurious to the European nations to force their governments to persuade the United States to drag the Israelis to the negotiating table. Sadat calculated that these limited aims posed no threat to Israel's vital interests and would not provoke the Israeli nuclear retaliation that he feared.

Sadat was aware that Jordan had suffered badly in 1967. It lacked an adequate air defence system and King Hussein would risk his throne if he intervened directly in an attack against Israel. Nevertheless, Sadat hoped to secure Hussein's good will, albeit without informing him of the war plans being drawn up in secret by Egypt, Syria and Sadat's Soviet advisers. Sadat and Syria's President Assad, while preserving their secret, also needed the help of other Arab states.

In 1972 Egypt's relations with Jordan were still badly strained – Nasser had deceived Hussein in 1967 – but Sadat secured substantial pledges of financial aid from oil-rich Saudi Arabia and Qatar and promises of troops and aircraft in any future war with Israel from Saudi Arabia, Algeria, Libya, Morocco, Sudan and Iraq. Most of the units pledged to Egypt and Syria were to arrive too late to change the course of the October War, although the Iraqi contingent was to play a significant role in the battle for the Golan Heights. Simultaneously, Sadat strove to improve relations with the West, opening communications with Henry Kissinger, the US Secretary of State, and in June 1973 restoring diplomatic relations with France, Britain and West Germany.

President Hafez al Assad of Syria. Born in 1924 of the Alawite clan, Assad joined the ruling Ba'ath party in 1958 and rose to become the commander of the Syrian Air Force. He was subsequently the Minister of Defence during the Six Day War He seized supreme power in October 1970 and began to rebuild the Syrian armed forces for the coming battle with Israel that erupted in October 1973. Photo taken in 1971 in Switzerland. (© Wally McNamee/Corbis)

PART I

THE SINAI

OPPOSING PLANS

In the early summer of 1971, the Egyptian military began to lay plans for a simultaneous two-front offensive. Careful analysis of the defeat in 1967 identified two key areas of Egyptian weakness: the ineffectiveness of the Egyptian Air Force when pitted against the IAF (the decisive factor in 1967) and the similar inferiority of the Egyptian armoured corps, both in the quality of its weapons and the training of its personnel. The IAF was thought to be at least ten years ahead of its Egyptian counterpart due in part to the outstanding performance of the McDonnell Douglas F-4 Phantom.

The Egyptians and Syrians believed that part of the solution to this quandary lay in the mobilization of aircraft and pilots from other Arab and sympathetic countries; an option that became increasingly attractive after the 1972 expulsion of the Soviet advisers. The Egyptians were to assemble an international air brigade that boasted elements from North Korea, Algeria, Libya and Iraq. The last supplied squadrons to both Egypt and Syria.

However, this barely ruffled the strategic surface. Even the evolving two-front plan left Egypt and Syria at a distinct disadvantage in the air. So the Egyptians and Syrians turned to ground anti-aircraft defences to redress the balance in the strategic equation. In the early 1970s Egypt and Syria built up the world's densest system of SAM-2, -3 and -6 missiles to protect their capitals and major cities, to cover the Golan Heights and both banks of the Suez Canal. A combination of the SAM-7 shoulder-fired missile and ZSU-23-4 self-propelled anti-aircraft guns would give their ground forces greater protection in the forward combat zone.

The Egyptians could not hope to match the Israeli expertise in armoured warfare. Rather they hoped to neutralize it by equipping their infantry with light anti-tank weapons ranging from the RPG-7 rocket launcher, through various recoilless rifles and anti-tank guns to the AT-3 'Sagger' wire-guided missile. It was anticipated that these weapons would enable the Egyptian infantry to hold their bridgeheads and inflict heavy damage on the counterattacking Israeli tank forces even before their own armour had been brought across the Canal.

Forty new battalions of engineers were formed to tackle the problem of the Canal crossing and amass the tools with which to cross a defended waterway.

The principal war leaders of the Egyptian forces confer on 15 October following the disastrous failure of the major Egyptian offensive to relieve the military pressure on their Syrian allies. President Anwar Sadat is in the centre flanked by Chief of Staff Lieutenant General Sa'ad Al Shazly (left) and Minister of War General Ahmed Ismail.

The Soviet Union and its allies supplied much of their assault crossing equipment, including PMP pontoon bridges and GSP and PT–S ferries. A junior Egyptian officer has been credited with the idea of breaching the embankment of the Bar–Lev Line by washing the sand away with 450 high-pressure hoses acquired from Britain and West Germany. The Egyptian Army practised canal crossings with remarkable rigour; some units rehearsed the operation over 300 times. At El Ballah, south of El Qantara, the Canal divides into two channels, one of which was entirely in Egyptian hands and provided an excellent training area.

The key to the two-front offensive, codenamed Operation *Badr*, was surprise. This would enable the Egyptians to gain and consolidate their limited objectives before the Israelis could react decisively. Under pressure in the Sinai and on the Golan Heights, the IDF would not be able to concentrate first against one enemy and then another as it had in 1967. Timing was of the utmost importance in this simultaneous attack, particularly on the Suez Canal. A steady current, especially strong during the spring tides, flows through the Canal from south to north to replace water lost in the Mediterranean by evaporation. The optimum time for an opposed crossing was the period of slack current during the neap tides. Sufficient daylight was also required to move the assault echelons across the Canal against the relatively light opposition from the Bar-Lev garrisons. Moonlight was needed to allow the bridge building in the first half of the night and darkness to hide the subsequent crossing of the armour and vehicles of the assault divisions. In addition, a convenient gap had to be found in US satellite coverage of the region. Finally, a sophisticated deception plan was initiated to mislead Israeli military intelligence.

The Israeli response

Under the strong leadership of Major General Aharon Yariv, Israeli military intelligence enjoyed an enviable reputation. However, in the spring of 1973 Yariv was replaced by his deputy, Major General Eli Zeira, an officer whose dogmatic approach was to have a significant bearing on the Israeli response to the Arab preparations for war.

Israeli military intelligence had calculated, correctly, that Syria would not make a move without Egypt, and the latter would not be in a position to launch an attack until 1975. This was when the Israelis estimated the Egyptian Air Force would have recovered from the 1967 losses and acquired an effective medium-range bomber force. However, Sadat could not afford to wait this long – the political pressure on him was too great. The arrival in Egypt in the spring and early summer of 1973 of 'Scud' battlefield support missiles provided a substitute for the medium-range bomber force. The Scud's range of 290km (180 miles) allowed it to engage civilian targets in Israel from Egypt.

Egyptian infantry scramble up the sand embankment of the Bar-Lev Line on 6 October at the outset of Operation *Badr*. The incline of between 45 and 60 degrees made the rampart impassable for all vehicles and extremely difficult for a heavily laden soldier to climb. (EGIO)

OPPOSITE

Aircraft losses during the Yom Kippur War remain contentious thanks to a significant amount of disinformation from the various combatants. However, subsequent analysis suggests that at the outset of the war the IAF had a frontline deployment of 309 combat aircraft; Egypt 490; Syria 265 with an additional 125 from Algeria, Iraq and Libya being committed over the course of the fighting. Overall losses during the 19 days of conflict were 103 Israeli combat aircraft or 35% of pre-war strength; Egypt 242 aircraft or 49%; 179 Syrian aircraft or 68% and 26% losses for the other Arab combatants. Other aircraft from war reserves and trainer types were also pressed into service during the conflict. The IAF lost a total of 110 aircraft during the war including five helicopters and two transport aircraft beyond the 103 combat aircraft. The two transport aircraft and one helicopter were lost due to flying accidents as were 13% of the overall Israeli aircraft losses. The IAF lost approximately 60 of its combat aircraft in the first four days of the war when the Arab air defence system was at its strongest due to a combination of SAMs and ground fire, particularly the ZSU-23-4 Shilka, as well as several to enemy ground attack aircraft during the initial Arab air assault against Israeli airfields in the Sinai. With the advent of Libyan Mirage 5 aircraft into the war, there were problems of identifying friend from foe and a few Israeli Mirage derivatives were destroyed by friendly fire, as were other aircraft. Accordingly, during the war all Israeli Mirages and Neshers were painted with a black-bordered yellow triangle on the tail as a recognition device. A greater number of Israeli aircraft were lost in air-to-air combat than the IAF has ever cared to admit. (EGIO)

A series of escalations and scares took place along the Suez Canal between December 1971 and May 1973. Israeli intelligence was thus accustomed to Egyptian concentrations and dispersals and the intelligence community became increasingly complacent as scare succeeded scare. Nevertheless, in May 1973 the Chief of the General Staff, Major General David Elazar, was sufficiently concerned to persuade the Israeli cabinet to order a partial mobilization. When nothing happened, Elazar lost the confidence of the cabinet and particularly that of Moshe Dayan, the Minister of Defense. Sadat, in their opinion, was indulging in brinkmanship. In fact, Sadat had postponed going to war to wait for the next propitious tides. The date finally chosen for Operation *Badr* was 6 October, which happened to be the date of the Jewish religious festival of Yom Kippur or the Day of Atonement. In the spring of 1973 Sadat gave an interview to the journalist Arnaud de Borchgrave of *Newsweek* in which he remarked: 'Everything in this country is now being mobilized in earnest for the resumption of battle.' The only person who seems to have appreciated the significance of Sadat's remarks was Henry Kissinger, soon to become the US Secretary of State.

The Egyptians capitalized on Israeli scepticism about their aims and capabilities. Western journalists were encouraged to file copy detailing Arab disunity and the lack of preparedness of the Egyptian armed forces. When, on 25 September, in a secret meeting in Tel Aviv, King Hussein gave a non-specific warning of an imminent Egyptian-Syrian offensive, Israeli intelligence did not give it much credence.

Israeli intelligence was also hamstrung by their view of Sadat as a weak man. Sadat had declared that 1971 would be a 'year of decision'. In November 1972 he had stated that within six months Egypt would be at war. Each passing deadline confirmed the Israeli view of Sadat as little more than a clown. Thus when, on 11 September 1973, Cairo Radio announced that Sadat was discussing with King Hussein 'preparations for the fateful battle with Israel' − a rare example from this period of an Egyptian intelligence blunder − it was drowned out by the 'mood music' of Israeli preconceptions. The CIA had provided a 40-page document detailing Egyptian military plans to the Israelis on 16 April 1972. The intelligence was staring the Israelis in the face, but there are none so blind as those who do not wish to see.

Nevertheless, the IDF had devised some plans to counter any Egyptian incursion. Despite the unresolved arguments within the high command as to the exact purpose of the Bar-Lev Line and whether it was to be held at all costs or act just as a trip-wire, the IDF believed that Egyptian preparations for any offensive would allow ample time for their reserves to be mobilized. The 252nd Armoured Division in the Sinai Peninsula had the task of containing the initial attack with the majority of its tanks held well back from the Suez Canal to

mount counterattacks as and when directed. Several tank companies were deployed in platoon strength to support the various forward fortifications along the Bar-Lev Line. This was the existing plan codenamed *Shovach Yonim* or Operation *Dovecote* that was drawn up in August 1970 when Major General Arik Sharon was GOC Southern Command. Sharon prepared various crossing points along the length of the Bar-Lev Line to allow a major counterattack within 48 hours of hostilities breaking out.

Selected crossing points were prepared by drastically thinning the sand ramparts of the Bar-Lev Line and creating massive marshalling yards, protected from artillery fire by sand berms. Tracks were prepared leading to the yards to allow heavy bridging equipment to be transported forward for a crossing of the Canal. As a firm believer in the concept of mobile armoured operations, Sharon had little time for the Bar-Lev Line and nobody in the high command persuaded him otherwise. Accordingly he allowed its fortifications to fall into a state of disrepair and only 18 of the 32 frontline strongpoints were manned

at the outset of war and then only by 436 reservists supported by 290 tanks, 12 artillery batteries with 52 guns and six anti-aircraft and two Hawk SAM batteries. Sharon's successor as GOC Southern Command, Major General Shmuel Gonen, tried to refurbish some of the defences along the Canal but it was 'too little, too late' against the powerful forces massing across the Canal.

OPPOSITE

In the euphoria of success, a T-55 of the Egyptian Third Army drives through one of the breaches in the sand ramparts of the Bar-Lev Line. The Egyptian High Command had estimated that 30,000 casualties were likely in the initial assault. In the event, just 208 Egyptian soldiers were killed with 20 tanks and five planes destroyed. Operation *Badr* was a huge success. (EGIO)

OPPOSING ARMIES

Egyptian forces

In 1973, the total strength of the Egyptian armed forces was 1,200,000 troops with 66,000 officers and 1,134,000 NCOs and enlisted men, with approximately half that number deployed for the coming offensive. They comprised 19 infantry brigades, eight mechanized brigades, ten armoured brigades, three airborne brigades, one amphibious brigade and 4,000 artillery pieces, 1,700 Main Battle Tanks (MBTs) and 2,000 other Armoured Fighting Vehicles (AFVs). The vital air defence contingent comprised 150 SAM batteries and 2,500 anti-aircraft guns. The Egyptian Air Force fielded 400 combat aircraft,

Egyptian combat engineers prepare a crossing point on the western bank of the Suez Canal. In the background is one of the breaches in the sand rampart on the Israeli side of the waterway that was created by high-pressure water hoses in a matter of hours. Using the latest Soviet PMP bridging equipment, the Egyptians were able to construct a pontoon bridge capable of bearing tanks and other heavy vehicles across the canal in under an hour. By midnight on 6 October, some 60 breaches had been made in the ramparts along the 161km (100 mile) stretch of the eastern bank of the canal. Within 24 hours the 2nd and 3rd Egyptian Armies were established in an almost continuous line along the whole length of the Canal with the bridgehead extending to a depth of up to 3.2km (2 miles) under an umbrella of anti-aircraft missiles and guns to thwart the inevitable Israeli counterattack. It was an astounding feat of arms by any standards. (© Genevieve Chauvel/Corbis Sygma)

ORDER OF BATTLE [1]
EGYPTIAN ARMY, OCTOBER 1973

GHQ
General Anwar Sadat, President of Egypt
General Ahmed Ismail Ali, War Minister
Lieutenant General Sa'ad Mohamed Al Hussani Al Shazly,
    Chief of Staff
Lieutenant General Mohamed Abd El Ghani Al Gamassy,
    Chief of Operations

Second Field Army (Northern Canal Zone) –
MajGen Mohamed Sa'ad Ma'amon[2]
2nd Infantry Division – BrigGen Hassan Ali Hassan Abu Sa'ada
4th Infantry Brigade
117th Infantry Brigade
120th Infantry Brigade

16th Infantry Division – BrigGen Fouad Aziz Ghali
3rd Infantry Brigade
16th Infantry Brigade
112th Infantry Brigade

18th Infantry Division – BrigGen Abdel Rab Al Nabi Hafez
134th Infantry Brigade
135th Infantry Brigade
136th Infantry Brigade
15th Independent Armoured Brigade (attached)

21st Armoured Division – BrigGen Ibrahim Oraby
1st Armoured Brigade
14th Armoured Brigade
18th Mechanized Brigade

23rd Mechanized Division – BrigGen Ahmed Aboud el Zommer
24th Armoured Brigade

116th Mechanized Brigade
118th Mechanized Brigade
129th Commando Brigade
182nd Parachute Brigade

Third Field Army (Southern Canal Zone) –
MajGen Mohamed Abd El Al Mona'am Wasel
4th Armoured Division
3rd Armoured Brigade
25th Independent Armoured Brigade

6th Mechanized Division
22nd Armoured Brigade
113th Mechanized Brigade

7th Infantry Division – BrigGen Ahmed Badawi Said Ahmed
19th Infantry Division – BrigGen Yousf Afifi Mohamed
25th Armoured Brigade (attached)

19th Infantry Division
130th Independent Marine Brigade

GHQ Reserve
3rd Mechanized Division + Special Forces + independent
armoured brigades of the Presidential Guard.

Foreign allied contingents operating with the Egyptian forces:
One Algerian armoured brigade
One Libyan armoured brigade
One Moroccan infantry brigade
One Sudanese infantry brigade
One Kuwaiti infantry battalion
One Tunisian infantry battalion

---

1   Both the Israeli and the Egyptian orders of battle have been drawn from many sources and they are both largely conjectural as neither the IDF
     nor the Egyptian armed forces have ever published official versions, and it is doubtful that they ever will.

2   Replaced 15 October by MajGen Abd El Munem Halil.

60 transport planes and 140 helicopters while the international Arab
contribution was one MiG-17 squadron, one MiG-21 squadron and one SU-7
squadron from Algeria, two Mirage 5 squadrons from Libya and one Hawker
Hunter squadron from Iraq.

In October 1973 five infantry divisions and a number of independent and
armoured brigades backed by three mechanized and two armoured divisions
were deployed along the Suez Canal. Each infantry division was three brigades
strong and supported by a brigade of 120 tanks. The tank brigade consisted of

Egyptian troops move through a captured stronghold or Maozim of the Bar-Lev Line. At the outset of the October War the Bar-Lev Line was manned by just 436 reservists of the Jerusalem Etzioni Brigade deployed in 18 Maozim and four observation posts. In addition, there were only 52 artillery guns and 290 tanks to defend the whole of the Sinai Peninsula – a total of some 18,000 men with fewer than 8,000 ready to respond to battle immediately. (EGIO)

three battalions each with 31 tanks, one battalion with each infantry brigade. Each infantry division also included one battalion of SU–100 self-propelled anti-tank guns and an anti-tank guided weapon battalion equipped with 314 RPG-7s and 48 Saggers. Each mechanized division included two mechanized and one armoured brigade, giving the division a total of 160 tanks. Both armoured divisions comprised two armoured brigades and one mechanized brigade, a total of 250 tanks per division. In the Suez Canal zone there were also independent tank brigades, two paratroop brigades and approximately 30 battalions of commandos and a marine brigade.

The Egyptian Second Army's 2nd, 16th, and 18th divisions were responsible for the northern half of the Canal from Port Said to the northern end of the Great Bitter Lake. Through the centre of the Great Bitter Lake ran the dividing line with Third Army's 7th and 19th divisions whose front ran down to, and included, the city of Suez. Each of the assault divisions was reinforced for the crossing by an armoured brigade, drawn in part from the armoured and mechanized divisions.

Israeli forces

In 1973 the Israeli active army numbered some 75,000 men, of whom one-third were regulars – 11,500 each in the army and air force and 2,000 in the navy. At any time some 50,000 conscripts were undergoing training and a varying number of reservists would be on duty. In the army up to 15 brigades would be operational, although not necessarily at full strength. On mobilization, Israel's armed forces grew to 350,000, and over 30 brigades could be deployed, grouped into division-sized task forces (Ugdas). In peacetime one ugda was based in Sinai and another on the Golan. The other ugdas were based on training establishments or other cadres and their commanders could be reservists. In the Sinai, an ugda was based around three armoured brigades each of three

Egyptian trucks and troops cause a serious traffic jam at one of the crossing points over the Suez Canal. During the first ten hours of the conflict on 6 October, Egyptian combat engineers blasted 60 holes through the sand ramparts; constructed ten continuous bridges and established 50 ferries to allow 500 tanks and mobile missile launchers across the Suez Canal. (EGIO)

ORDER OF BATTLE [1]
ISRAELI SOUTHERN COMMAND, OCTOBER 1973

Cabinet
Mrs Golda Meir, Prime Minister
General Moshe Dayan, Minister of Defence

Knesset
Legislative Assembly

Israeli Defense Forces GHQ
Lieutenant General David 'Dado' Elazar, Chief of Staff
Major General Israel 'Talik' Tal, Deputy Chief of Staff
Major General Eliezer Ze'ira, Chief of Intelligence

Southern Command
MajGen Shmuel 'Gorodish' Gonen[2]

Ugda Albert (252nd Armoured Division) – *MajGen Avraham 'Albert' Mandler*[3]
8th Armoured Brigade – Col Aryeh Dayan
14th Armoured Brigade – Col Amnon Reshef[4]
401st Armoured Brigade – Col Dan Shomron
460th Armoured Brigade – Col Gavriel Amir[5]
'Harel' Brigade – Col Avraham Bar-Am
plus Mech Inf & Paratroop support

Ugda Bren (162nd Reserve Armoured Division) – *MajGen Avraham 'Bren' Adan, GOC Armoured Corps*
217th Reserve Armoured Brigade – Col Natke Nir
460th Armoured Brigade[6]
500th Reserve Armoured Brigade – Col Aryeh Karen
+ Mech Inf & Paratroop support including 35th Paratroop Brigade – Col Uzi Yairi

Ugda Arik (143rd Reserve Armoured Division) – *MajGen (R) Ariel 'Arik' Sharon*
14th Armoured Brigade[7]
600th Reserve Armoured Brigade – Col Tuvia Raviv
'Haim' Brigade – Col Haim Erez
plus Mech Inf & Paratroop units including 243rd Paratroop Brigade – Col Dani Matt

Ugda Kalman[8] *(146th Reserve Armoured Division)* – *BrigGen Kalman Magen*[9]
11th Reserve Armoured Brigade – Col Aharon
'Tzvi' Brigade – Col Tzvi Rom
'Force Gonen' – Col Yoni Gonen
plus Mech Inf & Paratroop support
'Force Granit' – Col Israel Granit[10]

SHLOMO COMMAND – Southern Sinai District
MajGen (R) Yeshaya 'Shaike' Gavish

1 Both the Israeli and the Egyptian orders of battle have been drawn from many sources and they are both largely conjectural as neither the Israel Defense Forces nor the Egyptian armed forces have ever published official versions, and it is doubtful if they ever will.

2 Superseded from 10 October by LtGen (R) Chaim Bar-Lev as Commander, Canal Front.

3 KIA 13 October. Replaced by MajGen Kalman Magen.

4 Transferred to Ugda Arik.

5 Transferred to Ugda Bren.

6 Transferred from Ugda Albert.

7 Transferred from Ugda Albert.

8 Until 13 October, then Ugda Sasson.

9 Until 13 October then BrigGen Yitzak Sasson.

10 Created 18 October after Ugda Sasson crossed Suez Canal.

Of the 18 strongpoints in the Bar-Lev Line manned by the IDF at the outset of the war, all bar two had been evacuated or surrendered by 10 October by orders of Southern Command. The 'Quay' position opposite Port Tewfik surrendered on the 13th and 294 Israelis became POWs. But 'Budapest' on the Mediterranean coast refused to surrender and continued to defy repeated Egyptian attacks. Here, the commander of Budapest, Captain Motti Ashkenazi, is embraced after the position was relieved by Israeli troops; Ashkenazi subsequently led the movement demanding an inquiry into the conduct of the war, which became the Agranat Commission.

battalions with a total, at full strength, of 111 tanks per brigade. Infantry and artillery were allotted to the ugda as required for a specific operation or time frame – flexibility being the key rather than a strict order of battle. Few formations were at full strength; for instance the 252nd Armoured Division, the resident unit in the Sinai, had only 290 tanks at the outbreak of war. The Israeli Army fielded a wide variety of equipment, much of it acquired abroad and modified in Israel. Approximately half its tank fleet was British Centurions. There were also 600 M60s and up-gunned M48s from the United States; some 250 T-54/55s that had been captured in 1967 and 250 Super Shermans, converted from the American stalwart of World War II. Self-propelled (SP) 155mm guns, either American M109s or the locally produced Soltam, which was mounted on a Sherman chassis, provided the backbone of the artillery arm.

TABLE 1:
FORCE NUMBERS AT OUTSET OF CONFLICT

	Israel	Arab	Egyptian
Personnel	350,000	505,000	1,200,000
Tanks	2,000	4,480	2,200
APCs	4,000	4,300	2,400
Artillery	575	2,100	1,200*
ATGW	100	1,200	900
SAMs	75	1,250	850
AA guns	1,000	3,500	2,500
SA–7s	–	3,000	2,000
Aircraft	360	1,000	600

* Weapons of 100mm calibre and larger

The Israelis also fielded captured Soviet artillery and some long-range M107 175mm guns. Armoured personnel carriers were a mixture of World War II halftracks and modern US M113s supplemented with captured Soviet vehicles.

The IAF possessed about 360 combat aircraft, including 130 F-4 Phantoms, 170 A-4 Skyhawks and older Mirage jets. The navy possessed five submarines, 21 patrol boats and ten tank landing ships.

OPPOSING COMMANDERS

Israeli Commanders

Israel's political leader at the time of the Yom Kippur War was the formidable Prime Minister Golda Meir. Born in Kiev in 1898, her family emigrated to the United States when she was eight. She settled in Palestine in 1921 and became a leading figure in the Labour movement. She was Minister of Labour from 1949 to 1956 and Foreign Minister from 1956 to 1966. She became Prime Minister in 1969. Thereafter she created her own group of close advisers – the famous 'kitchen cabinet' – but her decision was final in most matters. Throughout the October War, she was the firm hand at the helm as those about her faltered and panicked and in the end the State of Israel was saved. But it was not enough to save her and she resigned as Prime Minister in 1974 following the findings of the Agranat Commission, even though it did not find her culpable for failing to appreciate Arab intentions leading up to the war. She died in 1978.

A leading lieutenant in Golda Meir's kitchen cabinet was General Moshe Dayan in his role as Minister of Defense. A founder member of the Haganah underground militia, he was imprisoned by the British but subsequently lost an eye fighting in the British Army in 1941. Thereafter he wore his trademark black eye patch and entered the Israeli parliament in 1959. In 1967 he was appointed Minister of Defense and masterminded the brilliant Israeli success in the Six Day War of 1967 that assured his international reputation as a soldier/statesman. He was again Minister of Defense between 1969 and 1974. The early Israeli reverses in the opening days of the October War acutely depressed him and his advice to Golda Meir sometimes bordered on the alarmist and reckless. He too resigned in 1974 following the publication of the Agranat Commission report.

Chief of Staff of the IDF was Lieutenant General David 'Dado' Elazar. Born in Sarajevo in 1925, he distinguished himself as a member of the Palmach during the War of Independence in 1948. He was an infantry brigade commander in the 1956 Sinai campaign, after which he became the commander of the Israeli Armoured Corps from 1957 to 1961. In 1962 he was

Lieutenant General David Elazar and Major General Ariel Sharon discuss their options two days after the Israelis established a bridgehead west of the Suez Canal. (© David Rubinger/Corbis)

promoted to major general and four years later took over Northern Command where he was responsible for the brilliant campaign to capture the Golan Heights during the Six Day War. In 1971 he became the Chief of Staff of the IDF. Hours before the outbreak of the October War, the Israeli cabinet ordered the partial mobilization of the reserves but Elazar, on his own authority, organized a general call-up; it was a crucial decision that did much to save the State of Israel. After the war, however, the Agranat Commission found him negligent in failing to read Arab intentions. He resigned as Chief of Staff on 2 April 1974 and the Labour government of 30 years fell soon afterwards. He died playing tennis in 1977.

Another victim of the Agranat Commission was the GOC Southern Command, Major General Shmuel 'Gorodish' Gonen. He was appointed to the post just months before the war as successor to Major General Ariel 'Arik' Sharon, so he had little time to impose his will. His situation was further compromised by the fact that his most experienced divisional commander in the Sinai, Major General Avraham 'Albert' Mandler, was due for replacement as war broke out. His authority was immediately undermined when the more experienced generals Adan and Sharon were committed to the theatre of operations as the commanders of reserve armoured divisions. Sharon in particular was disinclined to follow Gonen's orders and often bypassed his headquarters to confer with the IDF High Command. It was a recipe for

Major General Ariel 'Arik' Sharon briefs the Minister of Defense General Moshe Dayan in the Sinai Desert during the height of Operation *Abiray-Lev* or *Bravehearts/Valiant Men* – the Israeli crossing of the Suez Canal as the initial phase of Operation *Gazelle* to surround the Egyptian 3rd Army. Crouching beside General Dayan is Colonel Amnon Reshef, the commander of the 14th Armoured Brigade, wearing sunglasses, flak jacket and sporting a luxuriant handlebar moustache. Colonel Reshef's unit was involved in some of the fiercest fighting of the war from the initial Egyptian attack to the bloody battle of Chinese Farm. The success of Operation *Gazelle* did much to restore Israeli morale and by the end of the war General Ariel Sharon was being declared as 'Arik – King of Africa'.

disaster and the highly experienced General Chaim Bar-Lev, then the Minister of Trade and Industry, was returned to active military duty at Southern Command as the IDF's 'representative of the General Staff' to assist Gonen. In fact he became the overall commander on the southern front. Although personally competent and courageous, Gonen was relieved of his command by the Agranat Commission in 1974 and denied any further military command. Humiliated by the experience, Gonen went into self-imposed exile running a diamond business in Central Africa. He died in September 1991 and was returned to be buried in Israel.

The dire situation in the Sinai during the opening days of the war was principally salvaged by the superior training of the individual Israeli soldier and the outstanding tactical abilities of the officer corps in general and the divisional commanders in particular – men such as generals Adan, Mandler and Sharon. All were veterans, having fought in the previous Arab-Israeli wars from their days in the Palmach as junior officers to their present senior ranks. Tragically, Major General Avraham 'Albert' Mandler, a courteous, studious man and a gifted leader, was killed in action on 13 October. He was replaced by Major General Kalman Magen, a dynamic tank officer who had been severely wounded during the War of Attrition. In the October War he led his ugda, or division, across the Suez Canal into Egypt.

The principal commanders on the southern front confer with the Chief of Staff, Lieutenant General Elazar, on the second day of the war at Khiseiba. General Elazar is seated between Major General Shmuel Gonen (in spectacles), OC Southern Command, and Major General Avraham 'Bren' Adan, OC 162nd Reserve Armoured Division. Pointing to the wall map is the commander of 252nd Armoured Division, Major General Mandler. This gallant officer was killed on 13 October by Egyptian artillery fire.

The defenders of the 'Quay' Maozim surrender their position to the Egyptians on 13 October after a siege lasting a week. Of the 42 Israelis trapped in the stronghold, five were killed and 37 wounded – a casualty rate of 100 per cent. (EGIO)

As the commander of the 162nd Reserve Armoured Division, Major General Avraham 'Bren' Adan fought a distinguished war and led his division to the outskirts of Suez City to effect the envelopment of the Egyptian Third Army. As the commander of the Israeli Armoured Corps between 1969 and 1974, he oversaw the doubling in size of the IDF's tank force and the introduction of mechanized infantry. His mastery of mobile armoured operations was a decisive factor in the eventual Israeli victory on the southern front. His final military appointment in the IDF was as defence attaché in Washington DC.

Last but not least was Major General Ariel 'Arik' Sharon, the commander of the 143rd Reserve Armoured Division. In 1953 he founded and led the 101 Special Commando Unit that carried out retaliatory operations against the Arabs. In 1956 he commanded a paratroop brigade and fought in the Sinai.

Egyptian troops and armour advance on 7 October to expand their bridgehead eastwards into the Sinai Desert. Operation *Badr* required the five Egyptian infantry divisions to advance some 15km (9 miles) and then dig in so as to remain under the protection of the SAM missile umbrella and avoid retaliation by the IAF. (EGIO)

Later he attended the Staff College at Camberley in Britain before serving as an infantry brigade commander and then commander of the IDF's Infantry School. He was appointed commander of the IDF's Northern Command and in 1966 became Director of the Army Training Department. He commanded an armoured division in the 1967 war and in 1969 became GOC of Southern Command. A formidable figure, in every sense of the word, and never one for half measures, Sharon's career had been dogged by controversy. In June 1973 Sharon had retired from active service to enter politics. With the outbreak of war he swiftly returned to service. As a firm believer that the best form of defence was attack, he was soon bombarding his immediate superior, General Gonen, and the high command with demands to lead an assault across the Suez Canal. There is little doubt that some of his actions during the war amounted to gross insubordination, and in any other army than the IDF he would have been dismissed without question. He had the ear of General Dayan, however, and he escaped serious censure. Despite his overbearing manner, he was a brilliant field commander and leader of men – attributes that cannot be overestimated in times of war. His preparations for a counterattack across the Suez Canal as GOC Southern Command and his hard-charging attitude throughout the war were fundamental to the Israeli victory. He rightly became a hero to the Israeli people in a war that cost them so dearly.

Egyptian commanders

Arrayed against the Israelis was undoubtedly the best army ever fielded by the Egyptians. However, its doctrine was based on Soviet precepts and as such its officers did not have the breadth of experience nor the capacity for individual initiative displayed by their Israeli counterparts. In the set piece battle of the initial offensive they performed admirably. When driven by political imperatives the original concept of a limited bridgehead in the Sinai was abandoned, however, and the maintenance of an aim so critical to military success was abandoned with it. From that moment on Egypt's war aims were doomed. After 14 October the Egyptian commanders were denied their ability to command and their troops paid the price despite fighting stubbornly to the end.

Although overshadowed by the charismatic Gamal Nasser, President Anwar Sadat skilfully imposed his authority over the Egyptian political and military hierarchy. Many of Nasser's cronies and political appointees in the armed forces were weeded out and more officers were promoted on merit. Having decided on war, Sadat entrusted a select band of approximately 20 officers with the detailed planning for the coming conflict, while he continued to pursue the stalled diplomatic negotiations on the world stage. In March 1973 he assumed the post of Egyptian Prime Minister and military Governor General to consolidate his power before the war began in October. Turning once again to diplomacy in the aftermath of the war, Sadat visited Jerusalem in November 1977. A peace accord was signed with Israel at the US President's Camp David retreat in September 1978 whereby the whole of the Sinai Peninsula was to be returned to Egypt. In the same year, Sadat was awarded the Nobel Peace Prize. It was a triumph by both military and diplomatic means and did much to restore Egyptian self-esteem. But it did little to improve the lot of the Egyptian people and, in a rising tide of Islamic fundamentalism, Sadat was assassinated in October 1981 during a military review to mark the successful crossing of the Suez Canal at the outset of the October War.

The Egyptian Minister of War, and as such Moshe Dayan's counterpart, was General Ahmed Ismail Ali. As the army Chief of Staff in Sinai, he was largely responsible for the disastrous campaign of 1967, when the Israelis comprehensively outfought the Egyptian army and President Gamal Nasser sacked him. However, he had friends in high places close to the President and Ismail was appointed as Chief of Staff in March 1969. In September he was sacked once more following an Israeli commando raid that caused much embarrassment to Nasser – the so-called 'Ten-Hour War' of 9 September when two of the latest T-62 Soviet tanks were captured. Ismail now loathed Nasser and attached himself to Sadat when he became President in 1970. His reward was the post of Minister of War in October 1972 at a time when he had been

A battery of M50 self-propelled 155mm howitzers fires in support of Israeli operations in the Sinai Desert. At the time of the October War the Israeli artillery arm was in a state of transition and had only just begun to procure modern self-propelled artillery pieces such as the M109. Most of its self-propelled artillery was still based on the venerable M4A3E8 Sherman chassis with an open-top fighting compartment.

diagnosed with cancer. His illness was to have a significant effect on his performance during the October War, when he proved indecisive and plodding. Nevertheless he devised the basic Egyptian strategy of a limited offensive to establish a bridgehead across the Suez Canal after the power of the IAF and the Israeli armoured corps had been neutralized by defensive missile screens. He succumbed to his illness in December 1974.

Ismail was ably supported by his chief of operations, Lieutenant General Mohamed Abd El Ghani Al Gamassy. He was in charge of the detailed planning for Operation *Badr* together with the commanders of the various branches of the armed forces, including Director of Armaments and Organization Major General Omar Gohar; Commander of Air Defence Major General Mohamed Ali Fahmy; Air Force Commander Air Vice Marshal Mohamed

Mubarak (now President of Egypt), and the man given the vital role of building the bridges across the canal, Commander of the Engineers Corps Major General Aly Mohamed.

Arguably, Egypt's finest soldier in 1973 was the Chief of Staff of the Egyptian armed forces, Lieutenant General Sa'ad Al Shazly. Born in a Nile Delta village in April 1922, Shazly was the founder of Egypt's airborne forces and he was the commander of the first paratroop battalion between 1954 and 1959. During the next two years he was the commander of the Arab contingent of the United Nations forces in the Congo. It was there that he fell out with General Ismail and they cordially loathed each other thereafter. This did nothing to help the Egyptian cause during the October War. Shazly was one of the few officers to gain any credit during the Six Day War when he was able to

A Soltam 160mm self-propelled heavy mortar is prepared for action in the Sinai Desert. Another Israeli self-propelled artillery weapon based on the Sherman M4A3E8 chassis, this breech-loaded heavy mortar is capable of accurate indirect fire out to a range of 10,000m (10,900yds) with a total of 56 mortar rounds carried on board the vehicle.

save most of his troops from the debacle. Thereafter he was appointed commander of the Egyptian Special Forces from 1967 to 1969 and commander of the Red Sea District from 1970 to 1971, when he became Chief of Staff of the Egyptian armed forces in May 1971. During the October War he was the overall commander of the assault crossing of the Suez Canal. He subsequently argued against the major offensive of October 14 and fell foul of Sadat. He quickly realized the danger of the Israeli incursion into Egypt and demanded the recall of the armoured formations on the east bank of the Suez Canal. He was overruled by Sadat and after the war, in December 1973, was sacked. Sidelined, he was given the diplomatic role of ambassador to Britain and then Portugal.

Very little information is available on the Egyptian army's field commanders during the October War. The GOC of Egyptian Second Field Army was Major General Mohamed Sa'ad Ma'amon and Third Field Army was commanded by Major General Abd El Al Mona'am Mohamed Wasel.

The constituent units of Second Army, 2nd Infantry Division, which attacked on the axis Ismailia–Tasa, were commanded by Brigadier General Hassan Ali Hassan Abu Sa'ada. The 18th Infantry Division, commanded by Brigadier General Abdel Rab Al Nabi Hafez, attacked from El Qantara towards El Arish. Brigadier General Fouad Aziz Ghali's 16th Infantry Division operated on the Deversoir–Tasa axis.

The Third Army's 7th Infantry Division, tasked with attacking from Shaloufa towards the strategically important Gidi Pass, was commanded by Brigadier General Ahmed Badawi Said Ahmed. Attacking from the city of Suez towards the equally vital Mitla Pass was the Egyptian 19th Infantry Division under Brigadier General Yousf Afifi Mohamed.

THE OCTOBER WAR

On 13 September 1973 Syrian fighters were scrambled to intercept an Israeli reconnaissance aircraft photographing Soviet shipping approaching the Syrian port of Latakia. In the ensuing battle with IDF top cover, 13 Syrian aircraft were shot down with no Israeli losses. The Syrians' well-advertised plans to meet further aggression provided a convenient cover for their concentration of forces on the Golan Heights. However, by the end of the month this deployment was sufficiently disturbing to prompt Moshe Dayan to order another armoured brigade to the Golan.

On the southern front, the Egyptians concentrated their forces under cover of Exercise Tahir 73 (Liberation 73), the annual autumn manoeuvres. Reservists were called up towards the end of September with the promise of release by 8 October. Activity along the Suez Canal was kept as normal as possible: Egyptian soldiers continued to fish and to walk along the embankment without helmets; civilians went about their work as usual. Nevertheless, Israeli forces in the Bar-Lev Line noted an increase in activity. Reports came in of artillery moving up to forward positions and troops moving into previously unoccupied SAM positions. Minefields were being cleared and underwater mines blown up or sown in new areas. Earth-moving equipment was much in evidence, as was the opening of passages to the waterline. But to the Israelis in the Bar-Lev Line there seemed no pattern to this apparently random activity. Israeli intelligence also failed to attach significance to the fact that Tahir 73 was taking place in Ramadan, a time when Muslims ordinarily avoid strenuous activity during the daylight hours.

On 30 September the situation was discussed by the Israeli High Command, which received a soothing intelligence appraisal from Major General Zeira, who stated that the probability of war was low, a view which won majority approval. At this crucial point in the Egyptian build-up, events in Europe conspired to distract the Israeli leadership further.

On 29 September five Russian Jews were taken hostage by Palestinian gunmen on the Czech-Austrian border, in what became known as the Schonau Incident. As a result the Israeli Prime Minister, Golda Meir, was absent in Europe until 3 October.

On 1 October, purely as a routine precaution, Major General Avraham Mandler's 252nd Armoured Division in Sinai went to the first stage of alert along the Suez Canal. On the same day, after making a thorough analysis of Egyptian activity, a junior officer, Lieutenant Benjamin Tov, on the Southern Command intelligence staff at Beersheba, informed his branch chief, Lieutenant Colonel David Gedaliah, that an Egyptian attack was imminent. His conclusions did not fit the overall Israeli intelligence picture and were ignored. Indeed, Tov was removed from his post but was subsequently reinstated by the Agranat Commission and promoted to the rank of captain.

On the following day, Major General Shmuel Gonen, the recently appointed GOC Southern Command (the entire southern sector of Israeli-occupied territory behind the Suez Canal – the Negev and Sinai), made a tour of the Bar-Lev Line, where he ordered a higher state of alert and a review of Operation *Shovach Yonim* (*Dovecote*). Gonen also issued orders to speed up the assembly of a prefabricated bridge to be used in the event of an Israeli crossing of the

Canal – an indication of the unrealistic thinking that pervaded the Israeli High Command in the last days before the October War.

On 3 October Anwar Sadat informed Soviet ambassador Vinogradoff of the imminent offensive. A similar meeting took place in Damascus conducted by President Assad. Sadat received tacit support with the proviso that Soviet shipping would leave Egyptian and Syrian harbours and civilians would be flown out of Cairo and Damascus. These movements were noted by Israeli intelligence, which warned Lieutenant General Elazar of the imminence of war. Mossad supported this view, but military intelligence remained certain that the pressures of détente would maintain the status quo in the Middle East. Zeira reasoned that if the Egyptians were indeed preparing themselves for war, the Soviets would have informed the Americans who in turn would pass the information to the Israelis. Nevertheless, Zeira, who was recovering from a brief illness, was beginning to feel uneasy about the developing situation. He received two further warnings via Mossad that war was about to erupt. Again Zeira did not act on the intelligence, which he regarded as too vague. Nor did Dayan, to whom the intelligence had also been passed by Mossad.

On 5 October Brigadier General Kalman Magen arrived in Sinai to succeed Major General Mandler as commander of the 252nd Armoured Division. Mandler had in his hands an aerial reconnaissance report of a new Egyptian artillery concentration on the Canal and other indications of warlike intent. The two generals decided to postpone the handover, but their request for reinforcements and the implementation of *Shovach Yonim* were refused on the grounds that they would be too provocative. A staff conference of Southern Command, held in mid-afternoon, reviewed all the preparations that had been made and discussed all the relevant plans. A decision was taken to despatch half the staff to visit the Suez front.

On 5 October the Egyptians infiltrated several dozen reconnaissance teams, some dressed as Bedouin, across the Canal. They reported back, 'The Israelis are asleep.' One of these teams and their radio transmitter fell into Israeli hands, but their captors did not know what to make of them.

On the northern front on the night of 5 October, the Syrians also moved their artillery forward, but the significance of this development was not appreciated by Israeli military intelligence. Nevertheless, Elazar placed the active army on the highest state of alert. It remained the belief of the Israeli GHQ that the active army was sufficient to absorb the impact of any offensive launched by Egypt and Syria.

Elazar was in a difficult situation. In the first week of October 1973 he was convinced that he was being fully informed by military intelligence and could expect adequate warning to order a general mobilization of the IDF. On 3 October he had told Israeli journalists, in answer to their questions, that in the

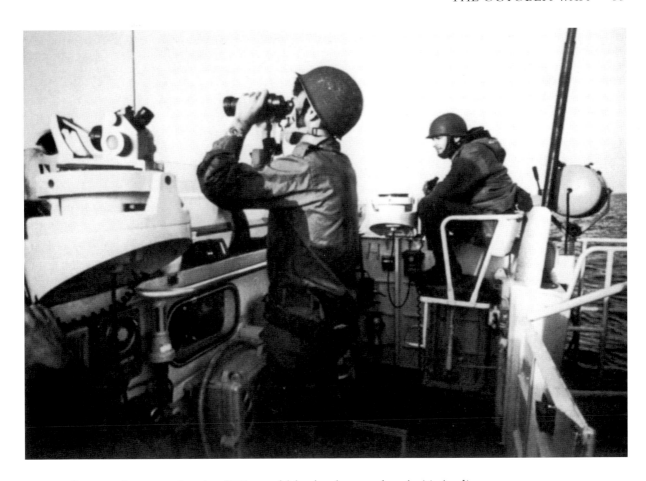

event of a complete surprise the IDF would be hard pressed to hold the line. After the war, Elazar told the Agranat Commission – established to report on the lessons of the October War – that a great deal of information about the probability of war was withheld from him. There were, he testified, items of information from Friday 5 October that indicated the imminence of war but which had not reached him until the morning of the 6th. Had he received this information, he would have ordered a general mobilization on Friday morning.

In peacetime Israel maintained a small cadre of regular forces along her borders with a large number of training and reserve units in the interior. The Israelis assumed that they would have at least 48 hours warning of an Arab attack, sufficient to call back their reservists from civilian occupations, fill out their skeleton formations and send them to the front. Mobilization was a well-rehearsed procedure and all reservists spent several weeks on duty each year.

Israel's Southern Command was about to take the full weight of the Egyptian onslaught. Its commander was General Shmuel Gonen, a soldier with a distinguished record. Gonen was not a glamorous martial figure like the dashing Moshe Dayan, being slight, intensely religious and somewhat pernickety in

Although the smallest element by far within the IDF, the Israeli Navy performed admirably during the Yom Kippur War and was the only service to escape severe criticism in the findings of the Agranat Commission into the conduct of the war.

A Sho't is re-armed with 105mm ammunition after a tank battle on Thursday 11 October. The prodigious consumption of ammunition during the war became critical for the Israelis after the first week and 105mm tank ammunition was a priority item when Operation *Nickel Grass* – the aerial re-supply from the United States – began on 13 October. The first C-5 Galaxy landed at Lod airport in Tel Aviv at 2201hrs Zulu carrying 97 tons of 155mm howitzer shells and 105mm tank ammunition. The first C-141 Starlifter landed at 2316hrs with more vital ammunition. Thereafter 4,000 tons of matériel were airlifted a day in six C-5 and 12 C-141 flights with all manner of ordnance and equipment – ECM pods to counter the SAM6, Shrike and Maverick missiles et al. A major propaganda coup was achieved when a C-5 Galaxy flew in an M60 MBT from a US base in West Germany and was off-loaded in front of world media representatives. Arab leaders were convinced that the United States was capable of replacing Israeli tank losses at will. In fact it was the only tank to be airlifted to Israel during the war. Indeed once the journalists had left the scene with their camera footage, the M60 was reloaded onto the Galaxy and returned to West Germany. Israeli tank losses were replaced from US stocks by sea some two months after the war ended. Operation *Nickel Grass* was vital to the Israeli war effort in October 1973 and in the words of Golda Meir – 'For generations to come all will be told of the miracle of the immense planes from the United States bringing in the material that meant life for our people.'

manner. Like Field Marshal Montgomery he abhorred his officers smoking. Nevertheless, he was technically competent and did not lack physical courage. He would, however, have his work cut out in the opening 48 hours of Operation *Badr*.

Operation *Badr*

At 0400hrs on the morning of 6 October, the ringing of his bedside telephone woke Major General Zeira. After a brief conversation he rang, in succession, Minister of Defense Moshe Dayan, Chief of Staff General David Elazar and Deputy Chief of Staff Major General Israel Tal. He told them that war would break out at around sunset that evening. Israeli intelligence had relayed details of Operation *Badr*, but significantly with the original H-Hour of 1800hrs.

Thirty minutes later the General Staff met and preliminary arrangements were made to prepare for mobilization, alert Civil Defence and evacuate the exposed settlements on the Golan Heights. Preparations were also made to launch a pre-emptive air strike against Syrian airfields and SAM sites. Shortly after 0700hrs, the commanders of both Northern and Southern Commands arrived at GHQ in Tel Aviv to be told by General Elazar to be ready for war at sunset and to be prepared to launch a major counterattack within 48 hours.

Shortly afterwards the Israeli inner cabinet was in session. Elazar urged full mobilization but Dayan was willing only to mobilize two divisions. The cabinet compromised with a mobilization of 100,000 men. At 1300hrs Elazar, acting on his own initiative, issued a far more widespread mobilization order. Tal gave orders that to speed the process, companies should be sent to the front as soon as they were ready rather than assembled in brigades and divisions. It was a critical decision, particularly in regards to the defence of the Golan Heights.

At this point Prime Minister Golda Meir vetoed any pre-emptive strike against Syria, having been warned by the US ambassador that American diplomatic and material support depended on Israel remaining the victim of aggression. At 1330hrs, only 30 minutes from H-Hour, Cairo Radio interrupted its programme with a spurious news flash that the Israelis had launched a raid on Zafarani on the Red Sea coast. This was followed half an hour later with an announcement that Egyptian troops were crossing the Suez Canal in reprisal. A substantial measure of surprise had been achieved.

At 1200hrs a warning had arrived at Major General Mandler's divisional HQ of an imminent artillery bombardment and instructing all forces to be on the alert. Mandler, who in 1967 had commanded an armoured brigade with distinction on the Golan Heights, was urged by his deputy to activate the *Shovach Yonim* plan and move his tanks forward to the Canal. Mandler issued the

An Egyptian MiG-17 attacking Israeli armour west of the Suez Canal, inside Africa. Despite being flown by Arab, Pakistani, North Korean, Cuban and even Russian pilots, the MiGs and Sukhois of the Egyptian Air Force were consistently outfought, suffering 172 aircraft lost in air-to-air combat.

At dawn on 14 October, following a massive air strike and artillery bombardment, 1,000 Egyptian tanks advanced out from under the protection of their SAM umbrella on three major axes. The Israelis were ready and by noon had destroyed 250 tanks and 200 other AFVs for the loss of just 20 of their own tanks. (EGIO)

order at 1345hrs after talking on the telephone to Gonen. In conclusion, Gonen observed that they had better move Mandler's tanks to the front now. Mandler replied with heavy irony, 'Yes, I suppose we had. We are being bombed at the moment.'

The crossing of the Canal had been preceded by an air assault. Some 200 Egyptian aircraft flew low over the Suez Canal and the Gulf of Suez to strike at Hawk SAM batteries, airfields, command posts, radar installations and supply bases. Also targeted was the strongpoint known as 'Budapest' on the Mediterranean coast east of Port Fuad. The attackers inflicted some damage but lost nearly 40 aircraft in dogfights and to ground fire. Simultaneously, two Egyptian Tu-16 bombers flew low over the Mediterranean to launch two AS-5 Kelt missiles at Tel Aviv in an attempt to deter the IAF from strategic bombing by sending the message that its own aircraft could hit civilian centres. One missile fell into the sea and an IAF fighter downed the other. A further 14 Tupolevs attacked targets in the Sinai Desert with Kelt missiles, with some success.

Along the Canal front, over 2,000 guns began a bombardment of the Bar-Lev Line. Howitzers and heavy mortars began to pour shells on its forts, minefields and barbed wire entanglements. 'Katyusha' rocket launchers and 'Frog' surface-to-surface missile batteries opened up. Their fire was supplemented by tanks that had climbed on to previously prepared positions atop the sand ramparts on the western bank of the Suez Canal to engage the

Israelis with direct fire. During the first minute of Operation *Badr*, 10,500 shells fell on the Israeli first line of defence.

Assault crossing

Every aspect of the crossing operation had been planned in the greatest detail. Ten bridges were to be thrown over the Canal: three in the El Qantara sector; three in the sector Ismailia–Deversoir; and four in the sector Geneifa–Suez. The first Egyptian wave was tasked with seizing and holding the earth and sand ramparts of the Bar-Lev Line. When the second wave arrived on the east bank, the troops of the first wave were to advance another 180m (200yds) and hold their positions. The third and fourth waves, due to arrive an hour after the opening of the assault, would join the first and second waves. The entire force would move forward as soon as the support units joined it. It was the task of the first wave of attacking infantry to advance up to 3km (2 miles), while specially trained infantry units dealt with the strongpoints. It was planned that each bridgehead would expand to a width of 8km (5 miles) and 5.6km (3½ miles) deep. With the arrival of tanks and artillery, they would then expand to 16km (10 miles) wide and 8km (5 miles) deep.

An M48 Magach rocks back on its suspension as it engages Egyptian forces with its 105mm main armament. Superior training, a flexible command structure and better equipment were the key elements in Israel's superiority in armoured warfare during the October War.

Shortly after the bombardment opened, commando units equipped with Sagger wire-guided anti-tank guided weapons (ATGWs) and rocket-propelled grenades (RPGs), crossed the Canal at a number of points, scaled the ramparts on the eastern bank and headed for the empty Israeli ramps to deny the IDF tanks their pre-planned firing positions. The Soviet-supplied Sagger (the NATO codename for the 9M14M Malyutka wire-guided anti-tank missile) could be carried by a single infantryman, was guided to its target by means of a sight and joystick and was capable of penetrating the thickest armour. When used in combination with the close-range RPG-7 unguided rocket-propelled grenade, the Sagger gave the Egyptian infantry a powerful counter to IDF armour whenever the latter attacked without infantry support of their own.

In the citizen army of the IDF, women perform a significant number of support roles including communications and intelligence analysis. Here a female soldier collates data at the Refidim administrative headquarters of Southern Command on 14 October 1973, the day of the major Egyptian offensive into the Sinai Desert. Refidim was the principal supply and command complex of the IDF in the Sinai and was a target for Egyptian fighter-bombers in the opening hours of the war.

EGYPTIAN ASSAULT CROSSING OF THE SUEZ CANAL, 6 OCTOBER 1973

An opposed crossing of a major waterway remains one of the most difficult military operations of all. In October 1973 the sand ramparts of the Bar-Lev Line comprised over 1.5 billion cubic metres of sand and rubble. They were quite impervious to conventional explosives and engineer earth-moving equipment would have taken days to create any passages through them. Several foreign observers believed the ramparts could only be breached by tactical nuclear weapons, but a group of Egyptian engineers thought differently. Having worked on the construction of the Aswan High Dam, they had found that high-pressure water hoses could move large quantities of soil and sand. Large numbers of generator-driven high-pressure pumps were acquired for the 'Cairo Fire Department' from Britain and West Germany. The first trials of this method were conducted in September 1969 and proved a capacity to shift 500 cubic metres per hour. Once the technique had been refined it was found a gap could be created in three to four hours. It was this method that was used to break through the great sand berms (left background) on 6 October, creating the gaps through which the Egyptian troops poured. The bottom of the gap was then levelled by bulldozers and lined with steel matting to allow the passage of tanks and other vehicles. As the engineers breached the ramparts, Egyptian artillery bombarded the Israeli strongpoints along the Bar-Lev Line (far left background) to prevent the defenders from observing or interfering with the crossing. At the same time Mi-8 helicopters

transported Egyptian Al Saaqa Commandos behind Israeli lines to disrupt the movement of reinforcements to the Canal. At 1430hrs the first troops landed on the east bank of the Suez Canal (centre background). In the first wave were 720 assault boats carrying 4,000 men. The gradient of the sand rampart was difficult for soldiers to climb with just their personal weapons and kit, so heavier weapons such as ATGW and anti-aircraft missiles were carried in four-wheel carts (right background) that were designed specifically for Operation *Badr*. Thousands of scooter wheels were purchased from Vespa and Lambretta of Italy and 2,240 carts went to war carrying 336 tons of Sagger ATGWs and Strela shoulder-launched, anti-aircraft missiles deep into the Sinai to counter the IAF and Armoured Corps. Tests demonstrated that the carts could be dragged up the sand berms relatively easily. Egyptian assault troops (right foreground) can be seen paddling across the canal to the rhythmic chant of 'Allahu-Akbar' (God is Great). They are equipped with a mixture of 7.62mm AKM assault rifles and Egyptian-manufactured 9mm Port Said submachine guns. They are also equipped with Soviet helmets and respirators but the rest of the uniform is of local manufacture, apart from the water bottle and its M1941 cover, which is of American origin. The OT-62 TOPAS amphibious armoured transporter (left foreground) acted as a rescue boat during the initial assault and supported the engineers by towing their generators and pumps across the Canal. (Kevin Lyles © Osprey Publishing Ltd)

At 1420hrs, as the Egyptian aircraft returned from their bombing sorties, the first wave of 4,000 assault infantry swarmed across the Canal in rubber boats, aiming for the 'dead' areas between the manned forts of the Bar-Lev Line, which were restricted to a field of fire extending to about 1km (0.6 miles) on either side. General Shazly later described the scene: 'The men of Wave One poured over our ramparts and slithered in disciplined lines down to the water's edge. The dinghies were readied, 720 of them, and, as the canisters began to belch clouds of covering smoke, our first assault wave was paddling furiously across the Canal, their strokes falling into the rhythm of their chant, "Allahu Akbar … Allahu Akbar [God is Great]."'

The Egyptians had anticipated that they would incur heavy casualties in this phase of the operation, and the need for personal sacrifice had been hammered home during the months of training. Fierce automatic fire from the forts of the Bar-Lev Line took its toll but the majority of Egyptian assault troops reached the eastern bank only six minutes after the guns had opened up. Flexible assault ladders were dragged up the sand ramparts and the infantry, accompanied by tank-killing squads and artillery observation parties, scaled the ramparts and began to push inland to establish a defensive front 3km (2 miles) from the Canal while specially trained units engaged the strongpoints in the Bar-Lev Line itself.

Six minutes later the second echelon companies of the assault battalions paddled away from the west bank of the Canal, to be followed 12 minutes later by battalion heavy-weapons teams and then, at H+40 minutes, a complete ammunition re-supply. One hour after the initial assault the remaining battalions of the assault brigades pushed off, followed within another hour by the leading elements of the second-wave brigades.

By 1500hrs Mandler was in no doubt that the Egyptians were launching a major attack all along the Canal front. Within another two hours it was also clear that the crossing of the Canal was a large-scale amphibious operation along its entire length. (Ironically, just such an operation had been the basis of an Israeli staff exercise in 1971.) The Egyptian infantry divisions were now well on the way to establishing a bridgehead up to 7km (4 miles) wide and were also using their high-pressure hoses to blast gaps through the sand ramparts to make vehicle exits for their mechanized and armoured formations. North of the Great Bitter Lake this had worked admirably. However, to the south of the lake, the hoses had reduced the clay-based ramparts to a glutinous slurry, eventually obliging the Egyptian engineers to bring up bulldozers and explosives. By 1615hrs eight infantry waves were across the Canal, ten brigades numbering some 25,000 men, concentrated in five divisional bridgeheads

In his headquarters, Major General Gonen anxiously tried to assess the situation as reports flowed back along the buried communication lines from the

18 manned fortifications in the Bar-Lev Line, which were garrisoned by 436 men of the 68th Infantry Battalion from the Jerusalem Brigade, mostly reservists completing their annual training. Where the troops had manned their firing positions, they were able to beat back the Egyptians, but the latter broke into the fortifications where the defenders had been ordered to take shelter on the assumption that the enemy had launched only an artillery attack. The Egyptian anti-tank teams, who had occupied the firing ramps, roughly handled the armoured forces rushed up to relieve the strongpoints. However, it should be noted that, in spite of fighting against overwhelming odds, not one of the Maozim was abandoned without orders. On the morning of 7 October the order was given for Israeli troops to evacuate the Bar-Lev Line; most did but some fought on.

While the Egyptians were blasting their way though the ramparts of the Bar-Lev Line, the Soviet-supplied amphibious vehicles and bridging equipment were brought up to specially prepared launching sites on the west bank. This

Half hidden in a hull-down position behind a pile of rocks, an M60 Magach engages enemy armour. It was from positions such as this that Israeli tanks broke up the great Egyptian offensive of 14 October by engaging at long ranges with heavy artillery support to suppress any Sagger teams. In this way the Israelis achieved an astonishing victory, destroying 250 tanks at a loss of just 20 to themselves.

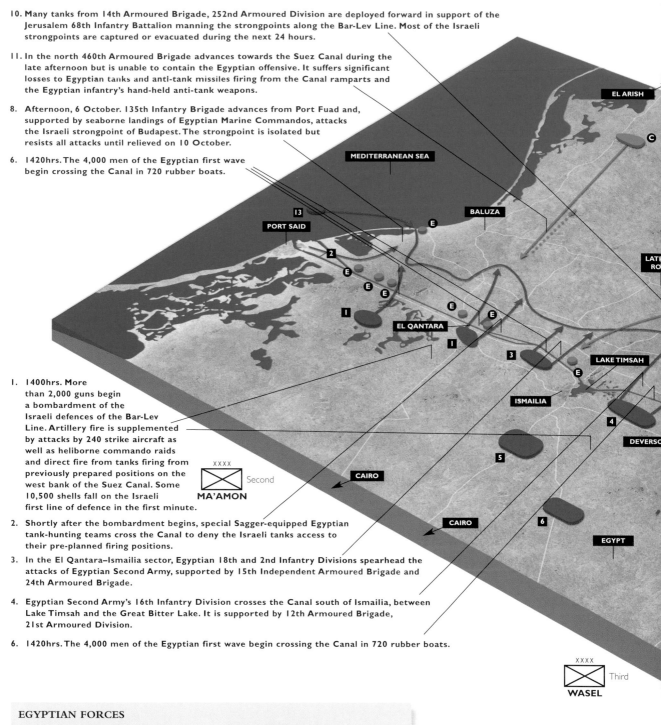

10. Many tanks from 14th Armoured Brigade, 252nd Armoured Division are deployed forward in support of the Jerusalem 68th Infantry Battalion manning the strongpoints along the Bar-Lev Line. Most of the Israeli strongpoints are captured or evacuated during the next 24 hours.

11. In the north 460th Armoured Brigade advances towards the Suez Canal during the late afternoon but is unable to contain the Egyptian offensive. It suffers significant losses to Egyptian tanks and anti-tank missiles firing from the Canal ramparts and the Egyptian infantry's hand-held anti-tank weapons.

8. Afternoon, 6 October. 135th Infantry Brigade advances from Port Fuad and, supported by seaborne landings of Egyptian Marine Commandos, attacks the Israeli strongpoint of Budapest. The strongpoint is isolated but resists all attacks until relieved on 10 October.

6. 1420hrs. The 4,000 men of the Egyptian first wave begin crossing the Canal in 720 rubber boats.

EL ARISH

MEDITERRANEAN SEA

BALUZA

PORT SAID

LATI RO

EL QANTARA

LAKE TIMSAH

ISMAILIA

1. 1400hrs. More than 2,000 guns begin a bombardment of the Israeli defences of the Bar-Lev Line. Artillery fire is supplemented by attacks by 240 strike aircraft as well as heliborne commando raids and direct fire from tanks firing from previously prepared positions on the west bank of the Suez Canal. Some 10,500 shells fall on the Israeli first line of defence in the first minute.

xxxx
Second
MA'AMON

CAIRO

DEVERSO

CAIRO

EGYPT

2. Shortly after the bombardment begins, special Sagger-equipped Egyptian tank-hunting teams cross the Canal to deny the Israeli tanks access to their pre-planned firing positions.

3. In the El Qantara–Ismailia sector, Egyptian 18th and 2nd Infantry Divisions spearhead the attacks of Egyptian Second Army, supported by 15th Independent Armoured Brigade and 24th Armoured Brigade.

4. Egyptian Second Army's 16th Infantry Division crosses the Canal south of Ismailia, between Lake Timsah and the Great Bitter Lake. It is supported by 12th Armoured Brigade, 21st Armoured Division.

6. 1420hrs. The 4,000 men of the Egyptian first wave begin crossing the Canal in 720 rubber boats.

xxxx
Third
WASEL

EGYPTIAN FORCES

Second Army – MajGen Ma'amon

1 18th Infantry Division – BrigGen Hafez
2 135th Infantry Brigade
3 2nd Infantry Division – BrigGen Sa'ada
4 16th Infantry Division – BrigGen Ghali
5 21st Armoured Division
6 23rd Mechanized Division

Third Army – MajGen Wasel

7   7th Infantry Division – BrigGen Ahmed
8   19th Infantry Division – BrigGen Mohamed
9   4th Armured Division
10 3rd Mechanized Division
11 6th Mechanized Division
12 130th Independent Marine Brigade
13 Egyptian Navy units

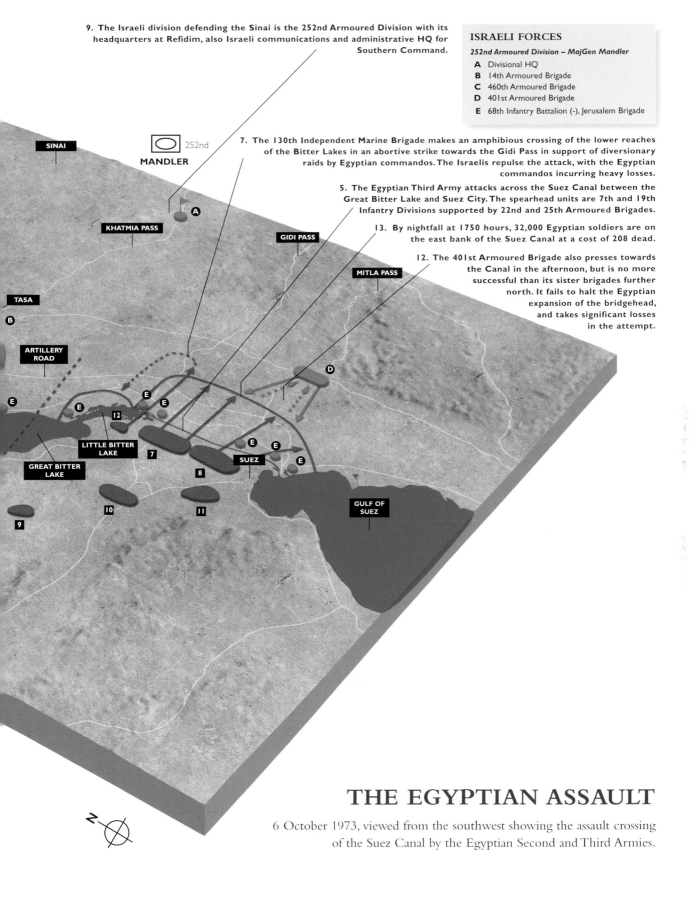

9. The Israeli division defending the Sinai is the 252nd Armoured Division with its headquarters at Refidim, also Israeli communications and administrative HQ for Southern Command.

252nd

MANDLER

7. The 130th Independent Marine Brigade makes an amphibious crossing of the lower reaches of the Bitter Lakes in an abortive strike towards the Gidi Pass in support of diversionary raids by Egyptian commandos. The Israelis repulse the attack, with the Egyptian commandos incurring heavy losses.

5. The Egyptian Third Army attacks across the Suez Canal between the Great Bitter Lake and Suez City. The spearhead units are 7th and 19th Infantry Divisions supported by 22nd and 25th Armoured Brigades.

13. By nightfall at 1750 hours, 32,000 Egyptian soldiers are on the east bank of the Suez Canal at a cost of 208 dead.

12. The 401st Armoured Brigade also presses towards the Canal in the afternoon, but is no more successful than its sister brigades further north. It fails to halt the Egyptian expansion of the bridgehead, and takes significant losses in the attempt.

SINAI

KHATMIA PASS

GIDI PASS

MITLA PASS

TASA

ARTILLERY ROAD

LITTLE BITTER LAKE

GREAT BITTER LAKE

SUEZ

GULF OF SUEZ

THE EGYPTIAN ASSAULT

6 October 1973, viewed from the southwest showing the assault crossing of the Suez Canal by the Egyptian Second and Third Armies.

equipment included 50-ton motorized rafts, each capable of ferrying four MBTs or up to ten trucks with four guns and trailers or 16 jeeps (the 96-ton rafts had twice this capacity); and PMP pontoon bridging trains which could be assembled in less than an hour. The bridges were assembled in prefabricated sections that slotted into each other, making them easy to repair if damaged by artillery or air attack. The Egyptians also brought up dummy bridges to absorb the attention of the IAF.

Within ten hours of the first crossing, the organic battalions of the infantry divisions were moving over the Canal to join their parent formations. They were to be followed within an hour by the divisional artillery and support elements. On the southern front, running from the Great Bitter Lake to the Gulf of Suez, the crossing was made by the Egyptian Third Army, commanded by Major General Wasel. Spearheading the assault were the 19th and 7th Infantry divisions supported by the 22nd and 25th Armoured brigades, the latter moving over the Canal on the morning of 7 October. Moving up behind them were the 4th Armoured and 6th Mechanized divisions. In the northern sector, from the Great Bitter Lake to El Cap, where the Canal ran on to Port Said through swampy ground, the assault of Major General Sa'ad Ma'amon's Second Army was led by three infantry divisions – 16th, 2nd and 18th – supported by the 14th, 24th and 15th Armoured Brigades and the 21st Armoured and 23rd Mechanized Divisions close behind.

The Canal crossing had gone like clockwork. In the planning stage the Egyptians had calculated that they might sustain up to 30,000 casualties in the initial phase. In fact, their losses amounted to little more than 200 killed. The commander of one of Third Army's two infantry divisions, which ran into determined Israeli resistance, later noted that he suffered 10 per cent casualties in the initial assault, a third of the figure he anticipated. A single Israeli tank had held up his men for 30 minutes before it was overwhelmed. To their amazement it was discovered that the entire tank crew were dead with the exception of one wounded man who had fought on alone. As he was borne away on a stretcher this brave soldier saluted the Egyptian general.

Not all Egyptian operations proceeded so smoothly. One of the subsidiary operations involved an eastward advance by the 135th Infantry Brigade 11km (7 miles) along the coast road from Port Fuad to link up with seaborne support to storm the Israeli strongpoint known as Budapest, situated on a sandbank on the edge of the Mediterranean. Budapest was manned by 18 men under the command of a reserve officer, Captain Motti Ashkenazi, and was the only position along the Bar-Lev Line to be reinforced by a platoon of tanks, in accordance with standing orders.

On the afternoon of 6 October the Egyptians attacked Budapest with a force that included 16 tanks, 16 APCs and jeeps mounting recoilless anti-tank guns. In

the ensuing clash, eight APCs and seven tanks were set ablaze. After the arrival of an Egyptian Marine Commando unit, Budapest was isolated and an Israeli relief force ambushed and destroyed. Ashkenazi was finally relieved on 10 October by a force personally led by Brigadier General Magen. However, the defenders of Budapest quickly found themselves surrounded once again by Egyptian commandos. After heavy fighting, the Israelis reopened the route to Budapest, which held out until the end of the war having withstood everything that the Egyptian armed forces could throw at it. It also earned the distinction of being the only frontline position in the Bar-Lev Line that did not fall to the Egyptians. Captain Ashkenazi subsequently became a leading member of the pressure group protesting the IDF's conduct of the war and a prime mover in the resignation of Minister of Defense Moshe Dayan.

The Egyptian commandos, who had been landed along the entire Sinai front, from Port Fuad in the north to Sharm El-Sheikh at the tip of the Sinai Peninsula, did not enjoy the same success as their army colleagues in the opening phases of Operation *Badr*. An attempt was made to cross the Great Bitter Lake by 130th Marine Brigade, employing PT-76 amphibious tanks. The aim was to

During the Yom Kippur War the IDF possessed only 570 artillery pieces with a calibre greater than 100mm whereas the Arabs had 2,055. After the heavy tank losses to Saggers and RPGs, artillery was increasingly used to counter the exposed ATGW teams. Here an M109 155mm self-propelled howitzer fires on Egyptian troops.

bypass Israeli forces and link up with heliborne commando forces in the area of the Mitla and Gidi passes. However, 14 of the commandos' helicopters were shot down by the IAF and those units that managed to survive the carnage were surrounded and captured before they could close the passes to the Israeli reinforcements rushing up from the east.

During the night of 6/7 October the Egyptians had pushed about 500 tanks across the Canal and a great quantity of artillery and APCs, much of it in the Second Army sector. In the southern sector little heavy equipment got across. Nevertheless, by late morning on 7 October five infantry divisions had crossed the Canal, each with a brigade of tanks and battalions of SU-100 self-propelled guns and BRDM mobile AT-3 Sagger launchers. To the north of the Great Bitter Lake, Egyptian infantry supported by tanks pushed into Sinai.

An Israeli Katyusha battery lays down a devastating curtain of fire during a bombardment of Egyptian positions. In the foreground, a battery of M50 155mm howitzers prepares to fire. (IDF)

Shovach Yonim

The Israeli High Command was unaware of the operational pause that the Egyptians were to impose after crossing the Canal. They feared that the Egyptians would bring their armoured and mechanized reserve across the Canal and drive for the vital Gidi and Mitla passes. When they failed to halt the Egyptians at the canal waterline, they resolved to stop them at the line of the Artillery Road (in fact the planned limit of advance in the first phase of Operation *Badr*).

However, on the evening of 6 October the Israelis were still in confusion. Early in the evening General Elazar described the situation as 'reasonable', a view prompted by a helicopter trip to the Gidi and Mitla passes made by Mandler's deputy, Brigadier General Pino. Elazar optimistically anticipated an Israeli crossing of the Canal the next day, even though the bridging equipment was not yet ready. The fog of war had enveloped the battlefield in the south.

At Mandler's headquarters there was similar confusion. Mandler's armoured forces were moving forward but with no clear picture of the developing battle. In the northern sector the 460th Brigade commanded by Colonel Gaby Amir was moving to block what was anticipated to be the main Egyptian thrust. Colonel Amnon Reshef's 14th Armoured Brigade was moving westward in the centre while in the south Colonel Dan Shomron's 401st Armoured Brigade was rushed through the Gidi Pass to a position south of the Great Bitter Lake.

Amir divided his force and attempted to reach two fortifications at Mifreket, on El Balah Island, and the stronghold east of El Qantara known as 'Milano'. He ran into fierce resistance and early on the morning of the 7th was ordered by Brigadier General Magen, who had assumed control in the northern sector, to withdraw his force and evacuate the fortification at Mifreket. In fighting his way through to Mifreket, Amir's brigade had been reduced to 20 tanks. Amir's battered force extracted itself to regroup.

In the central sector, Colonel Amnon Reshef, the commander of 14th Armoured Brigade, was denied his pre-planned positions on the Canal by Egyptian anti-tank units equipped with RPGs. Their fire was augmented by Saggers and Egyptian tanks on the west bank of the Canal, whose positions overlooked the approaching Israeli armour. On the 16km (10-mile) front Firdan–Ismailia, all but two of Reshef's tanks were knocked out. Throughout the night the two tanks held the crossroads at Firdan against a force of some 50 Egyptian tanks.

In the southern sector, Colonel Dan Shomron had been ordered not to move forward until the afternoon of the 6th, but at 1400hrs had come under attack by Egyptian warplanes. He divided his brigade of approximately 100 tanks, and at 1600hrs sent one battalion through the Mitla Pass, one battalion through the Gidi Pass and a third battalion through the Khatmia Pass, in case the Egyptians had blocked the two main routes into the Sinai.

Ammunition is the lifeblood of war and it was expended in far higher quantities than anyone had imagined or planned for during the October War. By the end of the great Egyptian offensive of 14 October, the IDF was critically short of 105mm tank ammunition; indeed its planned counter-offensive across the Suez Canal remained in jeopardy for want of ammunition until thousands of rounds were flown to Israel by the US Air Force at the outset of Operation *Nickel Grass*; one of the largest air re-supply operations in history.

Shomron, who in 1976 was the overall commander of the Entebbe raid, was responsible for a 56km (35-mile) front, stretching from the junction of the Great and Little Bitter Lakes south to Ras Masala, 19km (12 miles) south of Suez. In Shomron's sector the Israelis were facing some 650 tanks of the Egyptian 19th and 7th Infantry Divisions, 6th Mechanized Division and 4th Armoured Division, augmented by 130th Marine Brigade, tasked with the crossing of the Great Bitter Lake and blocking of the Gidi and Mitla passes. Shomron was outnumbered by a factor of over six to one.

Shomron's immediate objective was to link with the Bar-Lev fortifications besieged by the Egyptians. By the evening of 6 October he had achieved this objective. Only at Port Tewfik, on the breakwater opposite Suez and garrisoned by 42 regular army soldiers, was Shomron thwarted. The approaches to the 'Quay' fortification had been mined and were invested by thousands of Egyptian troops supported by tanks and artillery. Nevertheless, Shomron had been unable to obtain Mandler's agreement either to evacuate or reinforce the strongpoints and his losses had been heavy. By 0800hrs on Sunday 7 October, only 23 of his tanks were still 'runners'. Two-thirds of Shomron's losses in the entire October War had been

THE OCTOBER WAR • 71

incurred in the first night of action. He was now ordered to break all contacts with the Bar-Lev Line and concentrate on blocking the Egyptian advance.

Aware of his desperate situation – his three artillery batteries faced 75 batteries of Egyptian guns – Shomron concentrated his battered brigade and, husbanding his resources, hit the Egyptians in a long-range fire and movement battle, denying the enemy any chance to bring numbers to bear. It was not until 9 October that the Egyptians were in turn able to launch two mechanized brigades across the Artillery Road towards the Mitla Pass. Again Israeli tactical flexibility carried the day. Shomron counterattacked, destroying at least 20 Egyptian tanks and many APCs and forcing the Egyptians to withdraw.

On the morning of 7 October, however, the Israelis had little or nothing to celebrate. Two forts in the Bar-Lev Line obeyed the order to surrender. Five more had been abandoned, some of their garrisons making their way back to the Israeli lines on foot, others riding on the tanks sent to relieve them. Some platoons were ambushed and wiped out by Egyptian infantry as they headed for the Artillery Road. Of the 252nd Division's tanks, 153 (60 per cent) had been put out of action, many of them left stranded in the Egyptian bridgeheads, their burning hulks festooned with the guide wires of the Sagger missiles that destroyed them. They had inflicted losses on the Egyptians but had not disrupted the planned development of Operation *Badr*.

As the war progressed, the Israelis pressed into service all their tanks held in strategic reserve including the elderly World War II-vintage Shermans. Over the years, these Shermans had been heavily modified and were now armed with an innovative French 105mm gun firing high-explosive anti-tank (HEAT) ammunition. Despite their age, the Shermans proved effective both in the Sinai and on the Golan Heights against the Syrians and Iraqis.

There was confusion and a loss of morale in the units engaged in the opening phase of fighting. On his arrival at Tasa Base, situated on the Lateral Road 40km (25 miles) east of the Canal, Major General Sharon was dismayed at the apparent bewilderment of Israeli troops: 'Suddenly something was happening to them that had never happened before. These were soldiers who had been brought up on victories… It was a generation that had never lost. Now they were in a state of shock… How was it that [the Egyptians] were moving forward and we were defeated?'

In the late afternoon of 6 October the IAF had flown dozens of ground-support missions against the Egyptian bridgeheads. As darkness fell, it resorted to flares to locate and destroy the bridges. However, the IAF had only a limited ability to mount night operations, and these attacks did little to slow down the Egyptian timetable. Early on the morning of Sunday 7 October, the General Staff decided to disregard the Syrian offensive on the Golan Heights, where the IDF was believed to be holding, and throw the weight of the IAF against the Egyptians. Its Phantom and Mirage squadrons were given the task of destroying the anti-aircraft missile network between the Canal and Cairo, clearing the sky over the Suez Canal for ground-attack missions.

The Israeli jets took off at 0700hrs on the first stage of their mission, flew through the missile screen and hit a number of radar sites and airfields near the Canal and in the Nile Valley. They returned to their bases to refuel and rearm before launching massed attacks on the Egyptian missile umbrella in the Suez Canal zone. At this point they were abruptly switched back to the Golan front by Moshe Dayan, who, bypassing normal channels, told the commander of the IAF, General Benjamin Peled, that the 'Third Temple' (code for Israel) was in the utmost danger as Syrian tanks had broken through on the Golan and were plunging down the slopes towards the Jordan Valley. The IAF had to halt the Syrian armour. Dayan told Peled that the Sinai was mere sand; in the north Israeli homes were now in danger.

To the dismay of his senior staff, Peled turned the IAF back towards the Golan, leaving the Egyptian anti-aircraft network intact and the tank brigades without air support. Dayan compounded the strategic confusion that afternoon by recommending a withdrawal to a defence line on the Gidi and Mitla passes to Golda Meir, only to have the recommendation rejected by General Elazar.

By 0800hrs on 7 October the battle of the Suez Canal crossings had been won. According to General Shazly, Egyptian losses had been five aircraft, 20 tanks and 208 killed. In 18 hours the Egyptians had passed across the Canal 90,000 men, 850 tanks and 11,000 vehicles. Within another four hours, the Egyptian 7th Infantry Division and 25th Armoured Brigade had crossed with all their forces south of the Bitter Lakes.

Known as the Kurnass or Sledgehammer in Israeli service, the McDonnell Douglas F-4 Phantom was the Israeli Air Force's primary fighter-bomber during the October War. It was capable of carrying 7 tons of external ordnance including air-to-air missiles, bombs and ECM pods. The Phantom was used extensively against the Egyptian bridges across the Suez Canal in the first days of the war when they suffered severe losses; 33 Israeli Phantoms were downed during the war. After American promises that Israeli aircraft losses would be replaced on a one-for-one basis, 34 Phantoms were supplied to the IAF during the war with the first arriving on 14 October. With their darker USAF camouflage scheme, these reinforcements were known as Toad or Karpada in Hebrew and were committed to action as soon as possible. As Israel faced the prospect of defeat in the opening days of the Yom Kippur War, preparations were made to arm a squadron of Phantoms for a nuclear strike with 8 Kurnass to carry 20-kiloton weapons and five other aircraft acting as escorts. The implicit threat of nuclear warfare prompted the US government to mount Operation *Nickel Grass*.

The Israelis were still off balance and effectively without armour in the tactical zone. Egyptian military intelligence had forecast that the main blows of the IDF's mobilized reserves would fall within eight hours of the assault. But 18 hours had passed without any sign that the enemy's reserves had been committed. It now appeared that a counter-blow would not fall until 8 or 9 October. Shazly recalled: 'For both sides, Sunday was a race to prepare for that big battle. The very success of our deception operations had handed the enemy some advantages in this race. The principal benefit was that our deployments were fully revealed: the five sectors; the heavily reinforced infantry divisions in each; our tactics at the perimeters; the caution of our steady moves forward; the nature, density and effectiveness of our portable SAM and ATGW. The enemy could plan their counterattack on fairly full knowledge. Had their reserves been available in the later stages of our initial assault, by contrast, they would have attacked in considerable ignorance of our plans and of what our infantry could achieve.'

The next phase, up to 11 October, was to be devoted entirely to the defensive: consolidating and extending the long, shallow Egyptian bridgehead while inflicting maximum losses as the IDF counterattacked. Simultaneously the Egyptians would push down the coast of the Sinai towards Ras Sudur and Sharm El-Sheikh.

The first Israeli counterattack

The IDF High Command, dominated by veterans of Israel's Armoured Corps, were disciples of the doctrine of the concentrated armoured punch. This belief had not been dented by the setbacks of the first two days of battle. Rather Elazar and Gonen – now established in his advanced headquarters in Um Kusheiba – believed that the initial piecemeal commitment of armoured formations, in platoons and companies, had led to their being mauled by Egyptian armour, artillery and, in particular, infantry well armed and trained in the anti-tank role. Divisional- and brigade-strength blows delivered by the Israelis would be a different matter.

Elazar and Gonen persuaded a depressed Dayan to sanction a thrust in the Sinai by two fresh reserve armoured divisions, 162nd and 143rd, mobilized under the command, respectively, of Major General Adan in the northern sector of Sinai and Major General Sharon in the south. On the evening of 7 October, at Southern Command headquarters, General Elazar outlined the plan to destroy the Egyptian bridgeheads. The Israelis would roll southwards along the east bank of the Canal, leaving a distance of 3km (2 miles) between the Canal and the IDF right flank to minimize the threat of Egyptian anti-tank fire from their positions on the Canal ramparts. Adan's division was to strike from the area south of El Qantara at the Egyptian Second Army while Sharon's division was withheld in the Tasa area. If Adan's attack went according to plan, Sharon would launch an attack southward from the Great Bitter Lake against the Egyptian Third Army. However, if Adan's attack was in danger of failing, Sharon's division would be thrown in to support it. Elazar insisted that Sharon's division would initially act as a reserve to Adan's northern attack and would be activated on his approval alone. When ordering the offensive and subsequently, Elazar emphasized the objective of breaking up the Egyptian bridgeheads on the east bank. Gonen, in contrast, stressed exploiting success by crossing the Suez Canal. He told the IAF to stop the bombing of the Egyptian bridges immediately to the north of the Great Bitter Lake as they were to be used in an Israeli crossing. Neither Elazar nor Gonen were aware of the 'operational pause' built into Operation *Badr*. Their attack was, therefore, in part aimed at blunting Egyptian preparations to race for the Mitla and Gidi passes.

The SAM-3 'Goa' was a static anti-aircraft missile system that provided low- to medium-altitude coverage from 106m (350ft) to 4,550m (15,000ft) to supplement the high-altitude SAM-2 'Guideline'. Both missiles had a slant range of approximately 32km (20 miles). By the time of the October War, the Suez Canal, and the Egyptian Air Force airfields defending it, were protected by the densest integrated air defence system in the world, with some 150 SAM-2 and SAM-3 emplacements, together with 40 mobile SAM-6 'Gainful' batteries and numerous anti-aircraft weapons such as the highly effective self-propelled ZSU-23-4 'Shilka'. Furthermore, many Egyptian units were equipped with multiple shoulder-launched SAM-7 'Strela' weapons. Although the latter destroyed relatively few Israeli aircraft, they forced them to fly higher where they became vulnerable to the 'Gainful'/'Shilka' combination and at higher altitudes still to 'Goa' and 'Guideline' missiles. Once Israeli ground troops crossed the Suez Canal a priority task was to destroy these static missile sites to allow the IAF clear skies to undertake its multifarious missions.

There was another factor that was to compromise Adan's attack – the persistent belief that dash and drive would overcome Egyptian doggedness. Adan's division, brimming with confidence, set off with hardly any artillery support, as its self-propelled pieces and ammunition trains were still crawling across central Sinai. The IAF, torn between competing crises in the north and south, could only provide 62 ground support missions between 0800hrs and 1500hrs on 8 October.

Adan deployed along the main Lateral Road running east from Baluzi. The 460th Armoured Brigade, commanded by Colonel Gaby Amir, was to advance southwards between the Suez Canal and the Artillery Road, destroy the enemy in the area and reach the fortifications opposite Firdan and Ismailia respectively. On his left, and still west of the Artillery Road, Colonel Natke Nir's 217th Reserve Armoured Brigade was to drive south towards the Purkan fortifications opposite Ismailia. Colonel Nir was a remarkable character. He had been gravely wounded in the legs in the Six Day War and subsequently underwent over 20 operations. He had stayed on combat duty through sheer willpower, having to be hoisted into his tank, like a medieval knight onto his horse.

The 500th Reserve Armoured Brigade, led by Colonel Arieh Keren, was to advance south, east of the Artillery Road towards Matzmed, at the northern tip of the Great Bitter Lake, where a limited crossing of the Canal was to be attempted on Egyptian bridges if they could be seized intact. Once Adan had destroyed Egyptian forces east of the Canal, Magen's forces moving down from the north would mop up the survivors.

The Bell 205 helicopter was used in several clandestine missions against the Egyptian air defence system, including electronic warfare, the insertion of commandos behind enemy lines and as spotters for SAM missile launches to warn other Israeli Air Force pilots. At least two helicopters were lost on these hazardous missions.

As they drove south, however, Adan's forces held a course too far east of the Canal, along the Artillery Road, making no contact with the bulk of the forces holding the Egyptian bridgehead. The plan had been to roll up the narrow Egyptian bridgehead from its northern flank, where the Egyptians were least expecting a concerted Israeli thrust. But now they were moving across the front of the Egyptian bridgehead.

When he turned towards the Canal, Adan's attack developed from east to west. At about 1200hrs Amir's brigade was engaged by hundreds of Egyptian infantry who emerged from sand dunes to fire anti-tank weapons at short range. One Israeli officer recalled: 'In the distance I saw specks dotted on the sand dunes. I couldn't make out what they were. As we got closer, I thought they looked like tree stumps. They were motionless and scattered across the terrain ahead of us. I got on the intercom and asked the tanks ahead what they made of it. One of my tank commanders radioed back, "My God, they're not tree stumps. They're men!" For a moment I couldn't understand. What were men doing out there – quite still – when we were advancing in our tanks toward them? Suddenly all hell broke loose. A barrage of missiles was being fired at us. Many of our tanks were hit. We had never come up against anything like this before.'

Amir's leading battalions withdrew, leaving at least 12 blazing tanks behind. Meanwhile, Gonen's headquarters was labouring under the illusion that everything was going according to plan. At 1100hrs Sharon was ordered to move southwards to the Gidi Pass sector, ready to be unleashed against the Egyptian Third Army.

In the early afternoon Adan ordered an attack by Nir's and Amir's brigades towards the Firdan Bridge. They advanced against the Egyptian 2nd Infantry Division, which was reinforced by Second Army's anti-tank reserves, without supporting infantry. Nir's brigade got to within 1,000m (1,094 yds) of the canal when it was hit by anti-tank fire that destroyed 18 tanks. When he finally extricated his brigade, Nir had only four tanks with him.

It took Adan and Gonen some time to grasp the extent to which the Israeli plan had collapsed. It was only at about 1200hrs that Adan informed Gonen, 'We have taken a lot of casualties, a great many. Tanks are burning from missiles.' Still the penny did not drop. Forty-five minutes later, Adan was told that he had permission to cross the Suez Canal and establish a bridgehead on the western bank. At about the same time, Elazar approved a request by Gonen to allow Sharon's division to cross the Canal that afternoon and capture Suez City.

Eventually reality dawned. At 1400hrs Gonen realized that Adan's attack had failed and, with the Egyptians moving on to the counterattack, he ordered Sharon to return to the central sector. Thus Sharon's division had spent the best part of a day moving south and then north without exercising any influence on the unfolding battle. Had the Israeli attack been launched by two well-supported divisions in the Firdan Bridge sector, it might arguably have punched its way into a position from which it could have rolled up the Egyptian line. A weak frontal attack against a determined defence was doomed to failure.

It was now imperative that the IDF conserve its forces and allow time for the reserve army to deploy with all its supporting arms. Adan's cavalry charges had been launched unsupported and in insufficient numbers – he had at most 100 tanks – and there had been a fatal underestimation of the determination and efficacy of the Egyptian anti-tank defence. In the gloom that had settled on the Israeli High Command, it was impossible to appreciate the effects the fighting of 8 October had had on the Egyptians. Captured Egyptian documents later revealed that the Israeli counterattacks, however misconceived, had sapped Egyptian energy and disrupted the planned advance. In the northern sector, some Egyptian units had pushed into Sinai to a depth of 10km (6 miles), reaching the Artillery Road, but south of the Bitter Lakes, the Egyptians had fallen well short of that mark.

However, the mauling of Adan's division on the 8th had opened dangerous fissures in the Israeli High Command. Relations between Sharon and the GOC Southern Command, never particularly cordial, were now strained to breaking point. On the afternoon of 9 October, Sharon launched an attack to retake a second-line fortification that had fallen into Egyptian hands the day before.

Gonen ordered Sharon to break off the attack but the latter continued, prompting Gonen to ask Elazar to relieve Sharon of his command.

That day, one of Sharon's brigades, 14th Armoured Brigade commanded by Colonel Amnon Reshef, had penetrated the sector of the so-called 'Chinese Farm'. This was east of the Canal at the northern end of the Great Bitter Lake. It was an abandoned experimental agricultural station that, before 1967, had employed Japanese instructors. It had acquired its inaccurate nickname from the oriental characters the Japanese left on the walls. On 10 October the reconnaissance force was withdrawn, having satisfied itself that the area marked the boundary between Egyptian Second and Third Armies and constituted a weak link in the Egyptian line.

The fightback

On 9 October a subdued General Dayan briefed Israel's senior journalists. He indicated that he was considering an appearance on television to reveal the extent of IDF losses. Such was the air of depression he exuded that it was decided to replace him for the broadcast with General Aharon Yariv, the former Chief of Intelligence. Dayan had been badly shaken by the events of the last few days and was speaking of mobilizing high school students and men who had passed the age of reserve duty, and of the possibility that a new defence line might have to be established east of the Gidi and Mitla passes.

The pack was rapidly being reshuffled. General Chaim Bar-Lev, a former Chief of Staff and now the Minister of Trade and Industry, was asked by Elazar effectively to take over Southern Command from General Gonen as the CGS's 'representative'. Gonen was brave, technically competent and had performed with distinction as commander of the 7th Armoured Brigade in 1967. But as GOC Southern Command he had probably been promoted beyond his abilities. Moreover, he had previously commanded a division in Southern Command under Sharon. In 1973 the roles had been reversed and differences in personality had only exacerbated the tensions.

Predictably, the large, rumbustuous Major General Sharon was still making waves and urging for a crossing of the Canal at the earliest opportunity. On 12 October Bar-Lev made the first of several requests that Sharon be relieved of his command. Dayan, who it must be said did not have a good war in 1973, was nevertheless firm in his defence of Sharon, declaring that he did not know anyone who was a better field commander.

Meanwhile, the General Staff had to make hard decisions. It was now clear that the IDF was not strong enough to mount simultaneous offensives on both the northern and southern fronts. Nor, even when it had amassed sufficient strength, could it mount a frontal attack on the Egyptian bridgeheads. An indirect approach would have to be used to overcome the Egyptians. To add to

their anxious deliberations, General Peled warned Elazar on 12 October that by the 14th the IAF would reach a 'red line' in terms of pilots and serviceable aircraft and would not be able to support another ground offensive.

From 9 October the IDF set about stabilizing the front in the south. The Egyptians' high-water mark had been reached and they would make no further territorial gains on this front. The successive local attacks they made, sometimes in divisional strength, were contained, and their firepower countered by new tactics. The threat that the Sagger-armed infantry had posed in the opening exchanges was to be overcome by the use of coordinated smoke screens and concentrated artillery fire, together with supporting infantry.

Nevertheless, the fighting was fierce. On Wednesday 10 October the Egyptians launched five separate attacks on Adan's division while on the same day Sharon's division came under attack from the Egyptian 21st Armoured Division. Sharon's skilful manoeuvring enabled him to destroy some 50 tanks.

The outcome of the campaign now hung in the balance. Having stabilized the Sinai front, the Israeli High Command was considering a Canal crossing, an operation fraught with peril if Shazly continued to hold a substantial armoured reserve on the west bank of the Canal. During Operation *Badr*, the commanders of Second and Third Armies had crossed with approximately 1,000 of the tanks allotted to them, leaving an operational reserve of 330 west of the Canal, ready

This column of M-51 'Super Shermans' rolls across terrain typical of that in the area of operations in the Sinai Desert. Rolling sand dunes produced the ever-present clouds of dust to parch throats and clog engine filters; the latter had to be cleaned regularly to avoid damage to the engines.

to move against an enemy penetration. There was also a strategic reserve of 250 tanks in Egypt, 120 of which represented the presidential guard, a ceremonial formation that could be used only in the direst emergency.

Shazly anticipated a concentrated Israeli effort to penetrate his defensive line and roll it up from the rear. He was also mindful of the successful precedents for this strategy and of the risks he would run if he dissipated his operational reserve. Also nagging at Shazly were the losses he had suffered in a week of fighting. By the night of 13 October the Egyptians had lost 240 tanks. Shazly estimated that in the same period the Israelis had lost some 600 tanks, although the rate of IDF losses was now falling sharply as the Israelis made tactical adjustments. Moreover, the IDF was in a position to replace its armoured losses and deploy a numerically superior force. Shazly was confident that if he remained on the defensive and retained an operational reserve, he could hold firm on the east bank. But he knew that he did not possess the superiority needed for attack. Events were now to conspire to force Shazly to act against his instincts.

From 11 October Shazly came under increasing pressure from General Ismail to drive for the Gidi and Mitla passes. Shazly reminded Ismail of the fate that had befallen the 1st Mechanized Brigade when it was caught without air cover, but Ismail was unrelenting. He argued that the pressure on Syria must be reduced. Shazly replied that in Sinai the IDF still fielded eight armoured brigades and that the IAF could cripple the Egyptian ground forces if they 'poked their noses' beyond the SAM umbrella: 'Advance and we destroy our troops without offering any significant relief to our Syrian brothers.'

Matters came to a head during a conference held at 1800hrs on 12 October attended by Shazly and the commanders of Second and Third Armies. Ismail, on the instructions of President Sadat, overruled all objections. He told Shazly that a political decision had been made and he must obey. An attack would be launched from the bridgehead. Ismail's only concession was to postpone the jump-off time to dawn on 14 October. He added that the Egyptian bridgeheads were not to be weakened. Rather, the Egyptian operational reserves were to be committed.

In Israel the IDF had also been considering its options: a hazardous crossing of the Canal at a carefully selected Egyptian 'soft spot'; or perhaps, if an Egyptian second-stage offensive did not materialize, a ceasefire, even with Egypt holding its initial territorial gains, as a better option than a war of attrition that Israel could not sustain. These options were being considered at a meeting of the Israeli War Cabinet when military intelligence informed its members that the Egyptian armour on the west bank was on the move. It was crossing the Canal and an attack could be expected on 13 or 14 October. At a stroke the Egyptians had cut the Gordian knot of Israeli decision-making. The IDF and the politicians would wait for the Egyptian move and respond accordingly.

The Egyptian bridgeheads and SAM umbrella, 14 October 1973

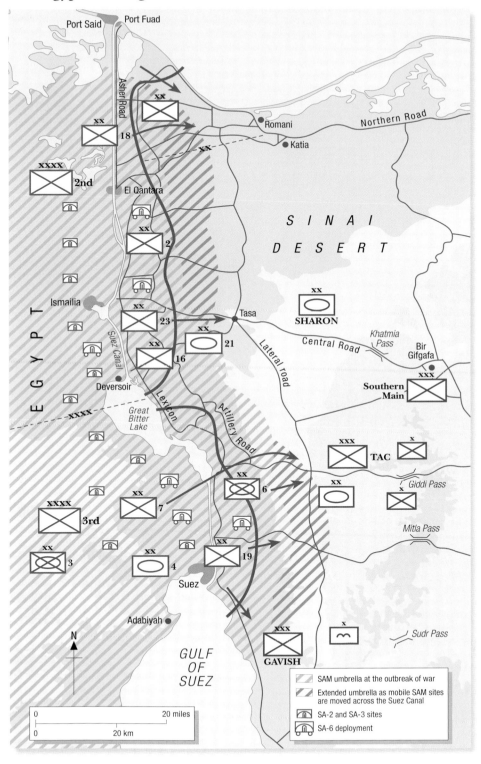

Shazly obeyed his orders with a heavy heart. The reserves, comprising the bulk of the 4th and 21st Armoured Divisions, crossed the Suez Canal, leaving an operational reserve on the west bank of a single brigade of tanks from the

The McDonnell Douglas Skyhawk was the principal ground-attack aircraft of the Israeli Air Force during the October War. Accordingly, it suffered the highest losses of any aircraft type when pitted against the sophisticated Egyptian and Syrian air defence systems. Of 103 Israeli combat aircraft lost, 53 were Skyhawks. Coincidentally, this was exactly the same as the number of Israeli pilots killed during the war.

4th Division. The movement was completed on the night of 13 October. Shazly felt that 'barring a miracle' the Egyptian attack stood not the slightest chance of success: 'The enemy had 900 tanks in his operational zone. We were attacking with 400. We were doing so, against well-prepared positions, in precisely the "penny packets" that had cost the enemy so dear over October 8–9. And we were condemning our tank crews to attack over open terrain dominated by enemy air power.' It should be noted that Israeli estimates of Egyptian armoured strength on 14 October were substantially higher than Shazly's gloomy figure, hovering around 1,000. There is clearly an element of special pleading in Shazly's post-war account of the campaign.

While Shazly agonized, Gonen made his dispositions of Southern Command. Armoured forces were to block the Egyptian thrusts on the Mediterranean coast and in the Gulf of Suez. Thereafter, the IAF, operating beyond the range of the Egyptian missile screen, would break up the attacking forces. If a frontal attack was launched in the centre and south, it was to be blocked by Mandler and Sharon. If the Egyptians threatened the vital supply base at Refidim (Bir Gifgafa),

An M38 Jeep of an armoured battalion's reconnaissance company leads an Upgraded Centurion across the desert sands towards the Suez Canal. It was just such a Jeep-mounted reconnaissance unit or 'Sayeret' that found the gap between the Egyptian Second and Third Armies that allowed Operation *Gazelle* to be launched.

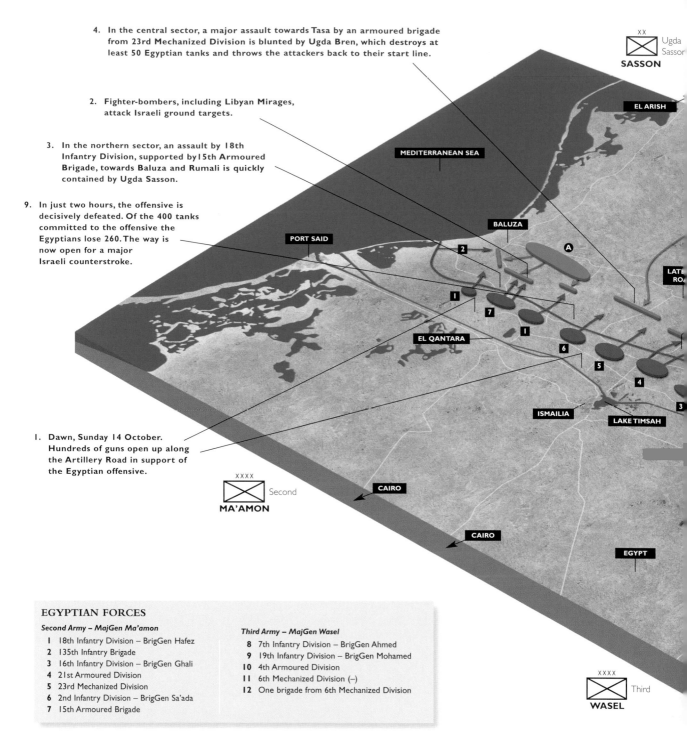

4. In the central sector, a major assault towards Tasa by an armoured brigade from 23rd Mechanized Division is blunted by Ugda Bren, which destroys at least 50 Egyptian tanks and throws the attackers back to their start line.

2. Fighter-bombers, including Libyan Mirages, attack Israeli ground targets.

3. In the northern sector, an assault by 18th Infantry Division, supported by15th Armoured Brigade, towards Baluza and Rumali is quickly contained by Ugda Sasson.

9. In just two hours, the offensive is decisively defeated. Of the 400 tanks committed to the offensive the Egyptians lose 260. The way is now open for a major Israeli counterstroke.

1. Dawn, Sunday 14 October. Hundreds of guns open up along the Artillery Road in support of the Egyptian offensive.

XX Ugda Sasson
SASSON

EL ARISH

MEDITERRANEAN SEA

BALUZA

PORT SAID

2

A

LAT RO

1

7

1

EL QANTARA

6

5

4

3

ISMAILIA

LAKE TIMSAH

XXXX Second
MA'AMON

CAIRO

CAIRO

EGYPT

XXXX Third
WASEL

EGYPTIAN FORCES

Second Army – MajGen Ma'amon
1 18th Infantry Division – BrigGen Hafez
2 135th Infantry Brigade
3 16th Infantry Division – BrigGen Ghali
4 21st Armoured Division
5 23rd Mechanized Division
6 2nd Infantry Division – BrigGen Sa'ada
7 15th Armoured Brigade

Third Army – MajGen Wasel
8 7th Infantry Division – BrigGen Ahmed
9 19th Infantry Division – BrigGen Mohamed
10 4th Armoured Division
11 6th Mechanized Division (–)
12 One brigade from 6th Mechanized Division

THE EGYPTIAN OFFENSIVE

14 October 1973, viewed from the southwest. Under political pressure as a result of Syrian reverses on the Golan Heights, the Egyptians emerge from the protection of their SAM umbrella in an abortive offensive.

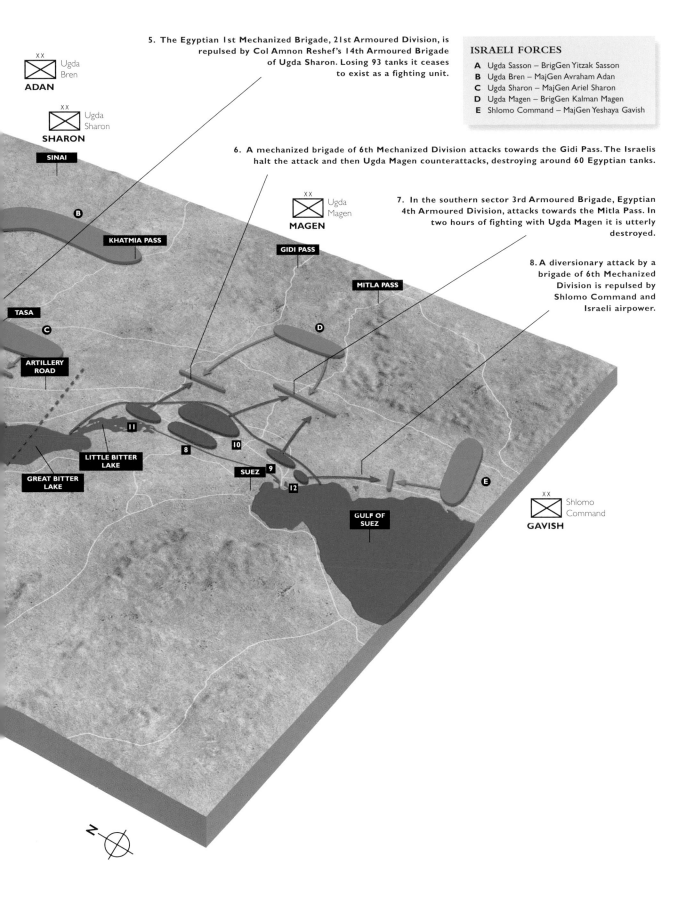

5. The Egyptian 1st Mechanized Brigade, 21st Armoured Division, is repulsed by Col Amnon Reshef's 14th Armoured Brigade of Ugda Sharon. Losing 93 tanks it ceases to exist as a fighting unit.

6. A mechanized brigade of 6th Mechanized Division attacks towards the Gidi Pass. The Israelis halt the attack and then Ugda Magen counterattacks, destroying around 60 Egyptian tanks.

7. In the southern sector 3rd Armoured Brigade, Egyptian 4th Armoured Division, attacks towards the Mitla Pass. In two hours of fighting with Ugda Magen it is utterly destroyed.

8. A diversionary attack by a brigade of 6th Mechanized Division is repulsed by Shlomo Command and Israeli airpower.

ISRAELI FORCES

A Ugda Sasson – BrigGen Yitzak Sasson
B Ugda Bren – MajGen Avraham Adan
C Ugda Sharon – MajGen Ariel Sharon
D Ugda Magen – BrigGen Kalman Magen
E Shlomo Command – MajGen Yeshaya Gavish

XX Ugda Bren
ADAN

XX Ugda Sharon
SHARON

XX Ugda Magen
MAGEN

XX Shlomo Command
GAVISH

SINAI

KHATMIA PASS

TASA

ARTILLERY ROAD

GIDI PASS

MITLA PASS

LITTLE BITTER LAKE

GREAT BITTER LAKE

SUEZ

GULF OF SUEZ

B

C

D

E

11

8

10

9

12

N

Among the most useful equipment captured by the Israelis from the Arabs during the Six Day War was the Soviet Katyusha BM23 mobile rocket launcher. These vehicles were used against their erstwhile owners during the October War to compensate for the lack of artillery assets in the IDF.

which lay 30km (19 miles) east of the Lateral Road, Adan's division, reinforced by Sharon, was to be held in reserve to execute a counterattack from the flank. One of Adan's brigades was moved to the area of Refidim.

On the morning of 13 October, Elazar flew by helicopter to Sharon's advanced headquarters to review the plans for the anticipated armoured battle and the Canal crossing that would follow its successful conclusion. Also flying to the meeting by helicopter, General Gonen was talking by radio to Major General Mandler when contact was lost. Mandler had been killed by Egyptian artillery fire. Brigadier General Kalman Magen immediately replaced Mandler.

On the night of 13 October the Egyptians preceded their attack by heli-lifting commandos to a point south of Tasa. The aim was to cause chaos in the Israeli rear but the commandos were quickly captured or killed. The main attack went in shortly after first light on the morning of Sunday 14 October when hundreds of guns opened up along the Artillery Road while fighter-bombers, including Libyan Mirages, attacked targets on the ground.

In the northern sector, the Egyptian 18th Infantry Division, reinforced by a brigade equipped with T62 tanks, attacked on the axis El Qantara–Rumali. In the central sector, Sharon's division bore the brunt of the Egyptian 21st Armoured Division and a brigade from the 23rd Mechanized Division driving out of the bridgehead along the central route leading from Ismailia. A thrust to the south by two tank brigades was aimed at the Gidi and Mitla passes. Farther to the south a task force made up of an infantry brigade and a tank brigade advanced towards Ras Sudar along the Gulf of Suez. In all, there were six separate Egyptian attacks: three mounted by General Ma'amon's Second Army and three by General Wasel's Third Army.

The attack precipitated an armoured battle that rivalled in size and savagery the great armoured clash of World War II at Kursk on the Eastern Front in the summer of 1943. Just as in that pivotal battle, the weather was heavy and humid. In the northern sector, Major General Adan's division, which Gonen had quickly ordered into action, threw the Egyptians back to their start line, destroying at least 50 tanks. In the central sector, Sharon meted out similar punishment. The tanks of Colonel Amnon Reshef's 14th Armoured Brigade had been astutely sited on high ground from which they engaged the headlong Egyptian charge at ranges as close as 91m (100yds). When the firing stopped, the Egyptian 1st Mechanized Brigade had lost 93 tanks and had ceased to exist as a fighting unit. This had been achieved at a cost to Reshef of just three tanks, all of which had been struck by missiles. Not one of Reshef's vehicles had been hit by Egyptian tank fire.

To the south of Sharon, Magen's division contained the Egyptian drive on the Gidi and Mitla passes and then counterattacked, destroying some 60 enemy tanks. A flanking Egyptian movement to penetrate the Mitla Pass from the south

An M-60A1 Magach tows a Unifloat bridging section to the 'Yard' at the outset of Operation *Valiant* – the Israeli codename for the assault crossing of the Suez Canal. In the winter of 1971/72, General Sharon organized a live-firing exercise to simulate a canal crossing by flooding a small valley in the northern Sinai in order to evaluate current combat engineering techniques. Although largely successful further bridging equipment was procured including the monstrous roller-bridge (see page 92) to span the Suez Canal in combat.

was broken up by a combination of paratroops and Magen's tanks. In two hours of fighting, 3rd Armoured Brigade of the Egyptian 4th Armoured Division had been utterly destroyed. The Egyptian armour that extricated itself from the debacle came under heavy attack from the IAF. In the northern sector, IDF forces were able to re-establish contact with the Budapest fortification.

The battle was a major turning point in the war. The Israelis estimated that they had knocked out some 260 Egyptian tanks for the loss of no more than 20 of their own. Magen summed up the day's action as a 'fine battle'. For the Egyptians the bright outlook on the morning of 6 October had now given way to the shadow of impending defeat. They had only just become acclimatized to the warm glow of victory. Once more they were out in the cold. General Bar-Lev commented in words that recall Wellington at Waterloo: 'The Egyptians are again acting in their traditional way, and we are resuming our old ways.'

The Egyptians had attempted to move missile infantry forward with their armour, riding in personnel carriers and trucks. This effort to extend the missile screen ended in disaster. It is one thing for well-dug-in infantry to fight armour from well-chosen positions. It is quite another to face well-handled tanks in a fluid battle of movement. Many of the burnt-out hulks that littered the desert were those of personnel carriers and rocket-launching vehicles, destroyed by the Israeli tanks at long ranges. In contrast, Israeli infantry knocked out many Egyptian tanks with American-supplied TOW missiles (although the US has always maintained that no TOW missiles were supplied to Israel before the last days of the war).

Nevertheless, it was on 13 October – the day on which the Israelis had broken the back of the Syrian assault on the Golan – that the US Air Force launched Operation *Nickel Grass*, a major airlift of armaments, ammunition and supplies, which by 14 November had flown in 22,395 tons of equipment to Israel. Political pressure from Jewish Americans, the Arab rejection of Western ceasefire proposals, and apprehension that Israel might still unleash its nuclear armoury had pushed *Nickel Grass* to the top of the US agenda. The significance of the airlift cannot be underestimated because it offset the Soviet resupply of Egypt and Syria, by air and from freighters in the Mediterranean. The planes were the Lockheed C-141 Star Lifter and the recently introduced Lockheed C-5 Galaxy heavy airlift transport, the strategic value of which was crucially demonstrated during *Nickel Grass*.

In addition to Operation *Nickel Grass*, the United States supplied 33,000 tons of equipment by sea, mainly tanks, that arrived in mid-November. During the war Israel also received 34 Phantoms, 36 A-4 Skyhawks and 12 C-130 transports. The Soviets mounted a parallel airlift to Egypt, commencing on 10 October. During the course of the war and its immediate aftermath, about 15,000 tons of war matériel were flown to Egypt and Syria, and a sealift of

63,000 tons, mostly tanks and artillery, reached the Arab states by 30 October. In all, the Egyptians and Syrians received some 1,200 tanks and 300 MiG-21 aircraft from the Soviet Union, a factor that helped to stave off collapse in the latter stages of the conflict.

The setback of 14 October was too much for General Sa'ad Ma'amon, the commander of the Egyptian Second Army. He suffered a heart attack, and was replaced by Major General Abd El Munem Halil. The long-awaited conditions to allow an Israeli counter-thrust had arrived. On 14 October General Elazar gave orders for a crossing of the Suez Canal to be launched on the following night.

Operation *Gazelle*

On the evening of 14 October General Ismail ordered the Second and Third Armies to pull back into their bridgeheads on the east bank. Shazly urged that the remnants of the 4th and 21st Armoured Divisions should be withdrawn across the Canal to re-form as a mobile reserve and restore the balance of the Egyptian forces if, as Shazly anticipated, the Israelis crossed the Canal. Ismail rejected this plea, considering that such a withdrawal would have an adverse effect on Egyptian morale. He knew that Sadat was to address the People's Council within 48 hours and would wish to speak from an apparent position of strength.

Both the prerequisites for an Israeli crossing had now been met; the commitment of the Egyptian armour and its defeat in Sinai; and the launching of Operation *Nickel Grass*. Bar-Lev aimed to surprise the Egyptians by exploiting the gap between the Egyptian Second and Third Armies, which had been detected on 10 October. The operation was to present a fascinating contrast between Egyptian and Israeli methods. Operation *Badr* bore the imprimatur of Egypt's Soviet military advisers: massive preparation and methodical development from a firm base with no precipitate exploitation to challenge Israeli armoured forces in a battle of manoeuvre. Years of planning and training had been devoted to the operation and each soldier had been drilled down to the last detail. The Israeli crossing, in contrast, was to be a pinpoint attack, beginning with a large-scale commando raid that would then expand into a fully fledged invasion. It was a high-risk operation, planned in haste, and relied on improvisation and local initiative to succeed. The Egyptians crossed in broad daylight after a massive bombardment. The Israelis would cross under cover of darkness and stealth would be the key.

There were three choices for the crossing site, all of which had been prepared before 1973 with bridging material pre-positioned and the canal ramp carefully thinned. The sites were opposite El Qantara, Deversoir and Kubri, the last 16km (10 miles) north of Suez. Bar-Lev chose Deversoir as it was close to the boundary between the Egyptian Second and Third Armies and the inviting gap between them; also the Israeli left flank would be protected by the Great Bitter Lake. The area north of the Great Bitter Lake had been the scene of earlier preparations for bridging the Canal undertaken during Sharon's time as GOC Southern Command. A large brick-surfaced marshalling yard some 300m (330yds) square and protected by sand walls, had been built to accommodate the heavy bridging equipment, and roads had been built around it for easy access. Two miles south of the yard was the metalled Akavish road, built by Israeli engineers to link the yard with the forward supply base at Tasa. The secondary Tirtur road, running dead straight from the 'Yard' and parallel to the Akavish road, led to the Matzmed strongpoint, an abandoned link in the Bar-Lev Line.

Since 7 October General Sharon had been champing at the bit to launch a crossing of the Canal. In his opinion, trenchantly expressed, it was the only way to secure the defeat of Egyptian Second and Third Armies. Now his division was given the task of leading the Canal crossing, codenamed Operation *Gazelle*, with a brigade of paratroops reinforced by tanks. Sharon's intuitive ability to quickly size up a complex operational situation would stand him in good stead in the coming battle.

Sharon's division had three tasks: first, to establish a bridgehead over the Canal at Deversoir; second, to protect the crossing place on the east bank from Egyptian intervention on either flank; and third, to clear the Akavish and Tirtur metalled military roads across the soft sand for the bridging equipment and follow-up troops. Adan's division, minus one brigade held in reserve, was to pass through Sharon's bridgehead and swing south to Suez City, hugging the Canal. Magen's division was to cross later to reinforce Adan's drive. Meanwhile, Sharon was to secure the crossing and protect the rear of the other two divisions on the west bank. The attack was to go in as soon as darkness fell, to enable the bridges to be in place before dawn. Diversionary attacks would be launched to the north and south.

Sharon drew up a complex plan for his four armoured brigades. Colonel Tuvia Raviv's 600th Reserve Armoured Brigade was to launch a frontal, diversionary attack along the Tasa–Ismailia road an hour before dark to pin down Egyptian 16th Infantry Division. Raviv's initial objectives were the 'Hamutal' and 'Machshir' sand hills. Thereafter he was to swing southwest to take 'Televisia'.

An hour later, Colonel Reshef's reinforced 14th Armoured Brigade was to make a flanking march through the sand dunes to the south of the Egyptian

A bearded veteran of 20 years, Colonel Dani Matt was the commander of the 243rd Paratroop Brigade that led the Israeli assault across the Suez Canal on the night of 15/16 October. The whole success of Operation *Gazelle* was due to the tactical and operational flexibility of the IDF officer corps and its senior NCOs. Despite their early reversals, the Israelis rapidly regained the initiative thanks to the military skills of their citizen army and ultimately gained victory.

ISRAEL'S MONSTER ROLLER-BRIDGE

One of the most curious structures ever to go to war was the articulated roller-bridge designed and constructed by the Israeli Engineering Corps prior to the October War. The original Israeli defence plan, codenamed *Shovach Yonim*, called for Israeli forces to go over onto the offensive as soon as possible and take the battle into enemy territory across the Suez Canal. Crossing sites were chosen and prepared to allow the swift construction of pontoon bridges. These bridges were held in reserve well back from the Canal. None of the standard types of bridging equipment was considered completely satisfactory, however. A legendary member of the Israeli Engineering Corps, Colonel David Laskov (who at the age of 70 was the oldest officer in the IDF at the time), found the solution. His design comprised over 100 metal drums filled with polyurethane foam, each 2m (6ft 6in.) in diameter, capable of floating and reaching the far bank of the Suez Canal as a single entity. It was 180m (200yds) long and weighed 400 tons. It took three days to assemble and could only be moved over the flattest of terrain and along well-prepared routes. This monster required 16 tanks to move it, 12 towing and four acting as brakes. It was so huge that it had never been tested operationally before the October War. Special roads called 'Akavish' and 'Tirtur' were constructed to allow Laskov's roller-bridge to reach the Canal at the chosen crossing point in the Deversoir area. The roller-bridge was fundamental to Israel's counterattack across the Canal in the Yom Kippur War,

originally codenamed *Abirei Lev*, but renamed Operation *Gazelle*. This took place in the early hours of 16 October but fierce fighting continued along the 'Tirtur' road and around the 'Chinese Farm', which delayed the arrival of the roller-bridge until the morning of 19 October. Here the roller-bridge is towed from the paved Akavish road across the southern slopes of Hammadia towards Tirtur on the early morning of 16 October. An M113 Zelda APC (right) is 'riding shotgun'. By October 1973 the IDF were equipped with 448 of the M113 family but many infantrymen preferred to ride on top of the vehicle rather than inside the cramped interior. On the thin-skinned M113 this also gave additional protection against mines. The bridge was towed by 16 M48 Magach tanks (centre foreground), but while negotiating one of the slopes of Hammadia the four braking tanks failed to slow the bridge sufficiently and it ran out of control, causing one of the roller connections to break. It took some hours for repairs to be made with the help of the accompanying M74 recovery vehicle (centre background). In the far left background combat engineers ride in an M3 halftrack and the taskforce also includes an Ambutank (left background), an armoured ambulance converted from an old M50 self-propelled howitzer. This extraordinary convoy was headed by six D-9 Caterpillar bulldozers to level the route where necessary and prepare the crossing point on the Suez Canal. (Kevin Lyles © Osprey Publishing Ltd)

positions blocking the Akavish and Tirtur roads until it hit the Great Bitter Lake. Thereafter it had a threefold task. First, to secure the 5-km (3-mile) sector of the Canal opposite Deversoir, including the marshalling yard with its concealed gap in the sand rampart giving access to the Canal. It was also to seize an Egyptian pontoon bridge to the north. Second, it was to afford the crossing area both depth and protection by securing Chinese Farm. Third, it was to clear the Tirtur and Akavish roads to allow access by bridging and wheeled vehicles. The bridging units had been concentrated 20km (12½ miles) to the east of Deversoir under the command of Sharon's deputy. A pontoon bridge was to be brought up the Akavish road and a prefabricated roller bridge along the Tirtur. The monstrous prefabricated bridge, which was some 180m (200yds) long and weighed 400 tons, was to be towed by 16 tanks.

Sharon's attached 247th Reserve Paratroop Brigade, commanded by Colonel Dani Matt and reinforced with ten tanks and some engineers, was to follow Reshef and cross at 2300hrs to secure two bridging and two rafting sites. The brigade was then to push on less than a kilometre (0.6 miles) to secure crossings

A Sho't and three M113 Zeldas cross the Suez Canal on a ferry pontoon comprising French-manufactured Gillois bridging units. Almost 100 Israeli combat engineers were killed in action in the construction of various bridges across the Canal for Operation *Gazelle*.

over the Sweetwater Canal, and to deny the Egyptians observation of the main canal bridging areas. Finally, Sharon's third armoured brigade, 421st, commanded by Colonel Haim Erez, was to follow Matt's paratroops to reinforce their bridgehead and to destroy Egyptian SAM sites. The gap created in the Egyptian air umbrella would give the IAF free rein to provide close air support.

Surveying his plans, Sharon could see that both the framework and timetable were wildly optimistic. The 24 hours between the end of the massive armoured battle in the Sinai and the crossing of the Canal scarcely allowed time for the issuing of his detailed orders and the regrouping and concentration of his formations. In effect, it left Sharon with three choices: he could postpone the attack until the night of 16 October; he could clear the crossing places on the east bank on the night of the 15 October and then cross on the night of the 16th; or he could plunge ahead with the crossing on the night of the 15th and simply disregard the timings.

Characteristically, Sharon chose not to share all his thoughts with Bar-Lev. Had he done so, it is almost certain that the operation would have been postponed for 24 hours. If Sharon had cleared the crossing places and then sat twiddling his thumbs for 24 hours, he would have given the Egyptians valuable time to reinforce the crossing area and render his operation extremely hazardous. Sharon decided to postpone the crossings until midnight and to muddle through.

At 1600hrs on 15 October Sharon despatched Raviv's 600th Reserve Armoured Brigade on its diversionary attack while Reshef's 14th Brigade and the divisional reconnaissance unit began their approach march. For some time Reshef advanced undetected. After reaching the 'Lexicon' road, which ran north–south 1km (⅔ mile) east of the Canal, the reconnaissance unit pushed on to take the Bar-Lev strongpoint at Matzmed. Reshef's brigade now divided into battalions before setting about its tasks, which included the capture of another Bar-Lev strongpoint, codenamed 'Missouri'.

As it moved north towards Missouri along the Lexicon road, the Israeli 18th Battalion came under fire from Egyptian infantry holding the Tirtur–Lexicon crossroads. Eleven tanks were knocked out by Egyptian Saggers, forcing 18th Battalion to divert to Missouri rather than attack the crossroads. The capture of the crossroads had been assigned to a company of the 40th Armoured Battalion, who were unaware that the administrative centres of Egyptian 21st Armoured and 16th Infantry Divisions were housed in the nearby Chinese Farm. Badly mauled by the fighting in Sinai on 14 October, the 21st Armoured was licking its wounds. A single Israeli company was now advancing into the middle of a huge concentration of tanks, trucks, guns, missiles, radar vehicles and thousands of troops. The Egyptians had also prepared positions in the Farm's irrigation ditches. A hail of fire shredded the Israeli company.

The 2nd Company of 40th Armoured Battalion was faring better as it cleared the Akavish road. Simultaneously, the divisional reconnaissance unit secured the strongpoint at Matzmed and the marshalling yard. Bridging equipment was immediately sent hurrying down the Akavish road, but as the Tirtur road was still unavailable as a secondary route, a huge traffic jam quickly developed. Matt's paratroop brigade was stuck at the rear of this snarl-up and by the time it reached the marshalling yard at the Canal it was hopelessly behind schedule. As the situation at Chinese Farm deteriorated, Sharon ordered Matt to cross the Canal.

Meanwhile, Reshef's 18th and 7th Battalions pushed north and ran into growing Egyptian resistance. The 7th Battalion was soon down to a third of its strength, and as the Egyptians readied themselves to counterattack, Reshef ordered a tactical withdrawal to form a line half a mile north of Chinese Farm where fighting continued throughout the night.

The 40th Infantry Battalion and 'Force Shmulik' (a paratroop unit supported by armour and named after a hero of the fighting on the Golan Heights) had also resumed the fight for Chinese Farm. Here the battle was no less desperate. According to one of the Israelis, 'Although it was night, after 15 minutes you could see everything like daylight'. Caught in interlocking fire from well-sited defensive positions in Chinese Farm's many irrigation ditches, the Israelis suffered heavy casualties and the Egyptians overran part of the force. The battalion commander, all his tanks and many of his men were lost in the fighting. By the morning of 16 October, Reshef's brigade had lost 60 tanks and over 120 men. Reshef was to lose more that morning securing the Tirtur–Lexicon crossroads.

After a failed attempt to take the position from the rear, Reshef changed his tactics. Rather than charge the Egyptian defences head on, he ordered his tanks to keep their distance and stay on the move while still laying down a barrage. In this way the Egyptians were worn down and the crossroads taken. The vital crossroads was now in Reshef's hands but he was still unable to clear Chinese Farm.

At first light on 16 October Reshef had surveyed the scene of the night's fighting from high ground. Below him was a panorama of smouldering tanks, abandoned workshops, missile transporters and field kitchens. Dead littered the ground, with Egyptians and Israelis often lying within a few metres of each other. In the fighting, Sharon's division had lost some 300 men killed and 70 tanks destroyed or disabled, the bulk of the casualties sustained by Reshef's 14th Armoured Brigade. Leaving a battalion to hold the line west of Chinese Farm, Reshef withdrew his brigade south to the shores of the Great Bitter Lake.

When Sharon inspected the results of the fighting at the Tirtur–Lexicon crossroads, he observed: 'I saw hundreds and hundreds of burned and twisted

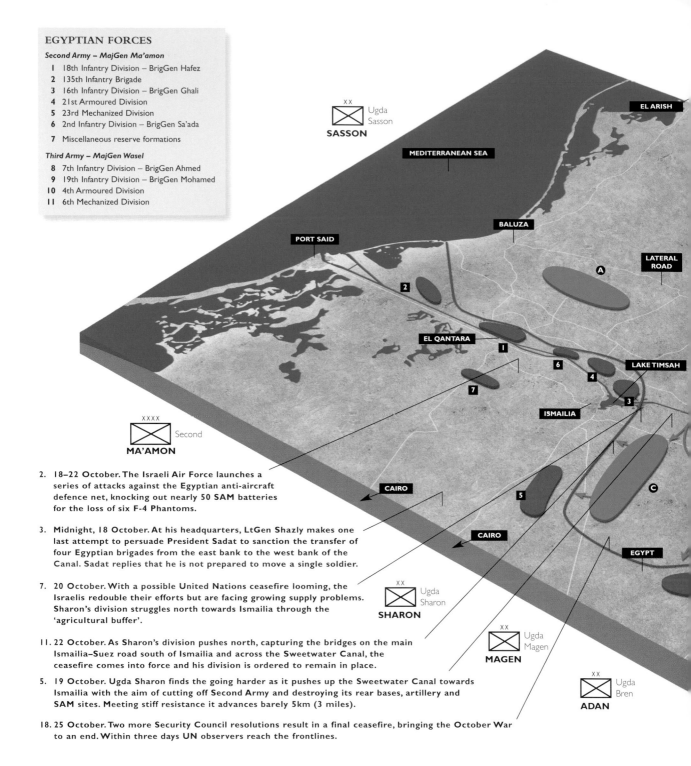

SASSON — Ugda Sasson

MEDITERRANEAN SEA

EL ARISH

BALUZA

PORT SAID

LATERAL ROAD

EL QANTARA

LAKE TIMSAH

ISMAILIA

MA'AMON — Second

CAIRO

CAIRO

EGYPT

SHARON — Ugda Sharon

MAGEN — Ugda Magen

ADAN — Ugda Bren

2. 18–22 October. The Israeli Air Force launches a series of attacks against the Egyptian anti-aircraft defence net, knocking out nearly 50 SAM batteries for the loss of six F-4 Phantoms.

3. Midnight, 18 October. At his headquarters, LtGen Shazly makes one last attempt to persuade President Sadat to sanction the transfer of four Egyptian brigades from the east bank to the west bank of the Canal. Sadat replies that he is not prepared to move a single soldier.

7. 20 October. With a possible United Nations ceasefire looming, the Israelis redouble their efforts but are facing growing supply problems. Sharon's division struggles north towards Ismailia through the 'agricultural buffer'.

11. 22 October. As Sharon's division pushes north, capturing the bridges on the main Ismailia–Suez road south of Ismailia and across the Sweetwater Canal, the ceasefire comes into force and his division is ordered to remain in place.

5. 19 October. Ugda Sharon finds the going harder as it pushes up the Sweetwater Canal towards Ismailia with the aim of cutting off Second Army and destroying its rear bases, artillery and SAM sites. Meeting stiff resistance it advances barely 5km (3 miles).

18. 25 October. Two more Security Council resolutions result in a final ceasefire, bringing the October War to an end. Within three days UN observers reach the frontlines.

OPERATION *GAZELLE*

18–23 October 1973, viewed from the southwest, showing the Israeli crossing of the Suez Canal and the breakout 'into Africa', undermining the positions of the Egyptian Second and Third Armies on the east bank of the Canal.

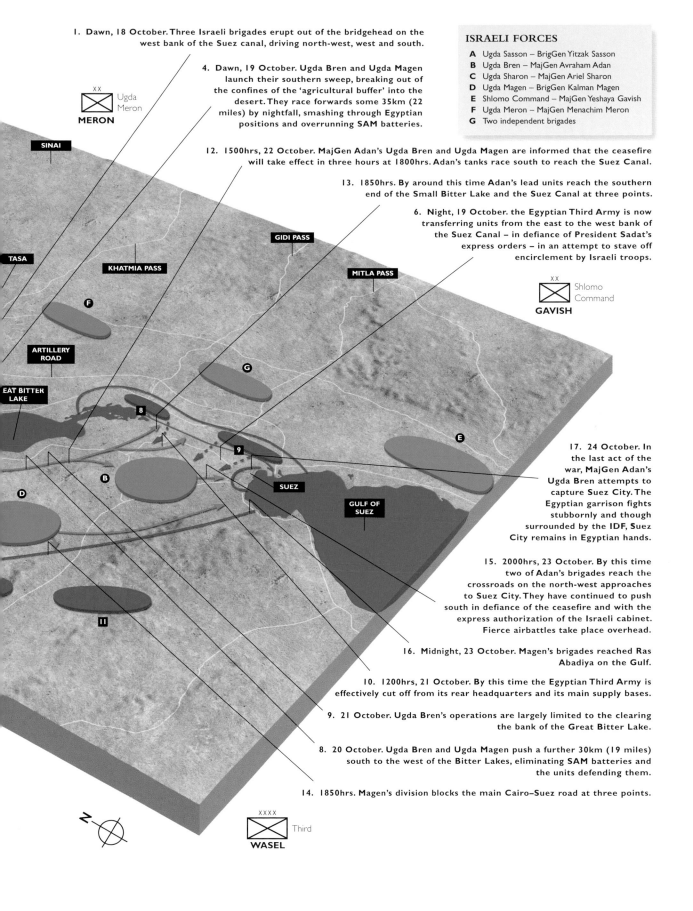

1. Dawn, 18 October. Three Israeli brigades erupt out of the bridgehead on the west bank of the Suez canal, driving north-west, west and south.

4. Dawn, 19 October. Ugda Bren and Ugda Magen launch their southern sweep, breaking out of the confines of the 'agricultural buffer' into the desert. They race forwards some 35km (22 miles) by nightfall, smashing through Egyptian positions and overrunning **SAM** batteries.

12. 1500hrs, 22 October. MajGen Adan's Ugda Bren and Ugda Magen are informed that the ceasefire will take effect in three hours at 1800hrs. Adan's tanks race south to reach the Suez Canal.

13. 1850hrs. By around this time Adan's lead units reach the southern end of the Small Bitter Lake and the Suez Canal at three points.

6. Night, 19 October. the Egyptian Third Army is now transferring units from the east to the west bank of the Suez Canal – in defiance of President Sadat's express orders – in an attempt to stave off encirclement by Israeli troops.

ISRAELI FORCES
A Ugda Sasson – BrigGen Yitzak Sasson
B Ugda Bren – MajGen Avraham Adan
C Ugda Sharon – MajGen Ariel Sharon
D Ugda Magen – BrigGen Kalman Magen
E Shlomo Command – MajGen Yeshaya Gavish
F Ugda Meron – MajGen Menachim Meron
G Two independent brigades

MERON

SINAI

TASA

GIDI PASS

KHATMIA PASS

MITLA PASS

ARTILLERY ROAD

GAVISH

EAT BITTER LAKE

SUEZ

GULF OF SUEZ

17. 24 October. In the last act of the war, MajGen Adan's Ugda Bren attempts to capture Suez City. The Egyptian garrison fights stubbornly and though surrounded by the IDF, Suez City remains in Egyptian hands.

15. 2000hrs, 23 October. By this time two of Adan's brigades reach the crossroads on the north-west approaches to Suez City. They have continued to push south in defiance of the ceasefire and with the express authorization of the Israeli cabinet. Fierce airbattles take place overhead.

16. Midnight, 23 October. Magen's brigades reached Ras Abadiya on the Gulf.

10. 1200hrs, 21 October. By this time the Egyptian Third Army is effectively cut off from its rear headquarters and its main supply bases.

9. 21 October. Ugda Bren's operations are largely limited to the clearing the bank of the Great Bitter Lake.

8. 20 October. Ugda Bren and Ugda Magen push a further 30km (19 miles) south to the west of the Bitter Lakes, eliminating **SAM** batteries and the units defending them.

14. 1850hrs. Magen's division blocks the main Cairo–Suez road at three points.

WASEL Third

vehicles... Here and there Israeli and Egyptian tanks had destroyed each other at a distance of a few metres barrel to barrel... Inside those tanks and next to them lay their dead crews... No picture could capture the horror of the scene.'

By 0030hrs on 16 October Matt's assault group, riding in halftracks, had entered the marshalling yard where something approaching pandemonium reigned. It was planned that once Matt had crossed the Canal and established a foothold, a battalion led by Lieutenant Colonel Dan would widen the bridgehead to the south while a battalion under Lieutenant Colonel Zvi would extend it northwards. A veteran of 20 years, Colonel Matt was a tall, bearded soldier, wounded many times in action, who had commanded a paratroop brigade under Sharon in the Sinai in 1967.

Progress to the marshalling yard had been agonisingly slow because of the massive traffic jam on the Akavish road. The soft sand on either side of the road, in which wheeled vehicles rapidly became stuck, only made matters worse. Because many of his troop-carrying vehicles were soft-skinned, Matt had also been forced to leave his brigade reconnaissance company and Dan's battalion at the rear of the column. As it moved forward behind a company of tanks, Matt's force came under artillery, missile and heavy machine gun fire from the Akavish–Artillery crossroads some 1,000m (1,094yds) to his north. A force he despatched to secure the crossroads was wiped out. Matt was crawling towards the Canal under intense fire and the schedule was slipping badly.

At 0135hrs the first wave of Israeli troops crossed the Canal in inflatable boats and set foot on the west bank. Brigade advanced headquarters crossed at 0240hrs, and within another three hours Matt's entire brigade was across and digging in. After engineers tore three large passages in the sand ramparts, tanks began to be rafted across the Canal. Within a short time 27 tanks and seven armoured personnel carriers (APCs) were on the west bank. There had been no Egyptian opposition. The paratroopers radioed Sharon with the codeword for success, 'Acapulco'. By 0800hrs Matt's bridgehead stretched 4.8km (3 miles) north from the Great Bitter Lake. As they pushed northwards, his men encountered pockets of surprised Egyptians who were dealt with in short order. The crossings over the Sweetwater Canal were secured, and Colonel Erez pushed westward with 21 tanks to destroy Egyptian SAM batteries.

With a foothold established, Sharon and Adan prepared to move the bulk of their divisions over the Canal. Sharon was convinced that the canal crossing was of far greater importance than the action at Chinese Farm and was eager in his situation report to minimize the losses sustained in the fighting in that sector. However, the Israeli High Command took a different view and was dismayed by even the modified casualty figures submitted by Sharon. Dayan went so far as to question the idea of crossing the Canal. Bar-Lev and Gonen took a

position summed up by the latter: 'Had we known that this would happen in advance, we probably would not have initiated the crossing. But now we are across we shall carry it through to the bitter end.'

Endgame

In an attempt to staunch its losses, the Israeli High Command ordered that no more tanks or men should cross the Canal until a bridge was in place. Sharon was given orders to clear Chinese Farm and Missouri while Adan kept the Akavish road open. Once again a major disagreement flared up between Southern Command and the explosive Sharon, who insisted that the breakthrough at the Canal should be exploited at all costs. Bypassing Gonen, Sharon appealed directly to Bar-Lev, who denied his request to continue the

Israeli paratroopers advance 'into Africa' accompanied by an M113 Zelda APC after the successful Israeli crossing of the Suez Canal in Operation *Gazelle*. Israeli paratroopers were commonly employed as assault troops for complex and dangerous missions and few were more daunting or decisive than Operation *Gazelle*. The Israeli crossing of the Canal was the key to the victory over the Egyptians in the October War.

advance. Bar-Lev considered that it would be reckless in the extreme to launch an attack across the Canal with an unsecured supply route while relying on vulnerable rafts and, in his opinion, Sharon's drive would grind to a halt within 24 hours.

Meanwhile, Adan reported that the Egyptians, transfixed by the bitter fighting at Chinese Farm, had left the Akavish road clear. The pontoon bridging equipment was slowly moved towards the Canal, screened by a battalion of the 35th Paratroop Brigade; fresh troops who had been rushed up from the south to take Chinese Farm. The paratroops held on for more than 14 hours less than 91m (100yds) from the Egyptians. The bridge reached the Canal on the morning of 17 October. But the paratroops had paid a heavy price – 40 were dead and some 80 wounded. The Egyptians still held Chinese Farm.

It remained abundantly clear that the Israeli forces on the east bank were in danger of being encircled. The Egyptian position at Chinese Farm kept the Tirtur road closed and threatened the Akavish road. The responsibility for

A Sho't churns up the sand as it advances across the desert. Despite being manufactured during the 1950s, the Centurion or Sho't was a firm favourite within the Israeli Armoured Corps during the October War because of its rugged reliability and its ability to sustain considerable battle damage and remain operational.

SHO'T TANKS OF UGDA BREN SAM-HUNTING IN AFRICA, 19 OCTOBER

The Israeli Air Force suffered heavy losses in the opening phases of the Yom Kippur War flying close air support missions to the ground forces. Ultimately these missions were halted due to the highly effective Arab air defences, and the army proved to have insufficient artillery to deal with the Sagger anti-tank teams that were inflicting heavy damage on the first Israeli armoured counterattacks. The IAF was seriously compromised until the Surface-to-Air Missile (SAM) threat was dealt with. Little could be done to counter this menace until the ground forces crossed the Suez Canal during Operation *Gazelle*. As soon as the first tanks had been ferried across the canal they were sent out in twos and threes to find the prepared SAM sites and destroy them. Colonel Haim Erez having crossed the canal on the night of 15 October, led a group of 20 tanks west hunting for SAMs. By midday on 16 October he was 12km (7½ miles) west of the Canal and, having taken the Egyptians by surprise, roamed unchecked for 24 hours. Here a trio of Upgraded Centurions (Sho't) of the 217th Reserve Armoured Brigade, commanded by the redoubtable Colonel Natan 'Natke' Nir, attack Missile Base 6214 some 2km west of the Vada'ut Road. The position was strongly defended by the Egyptians with Saggers and rocket-propelled grenades (RPGs). Three Israeli tanks were knocked out with three dead and 16 wounded, including the

battalion commander. Known as 'Guideline' within NATO and Dvina to the Soviets, the SA-2 missile (centre background) provided the low- to high-altitude coverage of the Egyptian air defence system. The SA-2 is a solid-fuel rocket that uses radio command guidance to reach its target. Guidance was provided by the 'Fan Song' radar detection system (far right background), which transmitted command signals to the missile. The latter's 129kg (286lb) warhead could be detonated by command or proximity fusing. The missile had a slant range of 45km (28 miles) and a ceiling of 18 km (11 miles). Although taken by surprise, several Egyptian SAM site crews had the presence of mind to at least attempt to fight back, and on more than one occasion the SA-2's launcher was depressed to the horizontal (right background) and the missile loosed off at the advancing Israeli tanks. Although no hits were achieved, the experience must have been somewhat unnerving for the Israeli tank crews and these doubtless qualify as the most expensive anti-tank rounds in the history of warfare. With the destruction of the SAM sites by Israeli armoured units, the IAF was given free rein at last and subsequently were able to provide highly effective close air support to the ground forces during the encirclement of the Egyptian Third Army. (Kevin Lyles © Osprey Publishing Ltd)

The ferocity of the fighting during Operation *Gazelle* is highlighted by these burnt-out wrecks of a T-55 and an M48 Magach, which are at little more than a barrel length apart. Of the 2,000 tanks employed by the IDF in the October War, half were damaged in battle with 400 being totally destroyed and 600 returned to service. Arab tank losses were 2,250 out of a total of 4,480.

taking this crucial position was passed to Adan. Gonen fretted that Sharon was still looking for a way to push more armour across the Canal, and even radioed one of Sharon's brigade commanders to forbid him to cross the Canal without direct orders from Southern Command.

Egyptian High Command initially brushed off the Israeli presence on the west bank of the Canal as a tiresome nuisance and Sadat airily dismissed it as a 'television operation'. On the afternoon of 16 October, Ismail and Shazly agreed that concerted action against the Israeli crossing would be taken the next day, but there agreement ended. Shazly urged a major westward shift of Egyptian forces to counter the Israeli thrust. Second Army's reserve, the 21st Armoured Division, could not easily be withdrawn and Shazly proposed that Third Army's 4th Armoured Division and the 25th Independent Armoured Brigade be used. A counterattack could be launched from the south-west towards the enemy crossing point. Simultaneously, 21st Armoured Division would move down the Canal bank to close the corridor to the Israeli crossing.

Ismail rejected the plan. He did sanction a southward thrust by the 21st Division but wanted the 25th Brigade to attack north from its existing positions in the Third Army bridgehead. Simultaneously, an infantry reserve held on the west bank, the 116th Brigade, was to attack due east towards the Israeli crossing. Shazly protested that it was reckless in the extreme to order the 25th Brigade to advance some 30km (18½ miles) with the Bitter Lakes on its left flank and its right flank open to enemy attack, but Ismail overruled him.

On the morning of 17 October the Egyptians steeled themselves to close the Israeli corridor and cut off all Israeli forces between Lexicon and the Canal. The Israelis guessed Egyptian intentions while the armoured formations were still moving into position. This enabled Adan and Sharon in the north to concentrate three armoured brigades against the Egyptian 16th Infantry and 21st Armoured Divisions while Lieutenant Colonel Amir Jaffe's battalion held the line west of Chinese Farm.

The Egyptian forces, already battered in the earlier fighting, stood little or no chance, but it seemed to the Israelis as if the sand dunes swarmed with Egyptian tanks. The Egyptian 16th Infantry Division took heavy casualties before breaking off and withdrawing. The 21st Armoured Division managed to cut the route to Deversoir from the east but then ground to a halt.

Meanwhile, the Egyptian 25th Armoured Brigade was driving north along the eastern shore of the Great Bitter Lake. The dust attracted the attention of the IAF, which confirmed about 100 T-62s, numerous APCs, fuel and supply trucks and artillery moving north. Battle was joined at 1200hrs when the tanks of Reshef's 14th Brigade opened fire at long range, knocking out the leading two tanks in the Egyptian column. Major General Adan ordered Colonel Nir to leave one battalion of his 217th Reserve Brigade in the area of Akavish–Tirtur and use the rest of his forces to lay an ambush to the east of Lexicon. He also ordered Colonel Arieh Keren to deploy his brigade to the east of 'Botzer' at the southern end of the Great Bitter Lake. To the north one of Reshef's units blocked the road at Lakekan; to the west was the Great Bitter Lake; between the lake and the road there was an Israeli minefield; to the east was Nir's 217th Reserve Brigade; and to the south-east Keren's 500th Reserve Brigade blocked the Egyptian rear.

Nir's brigade was the first to engage the Egyptians, forcing part of the 25th Armoured Brigade to leave the road. The Egyptians then blundered into the Israeli minefield near the lake. The survivors headed straight for the sand dunes, where Nir's tanks were waiting for them. Thirty minutes after battle opened, Keren's brigade moved from the Gidi road in a wide flanking movement towards Botzer. His armour opened fire on the Egyptians, now completely boxed in, and picked off tanks and vehicles, strung out along the shoreline, at will. Artillery support from Magen's division, to the south, added to the destruction of 25th Armoured Brigade. A few Egyptian tanks broke away in flight, pursued by Keren's armour, which itself became entangled in an Israeli minefield near Botzer.

Battle of Chinese Farm, 17 October, Phase 1

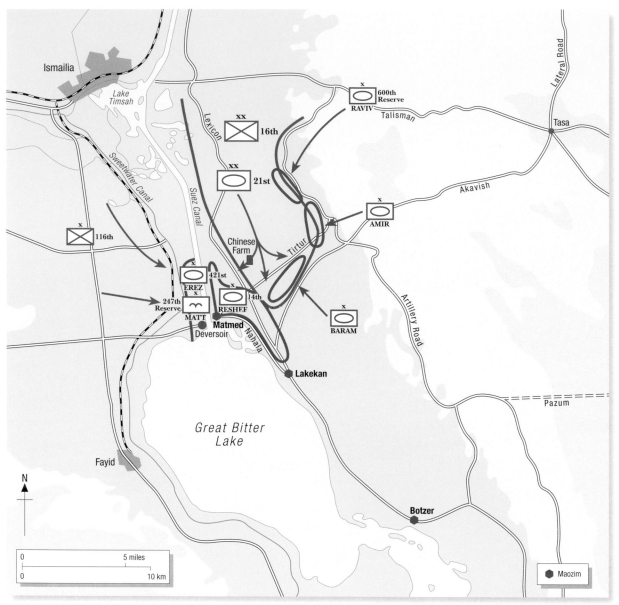

By 1730hrs the battle was over and 85 of 96 Egyptian T-62s had been destroyed. The brigade commander's tank and three others sought refuge in the Botzer fortification. All the Egyptian APCs and vehicles in the supply train were destroyed. The Israelis had lost just four tanks to mines in their pursuit of the fleeing Egyptians.

However, another furious row flared on the morning of 17 October at a conference at Adan's command post attended by Adan, Elazar, Bar-Lev and

Battle of Chinese Farm, 17 October, Phase 2

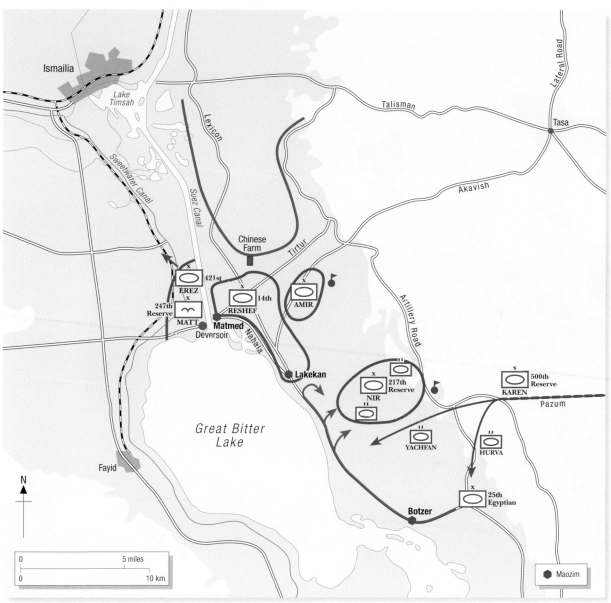

Sharon. The latter had once again proposed that his division cross to the west bank, while Adan dealt with the east bank. Adan pointed out that he had been fighting for 30 hours to clear Chinese Farm – a task originally allotted to Sharon – and accused Sharon of being a glory hunter. The high command ordered Sharon to clear and widen the corridor on the east bank before crossing the Canal. Relations between the IDF's senior fighting generals had hit a new low. General Elazar was, for the moment, able to pour oil on the

troubled waters by insisting that 'Sharon will continue with the task of consolidating the bridgehead, and Bren [Adan] will cross westward, according to the plan'. Sharon was unable, however, to subdue the Egyptian position at Missouri, nor did he enjoy unqualified success when the high command allowed him to cross the Canal.

At 1600hrs on 17 October, at the height of the armoured battle at Great Bitter Lake, Israelis engineers were laying a pontoon bridge across the Canal under air attack and heavy artillery bombardment. Sharon later described the scene: 'A tremendous Egyptian artillery barrage brought a curtain of shells crashing down on us... MiG fighters swarmed over the yard ... turning the compound into an inferno. With incredible courage, soldiers were standing outside in this storm of fire directing traffic... Others worked at ... assembling and launching their rafts... The chaos was mind-boggling.'

Colonel Matt's headquarters took a direct hit that wounded his deputy. Guns, mortars and Katyushas poured tens of thousands of rounds into the crossing areas. 'Frog' surface-to-surface missiles were added to the bombardment. The IAF, patrolling over the bridgehead, shot down large numbers of Egyptian fighter-bombers. The Egyptians resorted to throwing in helicopters on suicide bombing missions in which barrels of napalm were dropped on the crossing.

Matt's paratroops also came under attack from Egyptian commandos. The fighting was frequently hand-to-hand. In one incident an Israeli unit was cut off from the main body and surrounded by Egyptians. A four-hour battle ensued in which one Israeli officer, Captain Asa Kadmoni, fought with conspicuous gallantry, holding off attacks with grenades, a rifle and an anti-tank weapon. He had almost expended all his ammunition when a relieving force rescued him.

Colonel Haim Erez, a Polish Jew and exceptionally tough soldier who had arrived in Palestine in 1943 by way of the Soviet Union and Teheran, had crossed the Canal on the night of 15 October with 20 tanks and seven APCs. His force had headed west, hunting Egyptian SAM bases and destroying an assortment of enemy vehicles on the way. By 1200hrs on the 16 October Erez was 12km (7½ miles) west of the Canal. The Egyptians had been taken by surprise and for 24 hours Erez enjoyed complete freedom of movement, shooting up SAM sites and military columns. On the morning of 17 October, however, he came under attack from the Egyptian 23rd Armoured Brigade and took casualties before the Egyptians were driven off.

The Israeli sectional raft bridge on the Canal was completed late in the afternoon of 17 October, and before dawn on 18 October Adan had two brigades of tanks across. The prefabricated roller-bridge was operational by the early hours of 19 October. Within 24 hours a third pontoon bridge would also be carrying traffic across the Canal. Over 100 of Brigadier General Dan Even's engineers had been killed and many hundreds wounded in throwing the bridges across the Canal.

On the east bank Reshef's brigade had reorganized and, under Sharon's orders, attacked Chinese Farm, whose exhausted defenders finally yielded to a fierce assault. The victorious Israelis were confronted with a sobering sight: highly organized infantry and anti-tank defences with great quantities of anti-tank weapons – guns and Saggers – lying abandoned. Reshef forged on, driving north to widen the corridor. That afternoon Moshe Dayan arrived to inspect the battlefield accompanied by Sharon and Reshef. As he gazed on the scene of the bitterest fighting, he was clearly moved. Reshef observed, 'Look at this valley of death,' to which Dayan replied sotto voce, 'What you people have done here!'

Between 16 October and dawn on the 18th the Israeli bridgehead on the west bank remained about 1½km (1 mile) deep and some 4.8km (3 miles) from north to south, bounded on the east by the Canal, on the south by the Great Bitter Lake and on the west by the Sweetwater Canal, which channelled

PART II
THE GOLAN HEIGHTS

OPPOSING PLANS

Terrain is significant in any military operation but on the Golan it was fundamental both to the attackers and defenders and to a large extent determined the dispositions and plans of both sides. Rising above the Jordan Valley from the Sea of Galilee is an escarpment some 1,000m (3,280ft) high known as the Golan Heights. Covering an area of about 900 square kilometres (347 square miles), it rises steadily from south to north; its peaks looking down on the Upper Jordan Valley to the west and the Yarmouk Valley to the south. The latter forms the boundary with Jordan, which to the east gives way to extensive lava fields. In the distant past, this rugged terrain was shaped by volcanic activity. Lava, belching from craters, covered the high plateau with a coating of basalt. The largest volcanic cones, such as Tel Faris, rise to over 1,000m (3,280ft) above sea level. Dominating the northern end of the Golan is the peak of Mount Hermon, called Jebel Sheikh by the Arabs. This strategic high ground with its vital observation post was known as 'The Eyes of Israel' as it dominated the surrounding terrain, with excellent views of much of the northern Golan and deep into Syria.

In contrast to the Sinai in the south, the Golan is not good tank country. The going is better in the southern grasslands than in the north where large areas are rendered impassable to vehicles by basalt boulders and rock outcrops, while the Golan's many defiles represent perfect ambush country. The volcanic cones scattered across the heights also provide excellent observation posts and fields of fire. Many of them were integrated into the Israeli defence system on the Golan as natural firing ramps. Two of the dominant volcanic cones in particular, the 1,200m Mount Hermonit north of Kuneitra and the 1,250m (4,101ft) Tel Faris near the Rafid junction, were to play key roles in the October War.

The eastern boundary of the Golan, facing the Damascus Plain, ran in an irregular line along the edge of the United Nations' 'Purple Line' – a demilitarized zone established after the Six Day War and so called because of its colouring on the maps of the UN observers stationed there. Along the ceasefire line there was a narrow strip of neutral territory, less than 500m (547yds) wide, patrolled by personnel from the 16 UN observer posts built within the zone.

OPPOSITE

The Yom Kippur War was the closest the world came to high intensity warfare during the late 20th century. Casualties and matériel losses were high for all the combatants and particularly for the Israelis in the opening days of the war. The IDF lost 2,656 dead and 7,250 wounded during the war and the Arabs over 10,000 dead and over 20,000 wounded although the true figures will never be known. In just 19 days of warfare, the Israelis lost three times more men per capita than did the Americans in Vietnam between 1965 and 1975. Here, casualties of Strongpoint 116, the southernmost Israeli fortified position on the Purple Line, are treated by medics after they were evacuated by an armoured task force late on Monday 8 October. For over two days Strongpoint 116 resisted repeated ferocious assaults by the Syrians including ground, air and artillery attack. Bedraggled, the commander of Strongpoint 116, Lt Yossi Gur, is seen still clutching his loaded FN rifle as one of his men is given first aid. Gur was wounded in the right shoulder during the first evening of the war when he directed Israeli artillery onto his own position to beat off a Syrian attack. Having disabled two Syrian tanks with rifle grenades, Gur continued to command and fight between bouts of unconsciousness, propping his rifle on any nearby object and firing at the enemy with just his left hand. By such actions the Golan Heights were saved.
(© David Rubinger/Corbis)

A classic image of armoured warfare illustrates the principle of employing tanks en masse as a formation of Sho't Upgraded Centurions advances on Syrian positions. It also shows the normal posture of Israeli tank commanders in battle and how exposed they were to enemy fire, be it exploding artillery shells or Syrian snipers who were deployed on the battlefield with their Dragunov rifles with the specific task of killing Israeli tank commanders. Only Centurions and Shermans were deployed on the Golan Heights because experience had shown that the torsion bar suspension systems of the M48 and M60 tanks of US origin were less capable over rocky terrain. However, a few special-purpose variants, such as the M48 AVLB Bridgelayer, were used on the Northern Front.

A number of roads crossed the plateau and there was a network of tracks made by the IDF to aid the movement of military vehicles. There were two north–south roads. The first, set back from the Purple Line, ran for some 75km (47 miles) from Rafid in the south to Masada in the north. The second north–south road ran parallel to the 2,500km (1,533-mile) underground Trans-Arabian Pipeline (TAP), which carried oil from Saudi Arabia through Jordan across the Golan and into Lebanon where it terminated at the Mediterranean port of Sidon. The maintenance road, the TAP line road to the east of the pipeline, ran inside a chain-link fence. Running from west to east across the Golan were five roads that followed the easiest paths through the broken terrain from bridges over the River Jordan. The capture of these bridges was the principal objective for the Syrian Army in the Yom Kippur War.

After the Six Day War, the Israelis built a system of obstacles and fortifications along the eastern edge of the Golan plateau. To the west of the Purple Line was an anti-tank ditch, approximately 6m (20ft) wide and 4m (13ft) deep. On the western side, the spoil from the ditch was piled up to create an embankment shielding a network of concrete observation posts and strongpoints – 'Mutzavim' – built on volcanic hills or high ground, which afforded commanding views over the eastern approaches. Mutzavim actually means 'road block' although few if any were actually near a road. There were a total of 17 of these fortified positions, strung out at 4-km (2½-mile) intervals, each garrisoned by 10–30 troops, as well as intelligence and artillery personnel. Most of the positions were supported by a platoon of three tanks.

The number of infantry stationed on the Golan was commonly two battalions, with one to the north of Kuneitra and the other to the south. Positioned about 2,000m (2,186yds) to the rear were tanks and behind them four batteries of self-propelled artillery guns – a total of just 44 155mm howitzers. Their main role was to block roads and tracks and to bring down fire on the killing grounds into which Syrian armour and infantry were to be channelled by the minefields and terrain. In a measure much favoured by the IDF, special ramps specifically designed for the Centurion's ten-degree gun depression had been built on higher ground to enable the defending tanks to engage Syrian attackers from long range.

Behind the infantry defences along the Purple Line was the regular garrison brigade for the Golan, the 188th Barak [Lightning] Armoured Brigade with two tank and one mechanized infantry battalions. The brigade was commanded by

A solitary Centurion Sho't takes up position behind a wall of basalt rocks. Tank crews use any fold in the ground to minimize exposure to enemy observation or fire. This was particularly significant in the southern area of the Golan Heights with its open rolling terrain. At the outset of the battle, this was defended by just 33 Sho't tanks of the 53rd Mechanized Infantry Battalion commanded by Lieutenant Colonel Oded Erez against a force of some 250 Syrian tanks in the initial assault. This unit's ordeal in the Yom Kippur War is one of the most harrowing and courageous in the annals of modern warfare.

The eve of the war

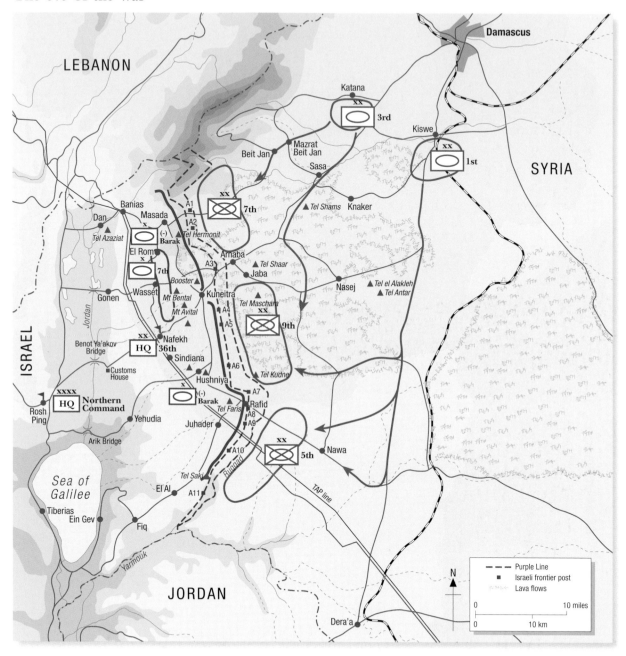

Colonel Yitzhak Ben Shoham with its headquarters at Camp Sa'ar [Storm] near Nafekh. The two tank battalions of the Barak Brigade possessed some 72 Upgraded Centurions, known within the Israeli Armoured Corps as the Sho't. These were deployed in support of the forward strongpoints along the Purple Line and, in times of tension, on the firing ramps to the rear.

Israel's overall strategy was simple – survival. It became an article of faith that military intelligence would give sufficient warning for the citizen army of Israel to be mobilized before war erupted. Thereafter, the aim was to mount a counter-offensive within 48 hours and take the battle to the enemy's territory in order to inflict heavy human and matériel losses to deter further attacks and preserve the integrity of the territories already occupied by Israel. In an area of approximately 48 x 24km (30 x 15 miles) there was little margin for error. It was a fine judgement as to how many troops and tanks should be stationed on the Golan to stem a Syrian invasion before the reserves could be mobilized, which would take approximately 72 hours. Too many was a waste of resources and a drain on the over-stretched economy and too few a recipe for disaster.

The plan of attack devised by the Syrians was heavily influenced by Soviet military doctrine – the accumulated result of 15 years of Soviet logistical and technical support and the schooling of Syrian officers at Soviet military academies. The aim was to capture the entire Golan Heights and reach the River Jordan within 36 hours. This was to be achieved by the onslaught of three

The BTR-152 was the first Armoured Personnel Carrier (APC) produced in quantity by the Soviet Union and it was exported in large numbers. This vehicle was the principal APC in the Syrian mechanized divisions.

An M50 155mm self-propelled howitzer fires in support of an Israeli attack on the Golan. One of the major lessons of the Yom Kippur War to all armies was the prodigious scale of ammunition expenditure during the heavy fighting. Artillery and mortars were quickly integrated into the fire plans of Israeli offensive operations to counter the menace of RPG and Sagger anti-tank teams, who found plenty of cover among the rocks of the Golan Heights to ambush Israeli tanks.

infantry and two armoured divisions, although the infantry divisions were heavily reinforced by an independent armoured brigade each as well as a significant mechanized infantry component.

The attack on the Golan was to be preceded by a short but intense bombardment delivered by all the available combat aircraft, artillery, tanks and heavy mortars. Moving forward on a broad front, to make their numerical superiority tell, the Syrians planned to force the Israelis into the widest possible dispersal of its forces on the Golan. The 9th Infantry Division was to drive west, to seize a line of hills south of Kuneitra and cut the Israelis' lines of communication. This was to be the preliminary to the concentration of an overwhelming mass of men, machines and firepower at two critical points where the Syrians would cut through the defences before the Israeli mobilization system could affect the battle.

In the north, the 7th Infantry Division was to launch holding actions all along its line and invest Wasset. Simultaneously, the Moroccan brigade, which was composed of trained mountain troops, was to operate on the foothills of Mount Hermon and pose a threat to Masada and Banias. Both formations were given limited objectives and orders not to advance further without orders from the Syrian High Command. In the south the penetration was to be made near Rafid by the 5th Infantry Division. The aim was to achieve a double envelopment of the greater part of the forces on Israel's northern front. Thereafter, the 7th Infantry Division was to drive west towards the Upper Jordan through El Rom and Wasset to the northern Jordan crossings while the 5th Infantry Division advanced on a parallel course towards the Arik Bridge, at the northern end of the Sea of Galilee. The plan was for both divisions to advance in two echelons, the breakthrough being exploited by the second echelon. In the event of a breakthrough, elements of 7th Infantry were to combine with the right wing brigade of 9th Infantry to encircle IDF forces in the area of Kuneitra.

Once the 5th Infantry Division had breached the Israeli defences southwest of Rafid, the way would be open for an advance by the 1st Armoured Division up the TAP line from south to north, the mirror image of the Israeli operation in 1967. The 3rd Armoured Division was to be held in reserve to follow on the heels of 1st Armoured Division, a striking example of the concentration of force. Once the breakthrough was achieved, there was to be a maximum effort by the Syrian airborne and armoured forces to seize the Jordan bridges. Heliborne troops were tasked with seizing the Arik and Benot Ya'akov bridges while the two armoured divisions, operating on separate axes – one down the Kuneitra–Benot Ya'akov road, the other down the Hushniya–Yehudia–Arik Bridge road – would race to link up with the airborne troops on the bridges to block the approach of the IDF reserve divisions.

Critical to the initial Syrian assault was a daring commando attack, at the northern end of the front, against the IDF's electronic intelligence base on Mount Hermon. In addition to its symbolic importance as 'The Eyes of Israel', the base monitored all Syrian air and ground traffic. The base was manned by some 40 intelligence and technical personnel and only 14 infantrymen. The task of taking the post was given to Syria's elite 82nd Parachute Battalion and Special Forces.

When the overall shape of Operation *Badr* had been hammered out, the focus had necessarily been on its initial stage – the crossing of the Canal by the Egyptians (and the deliberate consolidation of their position on the east bank while pressure was applied to the superpowers) and the breakthrough by the Syrians on the Golan. Enormous care was devoted to the planning of these moves as the preliminaries to the opening of an equally intense diplomatic

With vehicle recognition charts above his head, an Israeli soldier observes deep into Syrian territory from his observation post high above the Golan Heights on Mount Hermon. Known as 'The Eyes of Israel', its capture by Syrian commandos on the opening day of the war was a disaster for the Israelis and its recapture became a vital strategic objective before the UN Security Council imposed a ceasefire. Note the Nikon 'battleship' binoculars in the foreground that were developed for the navy of the Japanese Self Defence Force.

campaign. Nevertheless, both the Egyptians and Syrians had given some, although less detailed, thought to the second phase of operations. The Syrians had examined crossing the Jordan into eastern Galilee, but the thrust of all their planning with the Egyptians in 1973 had convinced them that a UN ceasefire would be imposed before this extended operation could be launched. The Syrians also had a healthy respect for the IAF and, like the Egyptian high command, were most reluctant to push out beyond their SAM umbrella. The recovery of all or most of the Golan would be reward enough for their endeavour. Syrian intelligence had correctly estimated that the Israelis had fewer than 200 tanks on the Golan to pit against a total of 1,300. This seemed a very safe margin when military doctrine demands that an attacking force outnumbers its opponent by a ratio of three to one.

OPPOSING ARMIES
Syrian forces

Identified Syrian formations on the Golan front were, from north to south, as follows: in the foothills of Mount Hermon was a Moroccan brigade; to the north of the Kuneitra–Damascus road was the 7th Infantry Division with an attached armoured brigade; south of the road and with a front extending from Kuneitra to just north of Rafid was the 9th Infantry Division, also with an attached armoured brigade; south and east of Rafid and north of the Yarmouk Valley was the 5th Infantry Division with a reinforced tank component and an attached armoured brigade. Behind these formations was a second

The Syrian Army also employed the eight-wheeled BTR-60 APC in significant numbers. This model is the BTR-60PB with an enclosed turret housing a 14.5mm KPVT heavy machine-gun and a co-axial 7.62mm PKT.

ORDER OF BATTLE
SYRIAN ARMY, OCTOBER 1973[1]

Cabinet & GHQ
Hafaz al Assad, President of Syria
Major General Mustafa Tlas, Minister of Defence
Major General Youssef Chakkour, Chief of Staff
Major General Abdul Razzaq Dardary, Chief of Operations
Major General Jibrael Bitar, Director of Intelligence
GHQ Forces
Assad Republican Guard Armoured Brigade
30th Infantry Brigade
90th Infantry Brigade
62nd Independent Infantry Brigade
88th Armoured Brigade
141st Armoured Brigade
1st Commando Group
82nd Parachute Battalion
Desert Guard Battalion

Western Syria
Latakia – Infantry Brigade
Homs – Infantry Brigade
Aleppo – Infantry Brigade

+ Moroccan Expeditionary Brigade
+ Saudi Arabian 20th Armoured Brigade (King Abdul Aziz Brigade)
+ Two commando brigades of the Palestinian Liberation Army

1st Armoured Division – Col Tewfiq Juhni
4th Armoured Brigade
91st Armoured Brigade
2nd Mechanized Infantry Brigade
64th Artillery Brigade

3rd Armoured Division – BrigGen Mustafa Sharba
20th Armoured Brigade

65th Armoured Brigade
15th Mechanized Infantry Brigade
13th Artillery Brigade

5th Infantry Division – BrigGen Ali Aslan
12th Infantry Brigade
61st Infantry Brigade
132nd Mechanized Infantry Brigade
50th Artillery Brigade
47th Independent Armoured Brigade (attached)

7th Infantry Division – BrigGen Omar Abrash[2]
68th Infantry Brigade
85th Infantry Brigade
1st Mechanized Infantry Brigade
70th Artillery Brigade
78th Independent Armoured Brigade (attached)

9th Infantry Division – Col Hassan Tourkmani
52nd Infantry Brigade
53rd Infantry Brigade
43rd Mechanized Infantry Brigade
89th Artillery Brigade
51st Independent Armoured Brigade

Iraqi Forces
3rd Armoured Division – BrigGen Lafta
6th Armoured Brigade
12th Armoured Brigade
8th Mechanized Infantry Brigade
+ Artillery Group

Jordanian Forces
40th Armoured Brigade – Brig Haled Hajhouj al Majali

---

1   Source: Colonel Trevor Dupuy, *Elusive Victory – The Arab-Israeli Wars 1947–1974* (Macdonald and Jane's, London 1978)

2   Killed in action on 8 October 1973. He was replaced by BrigGen Said Berakdar

echelon: 3rd Armoured Division deployed between Katana, its permanent camp, and Sasa; 1st Armoured Division deployed south and west of its permanent base of Kiswe.

A Syrian infantry division contained the following main combat elements: two infantry brigades, one mechanized infantry brigade, and one armoured brigade. The infantry and mechanized infantry brigades had three infantry battalions, a battalion of 40 tanks (T-54s or T-55s) and a field artillery battalion.

The armoured brigades fielded three 40-tank battalions. Other components of a Syrian infantry division included regiments of field and anti-aircraft artillery, a reconnaissance battalion and a chemical warfare company. Syrian brigades of all types had a troop of four PT-76 reconnaissance tanks per company and another for each battalion and brigade HQ.

These units gave the division a strength on paper of some 10,000 men, 200 tanks, 72 artillery pieces and approximately the same number of anti-aircraft guns and SAMs. The real figures at the beginning of October were, however, markedly different. Only the 5th Infantry Division had its full complement of armoured and mechanized vehicles; the 7th Infantry Division had only 80 per cent of its tanks and APCs and in the case of 9th Infantry Division the figure dipped to 50 per cent. Nevertheless, the designation 'infantry' is misleading, as these Syrian infantry divisions were essentially mechanized formations.

However, both Syrian armoured divisions, 3rd and 1st, were at full strength. Each of their two armoured brigades contained 120 tanks and, with a mechanized infantry brigade, they could put more than 250 tanks into the field with the same supporting units as an infantry division. For the attack on the Golan, Syrian forces numbered some 60,000 men, 1,400 tanks and 800 guns.

The Syrian Air Force, commanded by Major General Maji Jamil, had over 300 aircraft, including 30 Su-7 and 80 MiG-17 ground-attack aircraft, 200 MiG-21 interceptors and a small number of Il-28 light bombers. However, mindful of

The most powerful tank in the Arab armies during the Yom Kippur War was the T-62 with its formidable 115mm main armament and automatic loading system. Although it had been encountered before the war, the T-62 came as a rude shock to the Israelis as did the tenacity and determination of the Syrian crews who continued to attack despite appalling casualties.

the mauling it had received at the hands of the IAF on 13 September, the Syrians, like the Egyptians, integrated the air force with the SAM air defence system for the coming attack. West of Damascus they deployed about 100 SAM batteries and, in addition to divisional anti-aircraft weapons, some 30 anti-aircraft companies equipped with 160 guns, many of them ZSU-23-4 multi-barrelled, self-propelled anti-aircraft cannon.

Israeli forces

Against the formidable Syrian forces assigned to the attack on the Golan Heights, the Israelis deployed just a single under-strength armoured brigade, two infantry battalions and four batteries of self-propelled artillery. The reason for this alarming imbalance was simple – the Israelis did not believe the Syrians would attack without Egyptian co-operation and the Egyptians would not go to war for at least another three years. This was the received wisdom of the Israeli intelligence community and nothing would change this perception. Any Syrian incursion would be met by the full force of the mighty IAF that had paved the way for the stunning victory in 1967. By 1973, the air force absorbed 52 per cent of the Israeli defence budget and the other combat arms were being starved

The Israeli Artillery Corps was very much the poor relation of the IDF's various branches prior to the Yom Kippur War as, according to Israeli doctrine, it was the task of the air force to provide the majority of the fire support to the ground troops on the battlefield, once air superiority was achieved. As a result, there were too few self-propelled artillery batteries equipped with modern weapons such as this 175mm M107 gun bombarding Syrian positions.

Dishevelled and unkempt, an Israeli soldier sits cradling his Uzi sub-machine gun on a milestone just 58km (36 miles) from the Syrian capital of Damascus. The IDF has never been overly concerned with a soldier's appearance or smartness. Morale, thorough training, motivation and flexibility in combat are deemed to be of greater importance. In an essentially egalitarian society, rigid discipline is counter-productive within the citizen army known as Zahal. To paraphrase Clausewitz, the Zahal during the Yom Kippur War epitomized the soldier's readiness to serve and, in wartime, even to risk his life, closely interrelated with the will of the people as a whole to defend the integrity of its state and of its free and democratic constitutional order. (© Christian Simonpietri/Corbis Sygma)

of resources accordingly, particularly the infantry and the artillery branches. The infantry were equipped with outmoded personal weapons and the venerable M3 halftrack remained the principal battlefield transport as the M113 APC had been procured in relatively small numbers. Worse still the artillery had only a limited number of modern self-propelled guns such as the M107, M109 and M110. It

ORDER OF BATTLE
ISRAELI NORTHERN COMMAND, OCTOBER 1973

Cabinet Knesset
Mrs Golda Meir, Prime Minister Legislative Assembly
General Moshe Dayan, Minister of Defense

Israeli Defense Forces GHQ
LtGen David 'Dado' Elazar, Chief of Staff
MajGen Israel 'Talik' Tal, Deputy Chief of Staff
MajGen Eliezer Ze'ira, Chief of Intelligence

Northern Command
MajGen Yitzhak 'Haka' Hofi

Ugda Raful (36th Armoured Division) – BrigGen Rafael 'Raful' Eitan
188th Armoured Brigade 'Barak' – Col Yitzhak Ben Shoham
7th Armoured Brigade – Col Avigdor 'Yanush' Ben Gal
1st Infantry Brigade 'Golani' – Col Amir Drori
31st Parachute Brigade – Col Elisha Shelem

Ugda Laner (240th Reserve Armoured Division) – BrigGen Dan Laner
17th Reserve Armoured Brigade – Col Ran Sarig
679th Reserve Armoured Brigade – Col Uri Orr
+ Elements of the Barak Brigade from 7 October

Ugda Musa (146th Reserve Armoured Division) – BrigGen Moshe 'Musa' Peled
4th Reserve Armoured Brigade – Col Ya'akov 'Pepper' Hadar
9th Reserve Armoured Brigade – Col Mordechai Ben Porat
70th Reserve Armoured Brigade – Col Gideon Gordon
205th Reserve Armoured Brigade – Col Ben Yossi Peled

was the role of the air force to provide fire support to the ground troops and pound the enemy to destruction while the formidable Israeli fighters provided complete air superiority over the battlefield.

Thus the resident garrison on the Golan, supported by the overwhelming firepower of the air force, was deemed to be sufficient deterrent to invasion and more than adequate to counter any limited incursion. If war seemed imminent, the intelligence services would give at least 48 hours' notice during which time the well-oiled wheels of mobilization would be set in motion with reserves arriving at the front as war broke out. Reserve divisions would then be deployed to each of the fronts depending on the situation, be it Northern Command facing Lebanon and Syria, Central Command bordering Jordan or Southern Command in the Sinai against the Egyptians. Such was the theory but the Arabs had devised a counter to all these measures. The stage was set for war.

OPPOSING COMMANDERS

The fortunes of war are fickle and varied and the outcome of battle is most often dictated by the quality of the most basic component – the soldier. Whether commander or infantryman, the fate of nations can depend on his performance on the battlefield. The war on the Golan was just such an encounter with the survival of the State of Israel at stake. Although few individual actions can be genuinely considered fundamental to the outcome of a battle, there are particular decisions and particular events that can tip the balance. Predominantly it is the judgement of commanders that determines victory or defeat.

Syrian commanders

Early in 1973, General Ahmed Ismail, the Egyptian War Minister, began to hammer out a common strategy with his opposite number in Syria, Major General Mustafa Tlas. Tlas was one of the many politically conscious officers in the Syrian Army and he had visited Moscow, Peking and Hanoi. He had written books on guerrilla warfare and the campaigns of the prophet Mohammed. He had also been appointed as the overall field force commander on the Golan. Establishing his headquarters halfway between Damascus and the frontline in an attempt to coordinate the separate functions of political control and command in the field, Tlas fatally fell between two stools. Because he felt unable to leave his headquarters to visit his subordinate commanders and take personal stock of the situation, he was obliged to recall them at critical moments when they should have been controlling the tactical battle. It was to have a profound effect on the outcome of the war.

The Syrian Chief of Staff was Major General Youssef Chakkour, an Alawite; the director of operations was Major General Abdul Razzaq Dardary, whose deputy was Brigadier Abdullah Habeisi, a Christian more concerned with military strategy and tactics than political manoeuvring. To many officers in the higher echelons of the Syrian armed forces, a military career was simply a means of political advancement rather than the profession of arms in the defence of the state. There were of course some notable exceptions.

Major General Mustafa Tlas was the Syrian Minister of Defence and overall field commander during the Yom Kippur War. His decision to establish his field headquarters midway between Damascus and the frontlines so as to fulfil both his military and political functions was a major blunder. At critical stages of the battle, he ordered his field commanders to break off their operational duties to return to his headquarters, wasting valuable time when resolute decisions were required. Arguably this lack of flexibility in the command structure was to deny the Syrians victory in the war. Furthermore, once the initial assault of 6/7 October was blunted, the Syrian High Command had no alternative plan and the initiative passed to the IDF with the result that Israeli troops reached to within 32km (20 miles) of Damascus by the end of the war. Photo taken in 2000. (© International Picture/Corbis Sygma)

Brigadier General Omar Abrash, general officer commanding the Syrian 7th Infantry Division, was a graduate of the US Army Command and General Staff College at Fort Leavenworth. General Abrash led his division from the front and was directing operations at the anti-tank ditch as his forces opened the attack towards Kuneitra. In his path were the Centurions of the 77th Battalion of the 7th Armoured Brigade. Repeatedly, Abrash hurled his tanks at the Israeli positions with desperate gallantry. By the late afternoon of 8 October, the 7th Armoured Brigade was on the verge of collapse. At dusk on that fateful Monday evening, Abrash rallied his remaining tanks for one last attack relying on the Syrians' superiority in night-fighting equipment to overwhelm the Israelis. At that critical juncture, Abrash's tank was hit by an armour-piercing discarding sabot (APDS) round and burst into flames, killing the courageous commander. The attack was fatally postponed until morning, granting the 77th Battalion some vital respite and time for reinforcement. Lacking Abrash's dynamic leadership, the attack was contained after fierce fighting and the Syrian onslaught faltered, never to recover.

Israeli commanders

Major General Yitzhak Hofi was appointed general officer commanding Northern Command in 1972. Like so many officers in the IDF, he had acquired a nickname and was known as 'Haka'. A quietly spoken, dour man of few words, Hofi exuded an air of firm authority born of many years' experience of border fighting as a paratroop commander. During the autumn and winter of 1972/73, his command fought several bitter 'battle days' when the Syrians crossed the ceasefire line and clashed with Israeli forces. In the second of these battle days, the Syrians used Sagger ATGW missiles for the first time in large numbers, destroying several Israeli tanks. Hofi immediately issued his frontline troops with more mortars to counter the Sagger and on the next battle day they proved so effective that the menace was largely neutralized and very few hits were sustained. Hofi also launched a comprehensive overhaul of the military infrastructure of Northern Command, during which hundreds of kilometres of unpaved tracks were created, to speed the deployment of artillery and tanks across the Golan. At intervals along the tracks, tank ammunition (200 rounds per tank on the Golan as of 6 October 1973) was dumped to ease replenishment. The armoured mobilization centres were also moved closer to the frontline near the Sea of Galilee, including Rosh Pina, the Headquarters of Northern Command. Rigorous exercises confirmed that these measures cut mobilization times by up to half – this would prove crucial after 6 October. Simultaneously, the anti-tank ditch in front of the Purple Line was extended and deepened to slow any Syrian attempt at an armoured breakthrough and channel their tanks into prepared killing grounds. Only days before the war, further minefields were laid along the

Brigadier General Rafael 'Raful' Eitan was the commander of the inadequate forces tasked with defending the Golan Heights from Syrian attack. A tenacious character he refused to countenance retreat and handled his ever-diminishing units with adroit skill against overwhelming odds until sufficient reserves arrived on the Golan Heights to rescue the desperate situation. Photo taken in 1978. (© David Rubinger/Corbis)

Purple Line. Hofi's preparations in the months before the war were to play a vital part in the success of Israeli arms. Like his counterpart at Southern Command, Major General Shmuel Gonen, Hofi was to suffer intense pressure in the opening days of the war but, unlike Gonen, 'Haka's' reputation survived the October War intact. Hofi subsequently became the head of Mossad, Israel's Secret Service.

The forces stationed on the Golan were commanded by Brigadier General Rafael 'Raful' Eitan. Another taciturn man of stocky build and dark complexion, Eitan was first and foremost a farmer and happiest when tending his animals. After leaving the army in the early 1950s, he returned to farming. During the war of 1956, however, a friend reproached him, saying: 'They are killing Jews and you are milking cows.' Eitan rejoined the army as a paratrooper and gained a reputation as a ferocious fighter. He was considered by many colleagues to be a safe pair of hands but of no great intellect. He was shot in the head during the 1967 war; when he was subsequently promoted many thought it proved that you did not need brains for advancement in the IDF. He subsequently led the reprisal raid that destroyed 13 Arab airliners at Beirut Airport on 28 December 1968. After blowing up the planes, he calmly strolled into the transit lounge bar and ordered drinks for his men. As commander of the 36th Armoured Division or Ugda Raful, Eitan was temperamentally suited to the desperate defensive battle fought on the Golan – courageous with keen tactical skill and a refusal to countenance retreat. He remained at his underground bunker headquarters at Nafekh until Syrian tanks were literally at his door. His fellow commanders on the Golan were equally impressive.

As the commander of Ugda Musa, the 146th Reserve Armoured Division, Brigadier General Moshe 'Musa' Peled issues orders from his M3 halftrack command vehicle during the counterattack on the Golan Heights. After the Yom Kippur War, he became the commander of the Israeli Armoured Corps.

Brigadier General Dan Laner was an experienced officer whose war record stretched back to World War II. During the Six Day War of 1967, he led the attack that captured the Golan Heights. In February 1973 he was released from active service but in May, fearing the outbreak of war, Lieutenant General Elazar directed him to form and activate a new reserve division as soon as possible. On 6 October he rushed to the Golan Heights and quickly realized the gravity of the situation. Rather than waiting to mobilize his entire formation as instructed, Laner stood on the Benot Ya'akov Bridge acting as a military policeman and directing platoons and companies of tanks up the escarpment as soon as they were formed. It was to prove a vital measure in stemming the Syrian onslaught. That night, Laner suggested to Hofi that he take over responsibility for the southern half of the Golan while Eitan directed operations in the north. Hofi was quick to agree. It was this flexibility in command and control by the field commanders and the stubborn resistance of their men that allowed the Israelis to contain the Syrian onslaught. Laner's Ugda subsequently led the major thrust of the Israeli counterattack back to the Purple Line and into Syria. His appreciation of Iraqi 3rd Armoured Division's intentions and the trap he laid to destroy their offensive were masterly. Brigadier General Dan Laner is generally recognized as being the 'man of the match' in the war on the northern front. After the war, he returned to a well-earned retirement.

An equally formidable leader was Brigadier General Moshe 'Musa' Peled. Another farmer by birth, Peled was an outspoken, hard-bitten armour officer who was GOC of the 146th Reserve Armoured Division (Ugda Musa) following his appointment as the commandant of the Command and General Staff School of the IDF. Unlike many in the IDF high command, Peled was convinced that war would break out in 1973 and he trained his troops accordingly. Although due to take up a new appointment from 3 October, Peled immediately rejoined his division on Yom Kippur. As he drove to the depot at Ramle, his car was stoned by orthodox Jewish children for travelling on the holiest day of the year. The mobilization of Ugda Musa went to plan but much of its equipment was outdated including old Sherman and petrol-engined Centurion tanks. As a division of the strategic reserve, Ugda Musa was originally slated for service in Sinai, but on the second day of the war General Elazar ordered the division to the Golan Heights. Many of its tanks broke down en route for want of tank transporters. Once again a field commander took a decisive executive decision. Peled decided to commit his division along the road south of the Sea of Galilee towards El Al and up the Gamla Rise rather than, as his orders specified, over the Arik Bridge, which was the main line of communication for Ugda Laner. His prompt action did much to contain a dangerous Syrian thrust towards the heart of Israel. After heavy fighting in the southern Golan, Peled's division relieved Ugda Laner in the closing days of the war and was then transferred to the Southern Front in Sinai. After the October War, Peled became the commander of the Israeli Armoured Corps from 1974 to 1979 and did a fine job rebuilding the Heyl Shirion into a modern combined arms force equipped with the indigenously produced Merkava MBT, which incorporated many lessons from the high-intensity combat of the 1973 war.

When the Yom Kippur War broke out, the Israeli Armoured Corps still had 340 Shermans in War Reserve. So desperate was the situation on the Golan Heights that all but five were pressed into frontline service. These are the M51 version armed with the French CN 105 F1 gun. At 56 calibres and 6m (19ft 8in.) in length, the 105mm weapon was too large to fit into the existing T-23 turret due to the lack of space for the gun to recoil fully within the confines of the fighting compartment. Rather than modifying the turret, the gun itself was shortened by 1.4m (4ft 7in.) to 44 calibres and fitted with a large muzzle brake, thereby reducing the extent of recoil (becoming the CN 105 D1); however, this lessened the muzzle velocity from 1,000 m/sec (3,280ft/sec) to 800m/sec (2,625ft/sec) but still sufficient to destroy a T-55 or T-62 at normal combat ranges. Based on the Sherman M4A1 chassis with HVSS suspension and Cummins VT-8-460 diesel engine, the M51 proved to be a match for the Syrian tanks employed on the Golan Heights during the Yom Kippur War. (© Genevieve Chauvel/Corbis Sygma)

THE BATTLE FOR THE GOLAN

In the summer of 1973, the Soviet training mission moved into high gear as the Syrians struggled to absorb a flood of Russian hardware. One of the most significant additions to the Syrian arsenal was the arrival and installation of an extremely sophisticated air defence system. Soviet advisers and technicians undertook the task of integrating an array of SAMs with a range of altitudes and radar and optical fire-control systems backed by ECM. Soviet advisers also maintained a presence in every Syrian command post and combat formation in the battle zone. In the rear, Soviet technicians assembled combat aircraft shipped in by air and sea, including MiG-21s and Su-22s.

At the beginning of August, Egyptian and Syrian planning groups met in Alexandria to analyze the respective degrees of readiness of their armed forces and to assess the situation in Israel. However, the choice of Y-Day (*Yom* meaning Day in both Hebrew and Arabic) was a political decision to be made by Sadat and Assad; they opted for 6 October, when a range of factors operated in favour of Egypt and Syria.

For the Canal crossing, the Egyptians needed moonlight in the first phase of operations to help them establish bridges across the Canal. Later they needed darkness to push men and vehicles over to the east bank. In contrast, the Syrians argued for a daylight advance across the Golan plateau. The Egyptians needed favourable tides and currents in the Canal; the Syrians wanted to avoid the driving rain that usually enveloped the Golan plateau in November and the snow that blanketed Mount Hermon in December.

As 6 October, the tenth day of Ramadan, was the traditional anniversary of the battle of Badr won by the prophet Mohammed in AD 626, the military aspect of Operation *Spark* was assigned the codename *Badr* by the Egyptians and Syrians. S-Hour (*Sifr* is Arabic for zero) remained a matter of debate. The Egyptians wanted an hour in the late afternoon, the Syrians one early in the morning; both wanted the sun behind them shining in the eyes of the Israelis. It was not until 2 October in Damascus that Egypt's General Ismail secured a compromise from Assad. S-hour was set at 1400 hours.

In contrast to their indifferent performance during the Six Day War, most Syrian soldiers fought with tenacity and dogged determination during the opening days of the Yom Kippur War, although their training did not allow great tactical flexibility on the battlefield. Syrian marksmen and RPG teams repeatedly infiltrated the Israeli lines at night and exacted a fearful toll of Israeli tank commanders and vehicles. Once forced onto the defensive, the Syrian command structure suffered badly, with the wounded often abandoned on the battlefield. Nevertheless, when the Israelis invaded Syria itself, the Syrians put up stout resistance. The Israeli advance faltered with the IDF unwilling to be drawn into a battle of attrition when it was more important to transfer formations to the Sinai Front.

On 6 September, Ismail issued a Federal General Directive, placing both Egyptian and Syrian armed forces on a 'five-day alert' from 1 October. A week later, a fierce air battle took place over Tartous in Syria after Syrian MiG-21s scrambled to intercept IAF F-4 Phantoms and Mirage IIICs photographing arms deliveries by Soviet ships. In the air battle that followed, the IAF claimed 13 Syrian aircraft shot down while the Syrians admitted to eight and claimed five kills. There were in fact no IDF losses. During the engagement the Syrians were eager to unleash their SAMs, but the Soviet advisers refused to hand over the vital fuses they had retained; a wise decision as it turned out.

The Syrians' well-advertised plans to meet further aggression provided a useful cover for their concentration on the Golan. They also urged the Egyptians to advance the date of Operation *Badr*, but General Ismail insisted that the original timetable be adhered to. The deception plan was maintained to the last minute. On the southern front, the Egyptians concentrated under the cover of Exercise Tahir 73 (Liberation 73), the annual autumn manoeuvres, while continuing the dialogue with American and UN officials over a wide range of peace proposals. The Syrians also joined them in exploiting the news media to sow stories of 'business as usual'. For example, on 4 October Damascus Radio

announced that Assad would begin a nine-day tour of Syria's eastern provinces on 10 October. Meanwhile newspapers in both countries reported a deep political rift between Assad and Sadat.

Both Sadat and Assad also needed to 'deceive' their own troops, all the way up to senior field and staff officers. Very few of their soldiers knew that they were going to war until a few minutes before the offensive was actually launched. The highest-ranking Egyptian to fall into Israeli hands during the war, a colonel, told his interrogators that the first he heard of it was just after 1330hrs on 6 October when his commanding officer, a lieutenant general, rose from his prayers to inform his subordinate that war was about to begin – an announcement followed immediately by a flight of jets roaring overhead to bomb targets in Sinai.

Members of the Syrian Fedayeen guerrillas, the Saiqua, played a significant role in the deception plan to which Assad gave only reluctant consent. On 28 September, two Saiqua gunmen hijacked a train in Austria and took several Jewish passengers hostage. The resolution of this crisis proved to be a considerable distraction for the Israeli cabinet in the days leading up to the

With a crew of three comprising commander, gunner and driver as well as an infantry section of eight soldiers, the BMP-1 Infantry Fighting Vehicle (IFV) saw its combat debut during the Yom Kippur War. Armed with a 73mm smoothbore gun and a Sagger ATGW, the vehicle is fully amphibious and, for the first time, allowed the infantry in the back to fire their weapons from under armour, albeit in extremely cramped conditions. In Syrian hands, the BMP-1 did not prove very effective.

Based on the chassis of the PT-76 amphibious tank, the ZSU-23-4 proved to be a highly effective weapon system during the Yom Kippur War and inflicted significant losses on the Israeli Air Force in the early days of the hostilities. Its quadruple 23mm cannons were radar guided and normally fired bursts of 50 rounds a barrel to a combat range of 2,500m (8,200ft).

opening of Operation *Badr*. It also provided another cover for the Egyptian and Syrian mobilizations, as it could be plausibly argued that retaliatory measures by the IDF were now anticipated after the outrage in Austria.

On 3 October, the Soviet Union launched COSMOS-596, the first of a series of reconnaissance satellites, into orbit over the Middle East to cover Israel's northern and southern fronts. The Americans had launched a satellite performing the same function on 27 September. On the day of the Soviet satellite launch the Soviet Union began to withdraw Soviet personnel from Egypt, followed two days later by their personnel in Syria. On the night of 4 October, Syrian armour on the Golan moved from a defensive to an offensive posture.

The Syrian plan of attack

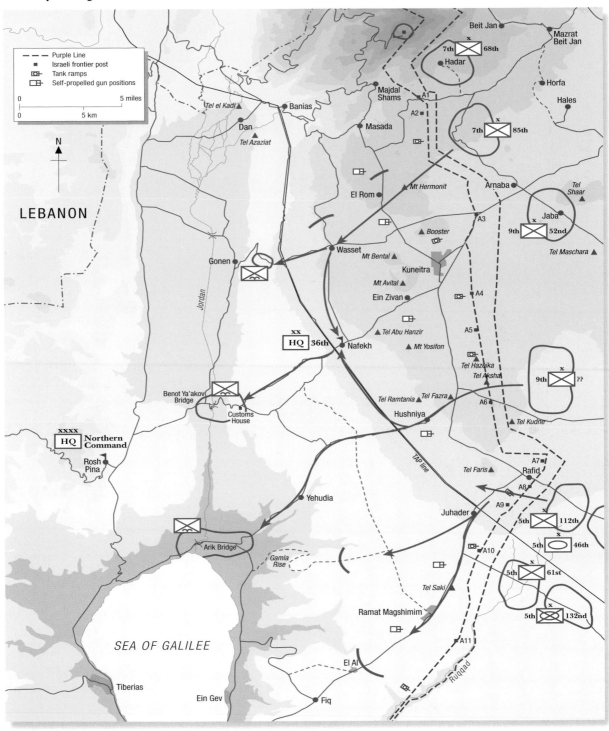

Purple Line
Israeli frontier post
Tank ramps
Self-propelled gun positions

0   5 miles
0   5 km

N

LEBANON

Tel el Kadi ▲
Banias
Dan ▲
Tel Azaziat ▲

Beit Jan ●
Mazrat Beit Jan ●
7th x 68th
Hadar ●
Horfa ●
Hales ●

Majdal Shams ●   A1
A2 ■
7th x 85th
☐ A2

Masada ●

☐

El Rom ●   ▲ Mt Hermonit
Arnaba ●
Tel Shaar ▲
A3
☐
x
9th x 52nd
Jaba ●
Tel Maschara ▲

Gonen ●
Wasset ●
Mt Bental ▲
Kuneitra
Mt Avital ▲
Ein Zivan ●   ☐ A4

Jordan

xx
HQ 36th
Nafekh
▲ Tel Abu Hanzir
▲ Mt Yosifon
A5
☐
Tel Hazeika
Tel Aksha
9th x ??

Benot Ya'akov Bridge
Customs House
Tel Ramtania ▲ ▲ Tel Fazra
Hushniya
A6 ■
▲ Tel Kudne

xxxx
HQ Northern Command
Rosh Pina ●
☐
A7 ■
Rafid ●
Tel Faris ▲
☐ A8
A9
Juhader ●
5th x 112th
5th ⬭ 46th

Yehudia ●
TAP line

Arik Bridge
Gamla Rise
☐ A10
☐
5th x 61st
Tel Saki ▲
5th x 132nd

SEA OF GALILEE

Ramat Magshimim ●
☐

Tiberias ●
Ein Gev ●
Fiq ●
El Al
A11
Ruqqad

אבירות

זהירות
מוטען חורג

One of the critical decisions that saved the Golan Heights from capture by the Syrians was the deployment of the regular 7th Armoured Brigade to Northern Command. At its base around Beersheba it had trained for desert warfare in the Sinai and as such was unfamiliar with the terrain on the Golan Heights. The 77th Battalion was the first of its units to be moved to the Golan, where it arrived on 4 October. It was to act as a reserve to the 188th Barak Brigade, under whose command it was placed. It had left its vehicles in the south and requisitioned replacements from Northern Command war stocks.

By September 1973 it was clear to the Israelis that a massive Syrian build-up was gathering momentum east of the Purple Line. Initially, Israeli intelligence chose to interpret this as no more than evidence of the training exercises that had taken place in previous years. However, from 20 September IAF reconnaissance photographs revealed that there were now three Syrian infantry divisions, with attached tank brigades, in their frontline and more mechanized and infantry units in the second line. An IDF intelligence estimate placed Syrian strength on the Golan at around 670 tanks and 100 batteries of artillery. Opposing this concentration on the other side of the Purple Line was one under-strength armoured brigade, the 188th Barak Armoured Brigade, and two infantry battalions.

The Israeli GOC Northern Command, Major General Hofi, was concerned by the Syrian concentration. At a meeting of the Israeli General Staff held on 24 September, Hofi pointed out that if it continued the Syrian build-up would be unprecedented in scale. The Syrians could attack without warning and with overwhelming force. In contrast to the Sinai, space could not be traded for time. Equally worrying was the introduction into the equation of the SAM batteries. The Chief of Staff, Lieutenant General David Elazar, echoed Hofi's concern. By contrast, the head of Israeli military intelligence, Major General Eliezer Zeira, was unruffled by the shape events were taking on Israel's Northern Front.

Ze'ira, who had only been in his post since the spring of 1973, subscribed to what the Israelis termed 'The Concept', a theory which ran as follows: Syria would only attack Israel in concert with Egypt; Egypt would not attack Israel until its air force had recovered from the catastrophe of 1967, a process that would take at least another five years; therefore there would be no war in 1973.

The Israeli Minister of Defense, Moshe Dayan, shared Zeira's optimism. Nevertheless, Dayan anticipated that the Syrians might respond to the air battle of 13 September and, with this in mind, on 26 September he placed the IDF on alert on both the Northern and Southern fronts, although this did not involve mobilization but simply putting Israel's active units on a war footing. On that day Dayan accompanied Elazar on a visit to Northern Command, during which he inspected a number of frontline positions. Hofi repeated his warnings as they viewed the concentration, which the Syrians were making only the most perfunctory efforts to conceal. Hofi drew Dayan's attention to the fact that in the Tel Kudne sector, on the Barak Brigade's southern front, there was a high

The 115mm smoothbore main armament of Syrian T-62s was able to penetrate all Israeli tanks at normal combat ranges with its fin-stabilized armour-piercing ammunition. Over 400 T-62s equipped the elite Assad Independent Armoured Brigade and the armoured brigades of the armoured divisions. Many were captured intact by the Israelis and converted for their own use. It was common practice for Syrian crews to cover the external fuel tanks of their Soviet designed tanks with sandbags in an effort to make them less vulnerable in battle.

THE SYRIAN OFFENSIVE

6–8 October 1973, viewed from the southwest showing the initial Syrian assault across the Purple Line and the breakthrough around Rafid and Hushniya.

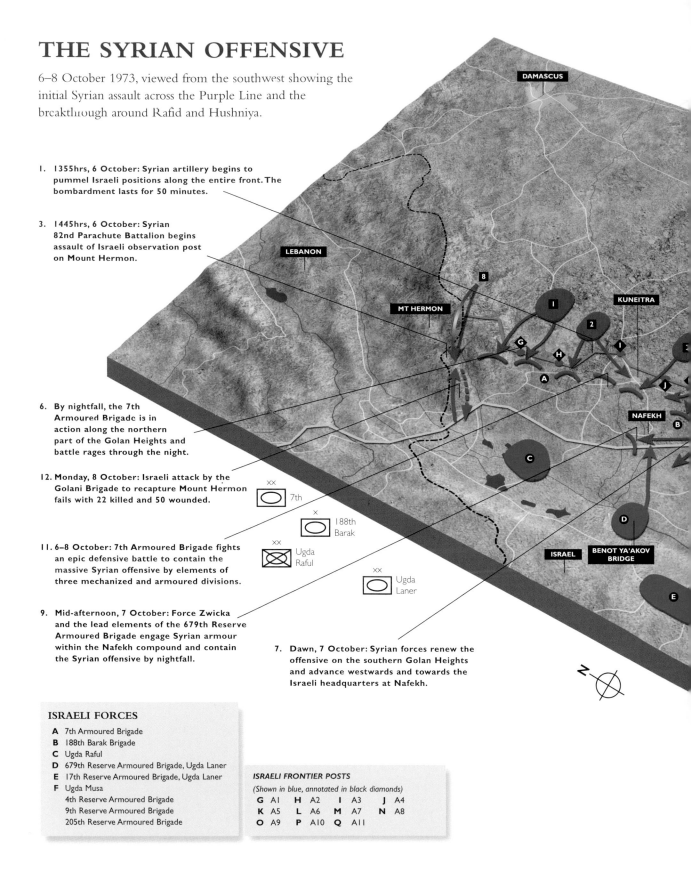

1. 1355hrs, 6 October: Syrian artillery begins to pummel Israeli positions along the entire front. The bombardment lasts for 50 minutes.

3. 1445hrs, 6 October: Syrian 82nd Parachute Battalion begins assault of Israeli observation post on Mount Hermon.

6. By nightfall, the 7th Armoured Brigade is in action along the northern part of the Golan Heights and battle rages through the night.

12. Monday, 8 October: Israeli attack by the Golani Brigade to recapture Mount Hermon fails with 22 killed and 50 wounded.

11. 6–8 October: 7th Armoured Brigade fights an epic defensive battle to contain the massive Syrian offensive by elements of three mechanized and armoured divisions.

9. Mid-afternoon, 7 October: Force Zwicka and the lead elements of the 679th Reserve Armoured Brigade engage Syrian armour within the Nafekh compound and contain the Syrian offensive by nightfall.

7. Dawn, 7 October: Syrian forces renew the offensive on the southern Golan Heights and advance westwards and towards the Israeli headquarters at Nafekh.

7th

188th Barak

Ugda Raful

Ugda Laner

DAMASCUS

LEBANON

MT HERMON

KUNEITRA

NAFEKH

ISRAEL

BENOT YA'AKOV BRIDGE

ISRAELI FORCES

- **A** 7th Armoured Brigade
- **B** 188th Barak Brigade
- **C** Ugda Raful
- **D** 679th Reserve Armoured Brigade, Ugda Laner
- **E** 17th Reserve Armoured Brigade, Ugda Laner
- **F** Ugda Musa
    - 4th Reserve Armoured Brigade
    - 9th Reserve Armoured Brigade
    - 205th Reserve Armoured Brigade

ISRAELI FRONTIER POSTS

(Shown in blue, annotated in black diamonds)

G	A1	**H**	A2	**I**	A3	**J**	A4
K	A5	**L**	A6	**M**	A7	**N**	A8
O	A9	**P**	A10	**Q**	A11		

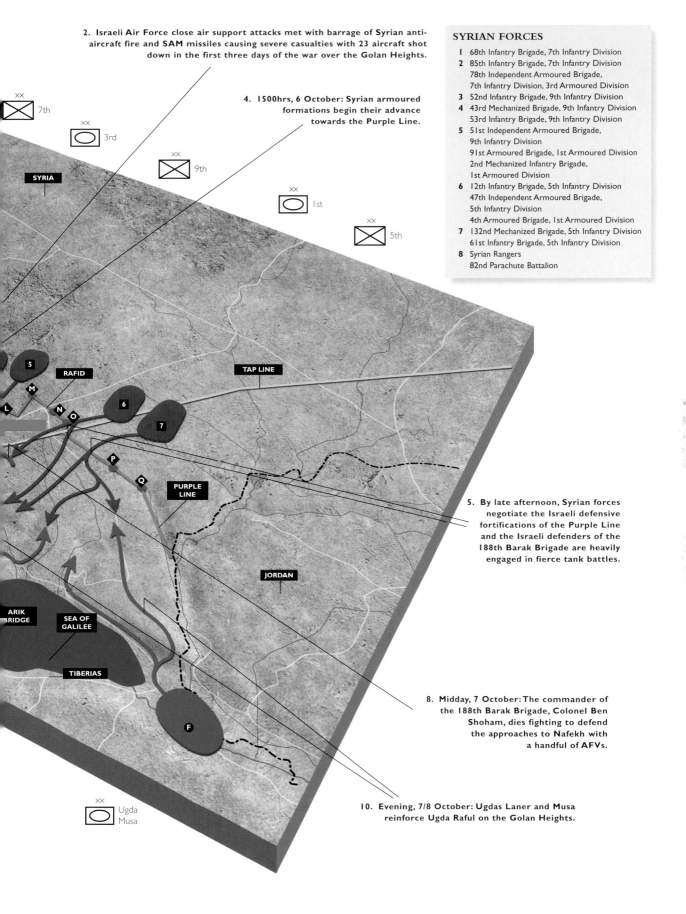

2. Israeli Air Force close air support attacks met with barrage of Syrian anti-aircraft fire and SAM missiles causing severe casualties with 23 aircraft shot down in the first three days of the war over the Golan Heights.

4. 1500hrs, 6 October: Syrian armoured formations begin their advance towards the Purple Line.

SYRIAN FORCES

1 68th Infantry Brigade, 7th Infantry Division
2 85th Infantry Brigade, 7th Infantry Division
   78th Independent Armoured Brigade,
   7th Infantry Division, 3rd Armoured Division
3 52nd Infantry Brigade, 9th Infantry Division
4 43rd Mechanized Brigade, 9th Infantry Division
   53rd Infantry Brigade, 9th Infantry Division
5 51st Independent Armoured Brigade,
   9th Infantry Division
   91st Armoured Brigade, 1st Armoured Division
   2nd Mechanized Infantry Brigade,
   1st Armoured Division
6 12th Infantry Brigade, 5th Infantry Division
   47th Independent Armoured Brigade,
   5th Infantry Division
   4th Armoured Brigade, 1st Armoured Division
7 132nd Mechanized Brigade, 5th Infantry Division
   61st Infantry Brigade, 5th Infantry Division
8 Syrian Rangers
   82nd Parachute Battalion

7th

3rd

SYRIA

9th

1st

5th

5

RAFID

TAP LINE

M

L

N O

6

7

P

PURPLE LINE

Q

5. By late afternoon, Syrian forces negotiate the Israeli defensive fortifications of the Purple Line and the Israeli defenders of the 188th Barak Brigade are heavily engaged in fierce tank battles.

JORDAN

ARIK BRIDGE

SEA OF GALILEE

TIBERIAS

F

8. Midday, 7 October: The commander of the 188th Barak Brigade, Colonel Ben Shoham, dies fighting to defend the approaches to Nafekh with a handful of AFVs.

Ugda Musa

10. Evening, 7/8 October: Ugdas Laner and Musa reinforce Ugda Raful on the Golan Heights.

concentration of field artillery, a significant indication of Syria's intention to launch an attack.

On the advice of generals Eitan and Hofi, Dayan then made two vital decisions. First he ordered that the single under-strength Barak Armoured Brigade garrisoning the Golan be reinforced by the 77th Battalion of the elite 7th Armoured Brigade, which was then stationed around Beersheba in southern Israel. The 7th Brigade had been formed in 1948 as the first armoured unit in the IDF and had spearheaded the Israeli thrusts in the Sinai in 1956 and 1967. Eventually, the entire 7th Armoured Brigade was mobilized for service on the Golan. To speed the transfer, the General Staff ordered the brigade commander, Colonel Avigdor 'Yanush' Ben Gal, to leave his own tanks at his training camp and take over tanks and heavy equipment from Northern Command's reserves. Dayan also sent artillery reinforcements north with 7th Armoured Brigade, which concentrated around the divisional headquarters at Nafekh.

By 2 October, Israeli intelligence was reporting an inexorable increase in Syrian strength immediately behind their frontline to 800 tanks and over 120 batteries of artillery. Three days later, on 5 October, the figures had risen again to 900 tanks and 140 artillery batteries. Northern Command intelligence also noted that the Syrian second line of defence was unoccupied, again prompting the conclusion that the Syrians were readying themselves for an attack. Meanwhile, the system designed to cope with the earlier flare-ups on the border swung into action. Leave was cancelled on the Golan and an emergency stand-to was implemented. The machinery of mobilization was checked and work redoubled on laying more minefields along the frontline.

On 5 October, Brigadier General Rafael Eitan, as commander of the 36th Division, was given permission by Hofi to move the entire 7th Brigade to the Golan Heights. It was to be concentrated as a reserve near Nafekh, poised to counterattack either north or south of Rafid. Hofi's staff believed that if the Syrians attacked, they would make their main effort in the centre along the Damascus–Kuneitra Road, enveloping Kuneitra from the north and racing on to seize the Benot Ya'akov Bridge over the Jordan River. In contrast, Eitan was anxious about a Syrian thrust south of Kuneitra over ground more favourable to armour.

It was the eve of Yom Kippur, the holiest of all days in Judaism. The IDF was now on the highest state of alert – 'Gimel–C' – for the standing army. The advanced headquarters of Northern Command was moved to the Golan and reserve units were ordered to be ready for mobilization at a moment's notice. Plans for the evacuation of civilians were readied. Artillery commanders were instructed to prepare targets and firing tables. After an intelligence briefing, Colonel Ben Shoham and the senior officers of the Barak Brigade met in an all-night conference in which they reviewed the situation running south from

Kuneitra to the Jordanian frontier. Meanwhile, the commander of the 7th Armoured Brigade, Colonel Ben Gal, accompanied his officers on a 'familiarization' trek over the northern sector of the frontline from the shoulder of Mount Hermon to Kuneitra. The two Israeli brigades on the Golan together fielded a total of 177 Centurion tanks.

On the night of 5 October, a huge weight of traffic struggled towards the Northern Front as personnel, vehicles and ammunition moved to the mobilization centres. As dawn broke on the 6th all seemed deceptively quiet. Northern Command's brigade commanders were summoned to an urgent meeting at Major General Hofi's headquarters to be informed of an imminent Syrian attack. Although all frontline units were in the highest state of alert it was, nevertheless, Yom Kippur and most soldiers were observing their devotions inside their bunkers, in their tank depots and at their machine-gun posts in the Mutzavim. Behind the steel doors of the observation post on Mount Hermon, now firmly locked, services were being held. Hofi informed his subordinates that a Syrian attack was expected at 1800 hours. It was not, however, thought this would be the preliminary to all-out war.

Tank crewmen of the 7th Armoured Brigade dismount from their Centurions armed with Uzi sub-machine guns. Originally the brigade was trained for deployment to the Sinai Desert but its brilliant commander, Colonel Avigdor 'Yanush' Ben Gal, had a premonition about the Golan Heights and ordered his battalion and company commanders to tour the frontlines behind the Purple Line in the weeks and days before the October War. It was a fateful decision which allowed the 7th Armoured Brigade to conduct arguably the greatest defensive battle in the annals of armoured warfare, notwithstanding the gallant stand of the 188th Barak Brigade.

The Syrian offensive

At 1345hrs spotters on Mount Hermon saw the Syrians remove the camouflage nets from the artillery pieces facing the Purple Line. Ten minutes later shells began to rain down upon Israeli positions along the entire length of the front. In the sectors chosen for the principal and subsidiary breakthroughs, on either side of Rafid and near Kuneitra, the Syrians had achieved a density of between 50 and 80 guns per kilometre, about half the concentration prescribed by strict Soviet doctrine but punishing nevertheless. The bombardment, delivered by artillery pieces ranging from 85 to 203mm calibre, had a numbing effect on the Israelis, sand-blasting the paint from tank hulls, cutting aerials and damaging optics. The bombardment, which lasted 50 minutes, was timed to coincide with the Egyptian crossing of the Suez Canal and was accompanied by air strikes against Israeli command centres and defensive positions.

At Nafekh, senior IDF commanders were attending an orders meeting at Eitan's HQ when it came under attack by Syrian fighter-bombers. As the officers gathered, they heard the roar of approaching aircraft immediately followed by a strafing and bombing attack. To the cacophony was added the crump of shells from Syrian artillery. This signalled the end of the orders group as battalion commanders hurried back to their units and Ben Gal hastily moved his brigade advanced headquarters out of the camp while the bombardment continued.

As Ben Gal's commanders returned to their units, their forward radio links confirmed that their deputies had already activated the IDF's contingency plans and the Centurions were lumbering towards their firing ramps to engage the dense columns of Syrian tanks and APCs that from 1500hrs were swarming towards the ceasefire line. Up to the moment when their engines roared into life, the crews of the Syrian armour had been receiving last-minute instructions from their Soviet advisers. Now the implementation of Operation *Badr* was in their hands.

Three Syrian divisions – 7th, 9th and 5th – moved forward behind a creeping barrage, bursting across the ceasefire line at pre-selected points to bypass the UN observation posts. The majority of the UN observer posts on the ceasefire line held out for the duration of the war; four were evacuated, three from the Israeli side and one from the Syrian. The observer officers in the posts on the Israeli side were able to maintain contact with UN headquarters in Jerusalem. One of these officers later likened the initial phase of the Syrian advance to a 'parade-ground demonstration'.

This was the fruit of months of careful preparation during which the Syrian tankers had honed tactics based on wave after wave of assaulting tanks rolling forward regardless of casualties and the progress, or lack of it, made by the wave in front. The assaults by the 7th and 5th Infantry Divisions were spearheaded by two slow-moving parallel columns of AFVs intermingled with command and

MAJOR SHUMEL ASKAROV, 53RD BATTALION, 188TH BARAK BRIGADE, IDF, DEFENDING MUTZAV 111 ON THE PURPLE LINE, EVENING, SATURDAY 6 OCTOBER 1973

At just 24 years of age, Major Shumel Askarov was the youngest deputy battalion commander in the Israeli Army. On the morning of 6 October, Askarov insisted on using his Sho't Upgraded Centurion to tour his command. At 1356hrs the peace and quiet of Yom Kippur was shattered by a massive Syrian artillery barrage and the exploding bombs of Syrian MiGs. Askarov immediately leapt into his tank at the Hushniya base and drove eastwards towards the Purple Line summoning other tanks of the battalion to follow him. Once at the Purple Line, his Sho't (centre) and a companion Centurion (left) mounted the tank firing ramps of Mutzav 111 overlooking Kudne. Askarov's vehicle bears the insignia of the 188th Barak Armoured Brigade on the rear hull, although this was not normally carried in combat for security reasons. The infantry strongpoint was defended by a platoon from the 50th Paratroop Battalion under the command of Sergeant Yoram Krivine. The hillock on which Mutzav 111 was situated offered a clear view far across the 1967 demarcation line. The Syrian bombardment had been under way for almost an hour when clouds of dust were clearly seen approaching from the east. Askarov had chosen the crew for his Sho't carefully and it included the finest tank gunner in the Barak Brigade, Yitzhak Hemo from the kibbutz at Kiryat Shmona. As his kibbutz was only a matter of miles behind the frontline, Hemo was fighting for his home and family. Within the first five hours of battle, Askarov and his crew destroyed 35 tanks and APCs including three of the vital MT-55/MTU-120 bridgelayers that were trying to span the anti-tank ditch to their front. Throughout

the late afternoon, the tanks of the Syrian 5th Infantry Division closed on Mutzav 111. Around 1900hrs Hemo destroyed a tank at a range of just 50m (55yds) and Askarov then swung the turret to engage a target just 30m (33yds) to their right. Both gunners fired at the same moment and both tanks were hit. Askarov was blown out of the turret and fell to the ground with wounds to the face and throat. He was rescued by the paratroopers inside the bunker (left) and evacuated to Safed hospital where he was operated on and told that he would remain in hospital for at least two weeks. Early on Monday morning, he discharged himself and returned to the desperate fighting on the Golan Heights, although he could not speak above a hoarse whisper. He rallied the remnants of the Barak Brigade and together with Colonel Yosi Ben Hannan, who had rushed back to Israel from his honeymoon in Nepal, Askarov scraped together some 13 battle-damaged tanks. This small force rushed to the front and arrived at a critical juncture when the hard-pressed remnants of the 7th Armoured Brigade were just about to be overrun. Both Ben Hannan and Askarov were wounded in the ensuing battle; the latter critically when a Kalashnikov round struck him in the head. Askarov was taken to the Rambam Hospital in Haifa where he was examined by four neurosurgeons. Three of them declared him beyond hope but the fourth surgeon, Yitzhak Shechter, persevered and performed an eight-hour operation that saved Askarov's life. Askarov was awarded the Medal of Gallantry, Israel's second highest decoration. (Howard Gerrard © Osprey Publishing Ltd)

support vehicles as well as towed and tracked anti-tank and anti-aircraft guns. In the vanguard were tanks designed to breach the minefields with rollers in front of their tracks. SU-100 SP guns, based on the T-34 chassis, were also in the vanguard, along with infantry armed with Saggers and RPG-7 rocket-propelled grenades and riding in APCs.

The 5th Infantry Division rumbled forward in good order, although its armour was soon bunched together in an unwieldy mass. The columns of the 7th and 9th Infantry Divisions respectively advancing north and south of Kuneitra, fell into confusion from the outset. The bridging tanks needed to cross the Israeli anti-tank ditches were stuck at the rear as road discipline disintegrated under the overwhelming pressure to get to grips with the Israelis.

The Israeli tank crews were ready and waiting. Firing from their ramps and trained to a high standard in long-range gunnery, they concentrated on the gaps that the Syrians had made in the minefields in the Israeli defences. They paid particular attention to the Syrian engineering equipment with accurate APDS fire aimed at the mine-clearing and bridge-laying tanks. One by one they were picked off at ranges of 2,000m (2,168yds) or more, while behind them a massive traffic jam was building up. In the confusion caused by the accurate Israeli fire,

Syrian tanks and APCs were forced off the road while frantic officers tried to restore order. Other tanks were ordered to smash straight through the minefields to clear a path for the bridge-laying armour moving up to deal with the anti-tank ditch. With the heavy losses of combat engineers, the Syrian infantry and tankers who reached the ditch were forced to leave their vehicles and, under heavy Israeli fire, begin to construct causeways with shovels. Eventually some bulldozers were brought up to fill in the ditch.

North of Kuneitra and south of the dominating Mount Hermonit was a ridgeline leading to another hill known to the Israelis as 'Booster', held by some tanks of the Barak Brigade's 74th Battalion, commanded by Lieutenant Colonel Yair Nafshi. The 74th Battalion, one of the two armoured battalions in the Barak Brigade, was strung out in platoons of three tanks to act in close support of the Israeli first line of defence and to deal with any breakthrough between them.

From the vantage point of Booster (known to the Arabs as Tel el Mehafi), Nafshi observed the advancing armoured columns of the Syrian 7th Infantry Division. Through the dust clouds raised by the Syrian artillery and armour, he could make out enemy bulldozer and MTU bridging tanks advancing at the head of the twin columns across a small dish-shaped valley. He ordered his tank crews to concentrate their fire on the bridging tanks. During the afternoon the Israeli tankers, firing at ranges of over 2,000m (2,186yds), accounted for all but two of the Syrian bridging tanks. The two that got away managed to reach the anti-tank ditch opposite Mount Hermonit. Meanwhile the plain below Booster was dotted with the burning hulks of Syrian tanks and APCs. It was the opening phase in a bitter battle for vital ground, which the Israelis were later to call the 'Valley of Tears'.

By the late afternoon of the 6th, Hofi concluded that the Barak Brigade was incapable of holding the entire Golan front against the weight of the Syrian onslaught, particularly south of Kuneitra. Accordingly, he ordered Ben Gal's 7th Brigade to transfer one of its battalions, the 82nd Battalion commanded by Lieutenant Colonel Haim Barak, to the Barak Brigade and simultaneously to take the responsibility for the line north of Kuneitra, assuming command of the Barak Brigade's 74th Battalion, which was already in the thick of the heavy fighting around the Booster feature. One of Ben Gal's battalions, the 71st under the command of Lieutenant Colonel Menachem Ratess, was to be held as a reserve. The 71st Battalion was a composite unit made up of students and instructors from the IDF Armour School that was attached to the 7th Armoured Brigade. Anticipating that he might lose control of this unit, Ben Gal collected a few tanks from each of his battalions to increase the size of his Sayeret reconnaissance unit to act as a brigade reserve force of about 20 tanks.

Meanwhile, Lieutenant Colonel Avigdor Kahalani's companies had moved east, under heavy artillery and air attack, to occupy blocking positions in the Booster sector. His tanks – now reduced to three companies, having lost one to

The Syrian breakthrough in the south, 6–8 October

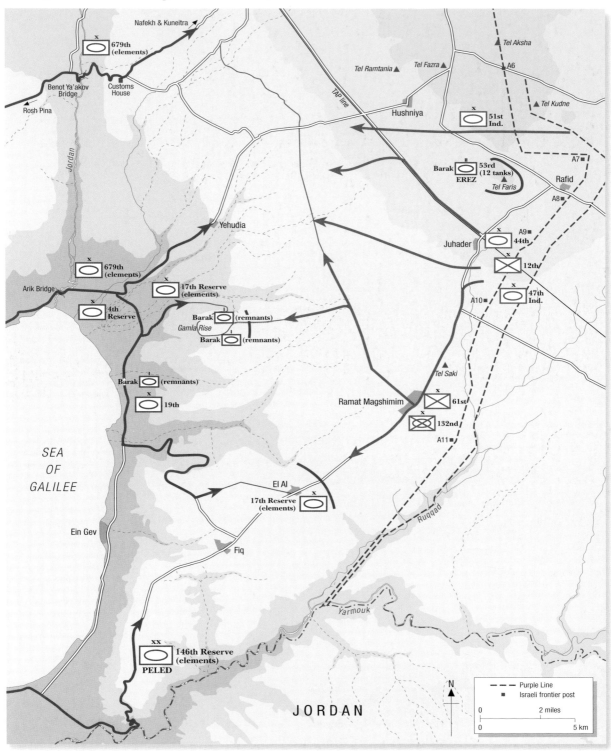

the brigade reconnaissance unit – took up their positions on the ramps overlooking the anti-tank ditch between Hermonit and Booster. Quickly deploying his tanks, designating fire sectors and co-ordinating direct and indirect fire, Kahalani swung his force into action. Battle was joined at odds of almost 15:1. It was to last for over 36 hours.

The capture of Mount Hermon

In the northernmost sector of the battlefield, Mount Hermon, the IDF suffered a potentially fatal reverse. The Syrians had originally planned to seize the Mount Hermon observation post at S-Hour, but there had been a delay in the briefing and organizing of the 500-strong 82nd Parachute Battalion tasked with the operation. It was not until 1400hrs that the Rangers reached the foot of the massif and began to scale it; 45 minutes later they were within 150m (164yds) of the observation post. Meanwhile, other paratroops had been inserted by helicopter below them to cover the road to Masada. As heavy artillery fire swept the fort and its surrounding defensive positions, the Syrians moved in cautiously, closing with the fort as most of its service personnel sought cover in the deep shelter at its heart. The Rangers had received the most detailed briefing for the

In the first hours of the war, the Syrians tried desperately to span the Israeli anti-tank ditch stretching along the Purple Line with vehicle-launched tank bridges. The withering fire from the Israeli Sho't tanks on their elevated ramps destroyed many of the specialized AFVs. It was not until nightfall that the Syrians were able to breach the defensive line and advance onto the Golan Heights in strength.

A PT-55 with mine-roller attachment moves along the road near UN Patrol Base 44 and Tel El Merhi after the area was handed back to the Syrians following the Israeli withdrawal on 15 June 1973. These specialized tanks and the MTU-55/MT-55 Bridgelayers were the priority targets for Israeli tank gunners during the first hours of the war to prevent them from breaching the anti-tank obstacles along the Purple Line. (United Nations)

operation and each section had a precisely allotted task. The drifting smoke of battle obscured the plain below them.

In their first attempt to rush the position with a frontal attack, the Syrians sustained 50 casualties. They regrouped and began sniping at the Israelis' outer positions while slowly working their way forward. Inside the observation post the non-combatants were frozen with fear and reluctant to come to the aid of the men of the Golani Brigade. At about 1700hrs the Syrians attacked again, coming in from the west with the sun dazzling the defenders. The Israelis withdrew from the outer defences into the main central position, which was shielded by a high wall. The Rangers, using ropes and grappling hooks, scaled this. Hand-to-hand fighting ensued in which the outnumbered Israelis were overcome. Eleven managed to escape, scrambling down the mountainside and the remainder were taken prisoner.

The Syrians then cleared the underground passages but were unable to break into the main sensor and communications centre, which was protected by its heavy locked steel door. They resorted to stern measures, beating an Israeli prisoner until he unlocked the door. The men inside the communications centre were then shot. On the morning of the 8th an attempt to recapture the Mount Hermon position with a detachment from the Golani Brigade ran into a Syrian ambush and was driven back with losses of 22 killed and 50 wounded. For the remainder of the war the Syrian Rangers, who were troubled only by intermittent air attacks and artillery bombardment, occupied the position. The post's sophisticated Japanese electronic and observation equipment was removed by the Syrians and given to the Soviet Union, much to their delight.

The turret crew of a Sho't peer apprehensively at the camera shortly before the war began. This crew is reputedly from the 74th Battalion of the Barak Brigade. After the war, the 7th Armoured Brigade gained much of the credit for saving the Golan Heights from the initial Syrian onslaught, but the Barak Brigade was equally worthy of praise as it fought to the last suffering the heaviest casualties of any unit on the Golan, with 112 soldiers killed in action.

In the open rolling terrain of the Golan Heights, tank crews used every fold in the ground to conceal themselves from enemy observation and direct fire. The rough basalt rock outcrops restricted the movement of tanks to a great degree and forced wheeled vehicles to use the roads and tracks almost exclusively. This left them vulnerable to enemy artillery fire directed by Syrian observers high above the Golan Heights on Mount Hermon, captured by Syrian Special Forces and paratroopers on the first day of the war. During the initial Syrian assault, ammunition supplies ran critically low in the defending Centurions. Troops in Jeeps and halftracks retrieved individual rounds from knocked out vehicles and distributed them to the surviving tanks despite the withering artillery fire.

The Syrians were now exerting intense pressure along the entire Israeli line. At about 1700hrs it became clear that the Syrian 5th Infantry Division was threatening to burst through the Rafid Gap towards Juhader. Colonel Ben Shoham hurried to Juhader along the TAP line to direct the battle and re-supply the Barak Brigade's hard-pressed 53rd Mechanized Infantry Battalion, commanded by Lieutenant Colonel Oded Erez. In his half-track, Ben Shoham took with him his operations officer, Major Benny Katzin, while his deputy, Lieutenant Colonel David Yisraeli, remained in Nafekh.

Ben Shoham's advanced headquarters reached Juhader only to come under intense artillery bombardment. The Syrians, who were monitoring Ben Shoham's communications network, kept him pinned down and he was unable to link up with Erez, who was himself surrounded. Ben Shoham now ordered supplies and ammunition to be brought up to re-supply Erez's tanks and APCs as, one by one, they slipped out of their positions to rendezvous with the logistics column. However, before this hazardous manoeuvre could be attempted a lone Syrian tank appeared, probing up the TAP line road.

The Syrian tank, which approached to within a few metres of Ben Shoham's halftrack, turned tail and fled. Ben Shoham decided that this was too close for comfort and that he and his ammunition supply convoy should return to Nafekh to organize a counterattack force. The Syrians now had 150 tanks in the area of

MAJOR QABLAN, SYRIAN 9TH INFANTRY DIVISION, DIRECTING SPECIALIZED AFVS CONFRONTING THE ISRAELI ANTI-TANK OBSTACLES BEHIND THE PURPLE LINE, EVENING, 6 OCTOBER 1973

In the organization of their land forces for the 1973 offensive the Syrians followed Soviet doctrine, deploying armour en masse. Each of the three attacking infantry divisions had an integral armoured brigade with 180 T-54/55 tanks. These were backed up by two armoured divisions, each with 230 of the latest Soviet tank design then exported – the T-62 with its powerful 115mm main armament. In addition there were another 400 tanks in independent brigades giving a grand total of 1,400 tanks. Syrian military intelligence had determined that the Israelis had only about 200 tanks on the Golan Heights giving the Syrians an overall 7:1 advantage; the odds were even greater at the actual point of attack. However, the nature of the terrain on the Golan Heights left the Syrians few choices for the axes of their offensive. Accordingly, the Israelis' main defensive line was situated on the high ground some distance behind the 1967 Demarcation Line. At those places of greatest threat, the Israelis had constructed an anti-tank ditch to delay the enemy's advance and to channel their AFVs into prepared 'killing zones'. The actual ditch was 5m (16ft 4in.) wide and 3m (9ft 10in.) deep with the spoil heaped up along the Syrian side of the ditch to a height of almost 2m (6ft 6in.). On each side of the ditch, mines were laid in a belt 3m (9ft 10in.) wide with anti-tank mines just 1m (3ft 3in.) apart. The dimensions of the ditch were specifically calculated to thwart the capabilities of Soviet tank-launched bridging equipment. The advance of the Syrian 9th Infantry Division has faltered at the edge of the anti-tank ditch barring the Jasim–Kudne road. The

force commander, Major Qablan (right), calls forward his specialized armour with a T-55 with KMT mine-roller detonating an anti-tank mine while an MTU-120 bridgelayer has just been hit by a Sho't of the 188th Barak Brigade on a firing ramp some 1,500m (1,640yds) to the west. Moments later the gallant Major Qablan's tank was hit by an APDS round and he was thrown from the turret before his tank exploded in a ball of fire. Above the battlefield, IAF Skyhawks fly a desperate close support mission to stem the Syrian assault only to be met by a volley of SAM-6 missiles and the concentrated fire of radar-guided ZSU-23-4 anti-aircraft guns (far left), which have hit one of the attacking aircraft. UN observers along the Purple Line recall that the first IAF planes appeared over the Golan Heights just minutes after war broke out when four Skyhawks flew in low around Mount Hermon. Before they were able to engage any Syrian targets, two were blown out of the sky by SAM-6 missiles. Although temporarily checked at the anti-tank ditch, the Syrian onslaught continued. As night fell, the Syrians brought up Caterpillar D-9 Bulldozers and quickly levelled the ditch. With no night-fighting equipment, there was little the defending Israeli tanks could do to stop them as the supporting artillery guns soon ran out of illuminating rounds. As the sun rose on Sunday 7 October, the tanks and APCs of the Syrian 43rd Mechanized Infantry and 51st Armoured Brigades resumed the offensive in overwhelming force against the dwindling numbers of the 188th Barak Brigade. (Howard Gerrard © Osprey Publishing Ltd)

Tel Kudne, 60 on the TAP line and a combined total of 140 around frontier posts A9 and A10, respectively north and south of the TAP line.

Unable to return directly to Nafekh, as the Syrians were infiltrating behind him, Ben Shoham had to make a detour by way of the Gamla Rise. The Barak Brigade had been badly battered and by late evening its remaining 15 'runners' faced 450 Syrian tanks. The Syrian infantry's Saggers and RPG-7s had inflicted much damage. The line south of the Juhader road crumbled as the survivors, in groups of twos and threes, concentrated on slowing the Syrian push up the TAP line road, which if successful could turn the entire Israeli position on the Golan.

The Syrian 5th Infantry Division continued to make progress after nightfall. It fanned out into three columns. The northernmost advanced along the TAP line before swinging west to Yehudia and the Arik Bridge, the southern column moved down the road from Rafid towards El Al while the third column peeled away to drive west from Ramat Magshimim. Ben Shoham gave orders for the evacuation of four of his eight frontline strongholds. The remainder were already enveloped and isolated.

The Syrians were well supplied with night-vision equipment for driver, gunner and commander and this soon began to tell. In the Valley of Tears, Kahalani's tankers were now unable to identify targets at long range. Artillery

A Centurion Sho't of the OZ 77th Battalion manoeuvres to another fire position covered by the gun of a companion vehicle. Commanded by the legendary Lieutenant Colonel Avigdor Kahalani, the 77th Battalion was called the OZ battalion: OZ being the Hebrew word for courage or valour while the number 77 is the numerical equivalent of the Hebrew letters of OZ. The other battalions within the 7th Armoured Brigade were the 71st Armoured Battalion under the command of Lieutenant Colonel Menachem Ratess; the 75th Mechanized Infantry Battalion – Lieutenant Colonel Yoss Eldar and the 82nd Armoured Battalion – Lieutenant Colonel Haim Barak. However, the flexibility of the Israeli command structure allowed battalions to be redeployed to other brigades. In addition ad hoc units were created to carry out particular tasks, acting as a brigade reserve for example.

illumination, called in to light up the battlefield, was sporadic – the artillery had only limited supplies of parachute illuminating shells and ammunition was running low. The IAF flew in to drop flares but these did little to dissipate the dark shadows on the floor of the valley. Such illumination as there was came from burning vehicles, and ranges closed to as little as 100m (109yds).

Syrian armour rolled forward, using coloured formation signs and flashing blinkers to mark the cleared mine corridors. Kahalani ordered his tank commanders to use their infrared sensitive binoculars to attempt to identify the Syrian formation lamps and infrared 'cat's eyes' winking across the Valley of Tears. The Israeli tank commanders used the Syrian lights to aim their guns, but without proper night-vision equipment, they were still unable to operate effectively at long range.

The fighting in the Valley of Tears was relentless. At 2200hrs the Syrian 7th Infantry Division put in another heavy attack, which was driven off after three hours of close-quarter fighting. The Israelis had also taken losses from the intense Syrian artillery fire. Nevertheless, the Syrians were still stuck fast in the

Israeli reinforcements move forward under intense artillery bombardment with knocked-out vehicles strewn beside the road. The view from this M3 halftrack command vehicle shows the vulnerability of the open-top APC to artillery fire and airburst shells, although many Israeli infantrymen preferred the old M3 to the cramped interior of the M113 Zelda.

OPPOSITE
One of the primary Syrian
objectives was the main Israeli
headquarters on the Golan
Heights at Nafekh Camp. In the
early afternoon of 7 October,
Syrian armour burst into the
camp causing General 'Raful'
Eitan to move his headquarters
staff rapidly northwards leaving
some administrative personnel
to fight off the Syrian onslaught.
These three officers formed
themselves into a bazooka team
and destroyed several tanks
including the one in the
background, hit as it mounted
a perimeter wall where its
engine remained running for
the next two days.

Valley of Tears. As dawn came up on 7 October, over 100 Syrian tanks lay damaged or destroyed on the floor of the valley.

At the same time, Ben Shoham received permission from Major General Hofi to take command of all the scattered forces in the southern Golan. South of Juhader, Lieutenant Colonel Oded Erez, commander of the Barak's 53rd Battalion, had called in air support. The four A-4 Skyhawks that flew in to bomb the Syrians were all downed by SAMs, exploding in full view of Erez's men. They were followed by a second flight of four, which lost a further two aircraft to Syrian missiles. Erez declined to call for any more air support. By 0800hrs, another Syrian breakthrough on the TAP line north of the 53rd Battalion removed any hope of their linking up with Ben Shoham and Erez was given permission to withdraw from Juhader and concentrate his force of 12 tanks and move to Tel Faris.

Ten kilometres (6 miles) to the southwest of Juhader, the Syrian 5th Infantry Division was exploiting the breakthrough it had made to Ramat Magshimim. As dawn came up, the Syrians enjoyed a magnificent view of the Sea of Galilee and of the town of Tiberias on its western shore. It seemed that victory was within their grasp. Aware that they were still meeting stubborn resistance to the north in the Valley of Tears while on the southern front the IDF forces appeared to be in disarray, the Syrian High Command now threw its weight behind the success in the south. It directed the 1st Armoured Division to exploit the breakthrough at Rafid and ordered the 15th Mechanized Brigade, 3rd Armoured Division, to move through the gap between Rafid and Tel Kudne. The Syrian Army was now deploying some 600 tanks in the southern Golan. All that opposed them was Erez's 12 tanks at Tel Faris, a few isolated units that had been cut off along the ceasefire line and a trickle of reserve units that were now beginning to arrive on the Golan.

Ben Shoham, still cut off from the remnants of his forces in the southern Golan, could see the dust clouds of the advancing Syrian columns. At his immediate disposal were one tank and a halftrack. Under fire from Syrian armour he headed for the Gamla Rise, which overlooks the eastern shore of the Sea of Galilee. On the way he gathered units straggling back to the Buteiha Valley and the Arik Bridge. Ben Shoham drove north past the Arik Bridge on a secondary road on the east bank of the Jordan and on to Nafekh, arriving there at about 0900hrs.

He was soon on the move again, setting out down the TAP line to link with his deputy, Lieutenant Colonel Yisraeli, who was now fighting alongside the redoubtable Lieutenant Zwi 'Zwicka' Greengold. It was at this point in the battle that the leading elements of the 679th Armoured Brigade began to arrive, having been rushed piecemeal to the Golan, and were organized into three-tank platoons, netted into a communications network and then sent down the TAP line route to bolster the Barak Brigade. Another ad hoc formation of six tanks

was ordered to advance parallel to the TAP line towards Hushniya, a ruined relic of the 1967 war dominated by a single bullet-scarred minaret, to counter a strong force of Syrian armour.

At about midday, this unit of six tanks reported that it had encountered a force of some 80 Syrian tanks, advanced elements of Syrian 1st Armoured Division, which had burst through the Rafid Gap and now presented a looming threat to the IDF headquarters at Nafekh. Radio contact with the ad hoc group was lost soon afterwards and within another 30 minutes alarming reports were coming in of Syrian tanks around Tel Abu Hanzir only 3km (2 miles) to the east of Nafekh. Immediately Eitan ordered Ben Shoham to withdraw down the TAP line to Nafekh and prepare a line of defence.

Eitan also ordered Lieutenant Colonel Yisraeli to cover Ben Shoham as he extricated himself. It was during the course of this fighting that Yisraeli was killed after his own tank ran out of ammunition and was shot up by Syrian armour. Unaware of the fate of his deputy, Ben Shoham continued to transmit orders to Yisraeli as he hurried back to Nafekh. He was barely 200m (219yds) from the base when he was killed by machine-gun fire from a disabled Syrian tank, as was his operations officer, Major Katzin.

T-55 tanks and BMP-1 Infantry Fighting Vehicles, probably of the Syrian 46th Armoured Brigade, lie burnt and abandoned along the Purple Line near Rafid, the victims of the deadly accuracy of the 188th Barak Brigade in the first hours of the war. (United Nations)

Within an hour of Ben Shoham's death, forward elements of the Syrian 1st Armoured Division attacked Nafekh, precipitating the evacuation of Eitan's advanced headquarters, racing out of the northern gate past blazing vehicles, to establish a new headquarters some 5km (3 miles) to the north. Syrian shells set the camp ablaze. Eitan later confessed that he had waited until 'it was no longer a disgrace to clear out; when the Syrian tanks had bypassed the camp on both sides.'

On Nafekh's southern perimeter was Lieutenant Colonel Pinie, deputy commander of the Brigade District, who had been ordered by Eitan to establish anti-tank defences around the camp. Now Syrian tanks were bulldozing their way through the perimeter fence and Pinie's men had fled. Beckoning two infantrymen guarding the southern gate with a bazooka, Pinie ran to some rising ground near the fence. Also with him were his operations and district assistant intelligence officers. For the operations officer, now siting the bazooka, it was a baptism of fire. Pinie acted as his number two while the intelligence officer manned a machine-gun.

A Syrian tank approached to within 200m (219yds) but with his third shot Pinie's operations officer scored a direct hit on the driver's aperture, forcing the crew to abandon their vehicle while the intelligence officer raked them with machine-gun fire. For two days the tank remained entangled in the fence, its engine still running. Shortly after the tank was abandoned, a series of explosions heralded the simultaneous arrival at Nafekh of two more Syrian tanks and the Israeli 679th Reserve Armoured Brigade, which Eitan had ordered down from the Kuneitra sector to hold the line at Nafekh. The Syrian tanks went up in sheets of flame and Pinie and his men raced to the southeast corner of the camp where a battle between Syrian and Israeli armour had erupted. Taking up position, they destroyed one Syrian tank and missed another with their last shell. As the Syrian tank's turret swung towards Pinie and his men, it was blown apart by a shell fired from the tank commanded by Lieutenant Greengold, who had been fighting continuously for almost 20 hours despite being severely wounded.

The intervention of the 679th Reserve Armoured Brigade, whose men had only hours before been going about their civilian lives, had proved crucial. Pitched into a high-intensity armoured battle, they had beaten off a Syrian advance that threatened to sunder the southern front in the Golan. By nightfall, the 679th Reserve Armoured Brigade had cleared the area around Nafekh and blunted another armoured thrust by the Syrian 7th Infantry Division, attacking west from Kuneitra.

For both Israel and Syria, the battle on the Northern Front had become a race against time. The Israelis knew that if they could not hold the Syrians until their reserve formations reached the Golan front, northern Galilee would be crushed by the weight of Syrian armour. The IDF was now so short of ammunition that Jeeps were scurrying from one disabled tank to another to collect unused shells. For their part, the Syrians were aware that the thin screen of tanks confronting them east and south of the Arik Bridge was all that stood between them and victory. By the afternoon of 7 October, a Syrian brigade was within 1,200m (1,312yds) of El Al and another, on the Yehudia road, was less than 10km (6 miles) from the Sea of Galilee.

However, the Syrians had taken heavy casualties, particularly when they had ventured out beyond their SAM umbrella, presenting targets to the IAF. Their tanks clung to the roads and made little or no attempt to camouflage or dig in. By late afternoon on 7 October, the Israelis estimated that they had destroyed some 400 Syrian tanks. Mindful of their defeat in 1967, the entire Syrian Army – from generals to the lowliest soldier – was determined not to retreat under any circumstances save orders from higher command. As a result, on meeting stubborn Israeli opposition, middle-ranking Syrian officers were loath to make any tactical withdrawals, even for the purposes of manoeuvring. They simply tried to batter their way through defences that, had they shown greater flexibility and co-ordination, could have been outflanked rather than out-fought. The IDF developed a grudging respect for Syrian courage, but in the final analysis Syrian tactical shortcomings would hand the initiative back to the Israelis.

The IDF, giving priority to the Northern Front, was now flying up replacement tank crews in helicopters that then returned with the wounded. Mobilization was moving into top gear, and the Deputy Chief of General Staff, Major General Israel Tal, made a key decision to commit reserve units as soon as they were assembled. Although this ensured their speedy arrival on the Golan, it was to cause considerable command and organizational problems.

However, the situation remained critical for the IDF. Early on 7 October Moshe Dayan, the Israeli Minister of Defense, made flying visits to the Southern and Northern fronts. He was alarmed by the situation in the north and returned to Tel Aviv to advise the Prime Minister, Golda Meir, that the IDF must withdraw from the Golan Heights to the very edge of the escarpment overlooking the Jordan Valley.

Golda Meir turned for advice to the retired Lieutenant General Chaim Bar-Lev, now Minister for Trade and Industry. Meir was well aware that a disaster in the north could have catastrophic consequences in Galilee. Bar-Lev donned a uniform and, with the agreement of generals Elazar and Dayan, hurried to Northern Command headquarters in Rosh Pina on the evening of 7 October. Elazar had authorized Bar-Lev to issue emergency orders in the name of the IDF should he deem this necessary.

Noting the unmistakable air of gloom that pervaded Hofi's HQ, Bar-Lev outlined the plans that had been made for the speedy mobilization and deployment of two reserve divisions, commanded respectively by Major Generals Dan Laner and Moshe Peled, and for the interim piecemeal commitment of mobilized reserves as they arrived. Then Bar-Lev drove to Laner's HQ – no more than three tanks and three APCs – at the Arik Bridge. Here he spoke briefly and persuasively to staff officers and senior commanders, instilling calm and confidence and issuing orders for a counterattack on 8 October. In morale terms, Bar-Lev's intervention was crucial.

On the evening of 7 October, Major General Laner had secured agreement to a division of responsibilities on the Golan with Eitan. The dividing line between their commands lay approximately a kilometre south of the Benot Ya'akov–Kuneitra road. Eitan was to be responsible for everything north of that line including the road, Laner for all operations to the south.

Laner had, as yet, no clear idea of what was happening on the ground for which he was now responsible, but from his forward command post, at the Arik Bridge, he realised that Syrian tanks were barely 5km (3 miles) away. His first action had been to send the 679th Reserve Armoured Brigade, under the command of Colonel Uri Orr, to support Eitan and relieve Nafekh. By nightfall, Orr had secured Nafekh after a tough encounter battle with the Syrian 91st Armoured Brigade, which was driven away to the east and south. Orr was now able to send fresh elements of his brigade north to take up position on the right flank of the 7th Armoured Brigade.

Laner began to reorganize his forces. The commander of the 4th Reserve Armoured Brigade was ordered to take the road south to Gamla Rise where he was joined by one of Barak's company commanders with two reserve tank companies; 19th Brigade was also ordered to move south to El Al with whatever forces were immediately available, where it was joined by another of Barak Brigade's reserve companies; 17th Brigade to the northeast, fewer than 50 tanks strong and locked in a desperate struggle on the Yehudia road, was reinforced with the tanks of a divisional reconnaissance unit bound for Eitan but commandeered by Laner. It had run into three Syrian tank brigades – 47th, 48th, 51st – and in a series of stiff actions on the Yehudia–Hushniya road, the brigade accounted for over 50 Syrian tanks before its commander, Colonel Ran Sarig, was wounded and evacuated to the rear.

Under heavy Syrian fire, Laner himself acted as divisional traffic policeman, sending units on their way as they arrived by platoons and companies. The situation remained one of great confusion. Only prompt thinking by Laner prevented Barak units on the Gamla Rise from firing on retreating troops of the Golani Brigade under the mistaken impression they were Syrian infantry.

By 1200hrs on the 7th, Laner had committed some 60 tanks on his front, a figure that had increased to 90 by dusk. Holding the last high ground just east of the escarpment, the tanks were now engaged in a desperate struggle with the armour of the Syrian 5th Infantry Division and its attached armoured brigade. By the end of the day the southern Golan from Nafekh to the Yarmouk Valley

Tlas was to compound this error by committing his reserve 3rd Armoured Division to the attack in the north, where the Israeli defence was holding, rather than reinforce success in the south. In fact, Tlas achieved the worst of all possible results by splitting the 3rd Armoured Division both to reinforce the 7th Infantry Division in the fight for Booster and to support the 9th Infantry Division in a bid to outflank Rafid and link up with the 1st Armoured Division. He had committed the cardinal sin of failing to maintain the operation's aim and was to pay dearly for it.

On the evening of 7 October, the leading units of Major General Moshe Peled's 146th Reserve Armoured Division were moving up the El Al road. Initially, there had been some disagreement within the Israeli High Command over the deployment of Peled's division. It had been proposed that the division should concentrate at the Benot Ya'akov Bridge. Peled had opposed this first option, on the grounds that he had few transporters. His division had already been travelling a long time on tracks and to reach the Benot Ya'akov would require yet more punishing track mileage. Peled urged that he be allowed to attack along the El Al axis, and the southern route was confirmed by Hofi with the backing of Bar-Lev. Barely 36 hours after the opening of the Syrian offensive, the IDF was about to launch a major counterattack.

The Valley of Tears

At 0800hrs on 7 October, the Syrians went on the attack again in the Valley of Tears. The 78th Armoured Brigade of the 7th Infantry Division advanced along a 3km (2 mile) front between Booster and Mount Hermonit, aiming to push a force up the wadi running along the base of Hermonit towards Wasset. Colonel Avigdor Ben Gal conducted a masterful defence, conserving his forces and always retaining a reserve. He stayed in constant touch with Eitan as the battle progressed. The 7th Brigade was soon fighting at ranges that varied from point-blank to 2,500m (2,733yds). The attack lasted some four hours and then the Syrians withdrew, leaving more mangled armour on the valley floor. Plumes of smoke hung over knocked-out tanks.

While the 71st Battalion remained in the northern sector, the 77th OZ Battalion was moved from south of Kuneitra to a central position overlooking the Valley of Tears at Hermonit. The battalion commander, Lieutenant Colonel Avigdor Kahalani, left a company behind in the Kuneitra sector, guarding the brigade's flank, and during the afternoon it came under heavy Syrian attack. Once again the Syrians were driven off, leaving 20 tanks behind them.

At 2200hrs, the Syrians launched a night attack in Ben Gal's central sector preceded by a massive artillery bombardment. The Syrian 7th Infantry Division had now been augmented by the 3rd Armoured Division, whose 81st Armoured Brigade was equipped with T-62 tanks. Kahalani had at his disposal some

40 tanks to pit against the Syrians' 500. Using its night-fighting equipment, the Syrian armour closed to ranges of 50m (55yds) while infantry equipped with RPGs attempted to infiltrate the Israeli lines. The fighting reached a climax at about 0100hrs on the 8th and then abruptly ceased as the Syrians scurried about the battlefield, attempting to evacuate their wounded and their damaged tanks. The Israelis laid down heavy artillery fire as their own tanks were refuelled and reloaded.

The Syrians attacked again at 0400hrs and, as the sky grew lighter, an increasingly nightmarish scene was revealed in the Valley of Tears. Many of the abandoned or wrecked Syrian tanks and APCs were between or behind the Israeli positions. The extent of 7th Armoured Brigade's plight was all too evident and Ben Gal ordered the brigade to fire at every moving target in sight.

The Syrians were suffering too. Brigadier General Omar Abrash, commanding the 7th Infantry Division, withdrew the battered units of his first echelon and committed the second echelon, planning to take advantage of the Syrian night-vision equipment. At dusk, while readying his armour for attack, Abrash was killed when his command tank took a direct hit. This setback

A Centurion lies burnt out and gutted after a massive internal explosion rent the tank asunder. This unmodified petrol-engined version of the Centurion was more susceptible to fire than the Sho't Upgraded Centurion with its diesel engine. Statistically, every Israeli tank deployed on the Golan Heights was hit one and a half times and 250 were knocked out, although all but 100 were subsequently returned to operational status.

undoubtedly dealt a severe blow to Syrian morale and the attack was postponed to the morning of 9 October. At about 0800hrs, after an accurate artillery barrage, the Syrians attempted to force their way through the Valley of Tears towards the high ground between Mount Hermonit and Booster.

The preliminary Syrian bombardment had been so intense that Ben Gal had ordered the tanks of the 77th Battalion to leave the ridge where they occupied a natural firing ramp and fall back 500m (547yds), anticipating that there would be sufficient time for them to regain their positions once the bombardment had lifted. But the Syrians moved too fast, seizing the crest where the 77th Armoured Battalion had been positioned and threatening a breakthrough. The outcome of the battle now hung in the balance. Suddenly a force of Syrian Mi-8 helicopters swooped over the armoured slogging match on the ridgeline, heading west to land a raiding party of commandos near El Rom. Shortly afterwards, Eitan received a report that a body of Syrian infantry was advancing to the north of El Rom. The drive on El Rom had also been joined by the T-62s of Assad's Republican Guard, which had pushed up the wadi below Hermonit and past the Israeli frontline. If the Syrian armour could link up with the infantry in the

With over 30 years in combat, the venerable M4 Sherman remained in widespread service with the IDF during the Yom Kippur War in many different variants such as this Makmat 160mm self-propelled mortar which is grinding its way towards the frontline on the Golan Heights with Syrian prisoners of war cowering in the foreground. With a range of 9,600 metres (10,493yds), the Soltam M66 160mm mortar was a potent weapon based on an M4A3E8 Sherman chassis fitted with a Cummins VT-8-460Bi diesel engine. The IDF employed heavy mortars as a cheaper alternative to conventional tube artillery. The outset of the Yom Kippur War saw only 11 artillery batteries with 44 self-propelled guns and insufficient ammunition to stem the Syrian onslaught on the Golan Heights. The problem was exacerbated by the breakdown of the field artillery computer direction system during the first afternoon of the war. However, mortars were essential to counter Syrian Sagger teams and snipers hiding in dead ground among the rocky outcrops. (© Christian Simonpietri/Corbis Sygma)

STAFF SERGEANT AMIR BASHARI, 2ND PLATOON, 3RD COMPANY, 77TH BATTALION, 7TH ARMOURED BRIGADE, IDF, OVERLOOKING THE VALLEY OF TEARS, EVENING, SATURDAY 6 OCTOBER 1973

The majority of the personnel of the 7th Armoured Brigade were young conscripts of 19 or 20 years of age who had never been in combat before. Although an elite formation within the Israeli Armoured Corps, the 7th Armoured Brigade had trained extensively for war in the Sinai Desert and was deployed to the Golan Heights just days before the outbreak of the October War. Staff Sergeant Amir Bashari was a veteran platoon sergeant in the 7th Armoured Brigade with only a matter of weeks left before his service was complete. As the commander of Sho't 'Beta 1' (right foreground) within 3rd or H Company of the 77th OZ Battalion, Bashari had commented to his company commander, Lieutenantt Avraham 'Emmy' Palant, and his battalion commander, Lieutenant Colonel Avigdor Kahalani, on the morning of 6 October that he was fed up with firing at barrels during gunnery practice. His years of experience were soon to be tested to the full. As the 7th Armoured Brigade deployed to the frontlines, H Company was transferred to the 75th Mechanized Infantry Battalion under the command of Lieutenant Colonel Yos Eldar at the Wasset Junction. Bashari and his platoon took up station near the commanding feature of Tel Hermonit. It lay right in the path of the advancing Syrian 7th Infantry Division (left background). H Company found itself fighting the Syrians at odds of over 15:1. Battle was joined with the Israeli tanks on their firing ramps subjected to devastating artillery fire. Bashari's gunner, Moshe Uliel, exacted a fearful toll of Syrian tanks but the odds were overwhelming. Despite coming under fire from the guns of numerous tanks and artillery

pieces, Bashari did not retreat. At 2130hrs, an artillery shell exploded on the exterior of his tank and Bashari was killed instantly, his body slumping inside the turret. Bashari was the first fatality within the 7th Armoured Brigade. Almost 60 per cent of the casualties within armoured brigades on the Golan Heights were tank commanders. It is standard procedure for Israeli tank commanders to operate with their heads out of the turrets for better observation. However, so many were decapitated by shell fire in the first day of the war that tank crews were ordered to wear their dogtags around their ankles so that headless bodies could be identified. The sight of their tank commander's headless torso collapsing into the fighting compartment was too much for most crews and many, understandably, abandoned their tank. Bashari's gunner and loader, Uliel and Ganani, jumped out of 'Beta 1' and took shelter among the rocks. When recovered, such tanks were virtually undamaged but the congealed blood splashed around the inside of the turret made it impossible for replacement crews to man the tank. The Israeli repair teams quickly found cleaning using diesel fuel overpowered the smell. This allowed the tanks to be returned to service as quickly as possible. Bashari was posthumously awarded the Medal of Gallantry. Bashari's Sho't is shown here with the insignia of the 7th Armoured Brigade on the rear hull although this was not normally carried in combat for security reasons. The registration number on this tank is not that of 'Beta 1' but of the Centurion memorial on the Golan Heights. (Howard Gerrard © Osprey Publishing Ltd)

El Rom sector, there was nothing to stand between them and Kiryat Shmona in northern Israel.

Ben Gal attempted to block the Republican Guards with the tanks of his 71st Battalion, which was holding the northern sector of the battlefield. Within minutes of engaging the Syrians, however, the battalion commander, Lieutenant Colonel Ratess, was killed. Ben Gal then ordered Lieutenant Colonel Kahalani, commanding 77th Battalion, to assume command of the remnants of 71st Battalion. Manoeuvring his 15 tanks on high ground overlooking the valley and firing from ramps, Kahalani's force halted the Republican Guard at ranges that never exceeded 500m (547yds). Some of the Syrian tanks managed to throw off the stranglehold and move behind the Israelis as the battle dissolved into a swirling melee of individual duels fought in a cauldron of smoke and flames laced with the reek of burning cordite. The Israeli tank crews had been in action for four days and three nights and, on average, were now down to their last four shells.

Ben Gal radioed Eitan that he did not think that 7th Brigade could hold on any longer. He had started the battle with 105 tanks and now had just seven left. Eitan tried to calm him, promising that he would soon be receiving reinforcements. The Syrians, sensing victory, were pushing past the line of abandoned Israeli ramps, but there now occurred another of those remarkable incidents on which the fate of armies turns.

When the war broke out, Lieutenant Colonel Yosi Ben Hannan, a former commander of the 53rd Battalion within the Barak Brigade, had been on his honeymoon in the Himalayas. On being told of the outbreak of war, Ben Hannan had used enormous initiative to fly back to Israel via Teheran and Athens, telephoning his family from the Greek capital to bring his uniform to Lod airport. From Lod, Ben Hannan had gone straight to the workshops behind the Golan front. Here teams were working round the clock on battle-damaged tanks. Ben Hannan collected 13 battleworthy vehicles and assembled sufficient crews to man them, including some wounded volunteers who had discharged themselves from hospital. With his small band of battered tanks, he headed for the 7th Armoured Brigade's sector.

Eitan had hastily placed Ben Hannan under the command of Ben Gal, who was on the point of ordering a withdrawal when his small task force arrived. Ben Gal's seven remaining tanks, now virtually out of ammunition, joined Ben Hannan's force as the latter went on to the counterattack, breasting the rise southeast of Booster to slam into the Syrian left flank. In the first clash Ben Hannan's force destroyed some 30 Syrian tanks. A report came in from A3, one of the Israeli strongpoints isolated but intact on the Purple Line, that the Syrian supply columns were pulling back. The Syrians, who had fought themselves to a standstill between Hermonit and Booster, began to withdraw under a huge pall

of dust while the Israelis tracked them in cautious pursuit. The arrival of Ben Hannan's tanks on the battlefield must have seemed to the battle-weary Syrians a preliminary to the arrival of yet more fresh Israeli reserve formations. Later Ben Gal observed: 'You never know the condition of the other side. You always assume he is in better shape than you. The Syrians, apparently, assumed that they had no chance of success. They did not know the truth, that our situation was desperate.'

The battle for the Booster feature was over. Eitan spoke over the radio to Ben Gal and his men, saying, 'You have saved the people of Israel.' The survivors of the 7th Armoured Brigade had been without sleep for 80 hours and had fought continuously for over 50 hours. They had lost all but seven of their tanks. In the Valley of Tears, however, they had knocked out 260 Syrian tanks and 500 other vehicles. The ground over which they fought – some 15km wide and 3km deep – had been rigorously prepared for battle and the range tables, ramps and alternative positions had been sited and constructed to enable a heavily

Lieutenant Colonel Avigdor Kahalani, the commander of the OZ 77th Battalion of the 7th Armoured Brigade, is caught on camera soon after the epic battle that arguably saved the nation of Israel. Behind Kahalani is the Valley of Tears where the Barak and 7th Armoured Brigades destroyed 260 tanks and an equal number of other AFVs in three days of intense armoured warfare. For his bravery and brilliant leadership, Avigdor Kahalani received Israel's highest gallantry award – the Medal of Valour.

A mortally wounded Israeli tank commander is gently lowered from the turret of his Sho't tank after he was struck in the throat by fragments from an exploding Sagger missile. Almost two-thirds of the Israeli Armoured Corps fatalities on the Golan Heights were tank commanders. Necessarily the brightest and the best within both the army and society, their loss was felt all the more keenly by the State of Israel. Israeli losses on the Golan Heights during the October War were 772 dead and 2,453 wounded in just 18 days of fighting.

outnumbered force to fight a holding action. Moreover, Ben Gal's handling of his mobile reserves was assured in retaining control of the high ground and the killing grounds in the valley below it.

Not even Ben Gal, however, could have anticipated the ferocity of the fighting, the odds at which it would be fought and the physical and moral demands it would make. The defensive nature of the battle exposed the IDF to the full fury of Syrian artillery, which took a punitive toll of the tank commanders of the 7th Armoured Brigade, while the Syrian armour's night-vision equipment gave it a huge tactical advantage that crucially it failed to exploit fully. The savagery of the battle also underlined the vulnerability of Israeli commanders as they directed the battle from open tank hatches under heavy fire.

The narrow margin of victory in the Valley of Tears was also a brutal reminder of the failure of the IDF to mobilize its reserves in time to meet the magnitude of the threat to Israel on the Golan. In the opening phase of the battle, the Barak and 7th Armoured Brigades were the only armoured elements of the IDF with which the Syrians had to contend. Had they been faced with all the brigades eventually dispatched to the Northern Front, the outcome would have been clear cut. There would have been a repetition of the Valley of Tears along the Purple Line.

The Israeli Air Force

The Israeli Air Force entered the war with every confidence that it could provide the essential close air support for the ground forces. It was to suffer a fearful shock as the first Skyhawk was downed by a SAM-6 missile within minutes. The comprehensive Arab air defence system caused heavy Israeli losses on both the Northern and Southern fronts – some 50 aircraft – in the first two days, amounting to almost 15 per cent of its frontline strength. The IAF kept flying by employing a wide variety of tactics and equipment including contour flying and evasive manoeuvring, the Sam Song warning system, flares, chaff and ECM to overcome the threat posed to low-flying aircraft by the SAM-6s and ZSU-23-4 self-propelled anti-aircraft guns.

Before the war, the IAF had not known the frequencies used by the SAM-6. It took some time to discover them and make appropriate adjustments to the ECM pods used by its aircraft, which succeeded in neutralizing the active radar mode but not the optical sight. The IAF's problems were compounded by the loss of the Mount Hermon observation post and radar station on the opening day of the war.

The losses sustained in the first two days of fighting forced the IAF to reduce the tempo of close air support and attempt to neutralize the SAM sites. It was a costly and brutal battle. In one operation alone the IAF lost six aircraft while destroying only one Syrian SAM site. On 8 October, the IAF began bombing Syrian airbases; within a week most of them were inoperable. On 9 October, in response to the Syrian firing of some ten FROG missiles at targets in Israel including the Ramat David airbase, the IAF launched a strategic offensive against Syria. First they destroyed the Barouk radar station in Lebanon, which was linked to the Syrian network, in order to open new attack routes and as a warning to other Arab neighbours of Israel. The IAF then launched a comprehensive attack on the Syrian oil industry and electrical power generating system. Also targeted were the oil port of Banias, the refineries at Homs and oil storage depots throughout Syria.

Israel later claimed to have attacked only strategic targets, but on 9 October a successful raid flown by eight F-4 Phantoms against the Syrian Air Force headquarters in Damascus also hit buildings nearby in the city's diplomatic quarter, causing a number of casualties. One of the Phantoms was lost during this mission and a second wave of F-4s was diverted, because of cloud cover over Damascus, to bomb Syrian troop concentrations near Hushniya.

On the morning of 9 October, when bad news was still coming in from the Northern and Southern fronts, the Israeli War Cabinet discussed a more drastic form of air attack – the possible use of nuclear weapons. Some accounts of this meeting allege that Dayan and Meir ordered the arming of Israel's missiles with nuclear warheads and that nuclear weapons were loaded onto a squadron

An Israeli F-1 Phantom plunges earthwards after being hit by Syrian anti-aircraft fire. On 7 October, six Israeli Phantoms were shot out of the sky by Syrian air defences and 33 Phantoms were lost during the course of the war. The Israelis lost 51 aircraft over the Golan Heights with most of the 51 downed in the first three days of the war. Total losses in the war amounted to 103 Israeli aircraft, of which just five were shot down in air-to-air combat according to IAF figures as against Israeli claims of 277 Arab planes destroyed in dogfights.

of F-4s at Tel Nof airbase in the heart of Israel. This may have been a stratagem to speed up the American resupply of the IDF. This operation got under way on the night of 13 October with the launching of a massive airlift.

Once it had recovered its balance one of the aims of the IAF was, as David Elazar put it, to force the Syrians to 'scream stop' by destroying the strategic infrastructure on which their war-making capacity depended. To reduce Israel's vulnerability it was axiomatic that their Arab enemies had to be dealt severe blows, the economic consequences of which would be felt for years.

Israel stabilizes the Golan front

On the evening of Sunday 7 October, Colonel Tewfiq Juhni, the commander of the Syrian 1st Armoured Division, established a supply and administrative complex in the area of Hushniya. Juhni was confident that an advance into Israel would be made on the following day. The Israelis had other ideas. When the sun came up on Monday the IDF was ready to seize the initiative. Major General Hofi, GOC Northern Command, planned to isolate the Syrian penetration with converging blows delivered by Ugdas Laner and Musa. It was the Israeli advance along the road towards El Al that alerted Colonel Juhni to the danger that now threatened his division.

Bombs rain down on the airbase of Nazaria as the Israeli Air Force strikes deep into Syria, seeking to emasculate its opponent. The Syrian Air Force mustered some 250 operational combat jets on six main airbases; all were subjected to concerted attacks by the Heyl Ha'avir or Israeli Air Force.

At 2000hrs on Sunday 7 October, Peled had briefed an orders group at Tzemach at the southern end of the Sea of Galilee. He planned to attack on two routes: the main effort was to be put in by the 9th Reserve Armoured Brigade along the El Al–Rafid road. The 205th Reserve Armoured Brigade would follow up this attack, while the 70th Reserve Armoured Brigade mopped up and shielded the right flank of the advance above the Ruqqad escarpment. On the left flank of the main effort, the 4th Reserve Armoured Brigade was tasked with advancing from the Gamla Rise at Givat Yoav through Mazrat Kuneitra to Hushniya. Peled's counterattack went in at 0830hrs on Monday 8 October. By noon, Ugda Musa had reached Tel Faris after heavy fighting, with some 50 Syrian tanks destroyed between Ramat Magshimim and El Al, a distance of some 9km (5½ miles).

The 205th Reserve Armoured Brigade then struck north, while the 9th Reserve Armoured Brigade refuelled and protected the left flank of the advance. Peled then ordered 19th Reserve Armoured Brigade to push up the lateral road that ran north from Magshimim to move on to the left flank of 4th Reserve Armoured Brigade and broaden the divisional front. By 1300hrs, Peled's armour had reached the point at Juhader intersected by the TAP line road. By this time the lead battalion of the 205th Reserve Armoured Brigade had advanced to Tel Saki on the road to Juhader. Here they ran into strong Syrian anti-tank defence consisting of hedgehogs of Saggers, tanks and anti-tank guns located on both sides of the road and covered by heavy concentrations of artillery fire. The lead battalion was pinned down by the weight of Syrian fire and the 205th Reserve Armoured Brigade was forced to launch a major attack to retrieve the situation.

The strength and depth of the Syrian defences surprised Peled and his brigade commanders. In the late afternoon, however, 9th Reserve Armoured Brigade, moving up on the 4th Reserve Armoured Brigade's left, burst through an anti-tank position that the Syrians had not yet completed. By the evening of 8 October the Syrians had withdrawn from Juhader, exposing the Syrian 1st Armoured Division's supply lines running south along the TAP line and forcing Juhni to commit an armoured brigade the next morning to secure the route.

Meanwhile, throughout 8 October, Major General Laner's division was fighting its way eastward against mounting opposition. The depleted 17th Reserve Armoured Brigade was slogging up the Yehudia road towards the TAP line through a succession of Syrian ambushes and had been reduced to one tank battalion and an attached reconnaissance unit destined for Ugda Raful. To the north, the 679th Reserve Armoured Brigade was locked in battle with Syrian forces pressing up the TAP line to overrun Nafekh.

Laner was exerting pressure on Juhni's 1st Armoured Division, which was still moving northward along the TAP line road and westward towards the Jordan.

Juhni was an able and hard-driving commander and, in contrast to the generally cautious performance of the Syrian Army, had subordinates who were not afraid to use their initiative. Colonel Shafiq Fayad, commander of the 91st Armoured Brigade, was one such. He had bypassed the stubbornly defended base at Nafekh to strike west across country and push his forward elements to within reach of Snobar, the main IDF supply depot on the Golan escarpment. Some of Juhni's forward elements almost reached the old Customs House only 5km (3 miles) from the River Jordan. This was the deepest Syrian penetration of the war and just a ten-minute tank drive from the Benot Ya'akov Bridge.

The fighting for the TAP line was intense. Moving south down the TAP line road, the 679th Reserve Armoured Brigade, reinforced by a company detached from the 7th Brigade to the north, drove the Syrians from Sindiana and by nightfall controlled the TAP line road around Nafekh. There was more hard fighting for the 679th Reserve Armoured Brigade on the morning of 9 October

An M38A1 Jeep of a reconnaissance unit leads an M50 Sherman of the 9th Reserve Armoured Brigade along the shoreline of the Sea of Galilee as the brigade grinds its way up to the Golan Heights. The ancient Sherman is armed with a French 75mm gun and is equipped with a simple searchlight for night fighting but is without the infrared capability of the Syrians.

Israeli armour advances alongside the chain-link fencing of the TAP line road. This was one of the main Syrian axes of advance in the opening battles of the war. The attack was only thwarted by the tenacity and courage of a handful of Israeli tank crews during the first desperate night of the war.

when the Syrians counterattacked after a heavy artillery bombardment. The Syrian assault was broken up at long range by Israeli tank fire. That afternoon, as the 17th Reserve Armoured Brigade closed on the TAP line from the west, the 679th Reserve Armoured Brigade moved on Hushniya, the headquarters of the 1st Armoured Division that was defended in depth by tanks, anti-tank guns, missiles and infantry armed with RPGs.

As night closed in on 8 October, Colonel Uri Orr took Tel Ramtania, a heavily fortified spur of the Hushniya defensive box. Orr's brigade had taken heavy losses in a day of continuous fighting that had seen the birth of a new esprit de corps. By the evening of Tuesday 9 October, Laner had shut the northern and western pincers on the Syrian concentration at Hushniya. The 679th Reserve Armoured Brigade looked down on it from Tel Ramtania and the 17th Reserve Armoured Brigade was on the TAP line road, refuelling and poised to move east. Peled was to close the trap from the southeast.

In the small hours of 9 October, Peled briefed his orders group on their line of advance. The 205th Reserve Armoured Brigade was to advance on the Syrian border, keeping the Rafid–Tel Faris road on its left; the 14th Reserve Armoured Brigade was to press on to the left of the El Al–Rafid road; and 19th Brigade was to drive on Hushniya. Peled intended that his division's impetus would carry him across the ceasefire line, taking Tel Kudne in the process. It was the first time since his division had joined the battle that Peled was able to brief all his subordinate commanders, an indication that order was being restored to the battlefield.

When the attack went in at dawn, Peled collided with the Syrian 46th Armoured Brigade covering the southern flank of the 1st Armoured Division, now fighting for its life around Hushniya. On his right flank, amid emotional scenes, Peled had linked up with the garrisons of those IDF strongpoints that had held out since the beginning of the war. Meanwhile the 9th Reserve Armoured Brigade was swinging northwest to close on Hushniya. Linking with Ugda Laner advancing from the west, the Israelis reached the high ground southeast of Hushniya by mid-morning on 9 October. Heavy fighting ensued with a Syrian force of some 50 tanks augmented with anti-tank guns and missiles. The Israelis suffered heavy losses and the attack was brought to a halt.

To the south, better progress was being made against the 46th Syrian Armoured Brigade by the 205th Reserve Armoured Brigade, which by 1200hrs had reached the area of Tel Faris. However, the 205th Reserve Armoured Brigade was in a dangerously exposed position. Syrian armour was being fed across the Purple Line, and Peled's division was now straddled alarmingly across its three principal axes of advance.

The Syrians, however, were also facing tough choices. The 91st Armoured Brigade had been pummelled by the 679th Reserve Brigade and was no longer an effective fighting formation. North of Kuneitra, the Syrians were unable to break through. Before developing this phase of operations, Juhni, commander of the Syrian 1st Armoured Division, had established his divisional supply system around Hushniya as a preliminary to breaking in to Israel itself. However, he was now threatened by Laner's forces from the west and north and Peled's forces from the south. The tables had been turned on Juhni, and his division was threatened with envelopment.

The Syrian plight was compounded by the increasing effectiveness of the IAF, which had largely overcome the Syrian SAM threat and brought the Hushniya pocket under effective bombardment. Juhni ordered his forces to attack Peled's arm of the pincer to break the stranglehold. Peled, meanwhile, ordered the 4th Reserve Armoured Brigade to make an all-out attack in the centre in which it seized control of the Hushniya–Rafid road, easing the pressure on the left flank of 205th Reserve Armoured Brigade, which overran Tel Faris and gained an excellent observation post. The tactical advantage this conferred was, however, mitigated by the fact that a small number of Syrian troops managed to remain in hiding on Tel Faris and were able to direct Syrian fire until 11 October, when they were eliminated. Peled's attack was, nevertheless, developing according to plan, and he now ordered the 9th Reserve Armoured

Brigade to move on Hushniya with close air and artillery support. The attack broke through the Syrian positions, taking the high ground at Tel Fazra, but again encountering stubborn Syrian resistance. After darkness fell, the Syrians began to infiltrate back, and the fighting became confused. The Syrian 15th Mechanized Infantry Brigade, detached from the 3rd Armoured Division and moved to reinforce the main effort in the south, tried to punch its way through to the 1st Armoured Division in the Hushniya pocket but was blocked at Tel Faris by the 205th Reserve Armoured Brigade.

Peled held an orders group in the small hours of Wednesday 10 October and reaffirmed the overall aim of seizing Tel Kudne, the Syrian forward HQ some 15km (9 miles) to the northeast of Tel Faris, which was now held by the 205th Reserve Armoured Brigade along with the Rafid crossroads. Although Peled was still baulked in the area of Hushniya, where the 9th Reserve Armoured Brigade was heavily engaged, he was moving steadily up to the ceasefire line.

Peled's thrust on Tel Kudne ran into determined Syrian opposition. He was ordered by Hofi to remain on the defensive, to provide the anvil against which the Syrian pocket could be crushed by the hammer of Laner's division attacking from the north with 679th and 17th Reserve Armoured Brigades. When Laner and Peled's forward units met near Hushniya, the entire area became a vast

tank–killing ground. Two brigades of the Syrian 1st Armoured Division had been destroyed, turning the Hushniya pocket into a colossal mechanical graveyard of burnt-out tanks, artillery, APCs, trucks and stores. The remnants of the Syrian Army streamed east over the ceasefire line, and by nightfall there was not a single Syrian unit on territory west of the Purple Line.

On the Golan plateau, the Syrians had left behind some 870 tanks, many of them T–62s, hundreds of guns and APCs, thousands of vehicles and enormous quantities of equipment. The carefully prepared Soviet-style offensive, launched on 6 October, had ended in crushing defeat and the Syrians were back on their start line.

The Israeli counterattack

On the night of 10 October, the Israeli cabinet, advised by its Chief of Staff General Elazar, had to decide whether to exploit its success against Syria or to concentrate against Egypt. The General Staff was also considering its options. There were several trenchant arguments in favour of adopting the first course of action. First, if the Syrian Army could be broken, it would then be safe to concentrate against Egypt, mainspring of the Arab alliance. Second, on 10 October Iraq had sent two armoured divisions to help the Syrians and had moved approximately 100 warplanes to advanced bases in western Iraq. There was also still a possibility that Jordan might intervene. On 10 October, Jordan had announced that it was calling up reservists and mobilizing its resources for the 'war effort'. The IDF defences along the River Jordan had been stripped and were now manned by a skeleton force. Finally, the Soviet Union was re-supplying the Syrians, who had to be deterred from launching another offensive.

There were two reasons for not advancing into Syria. First, any Israeli threat to Damascus might provoke Soviet intervention. Second, the IDF ran the risk of being drawn into a battle of attrition in the deeply echeloned Syrian defensive system and the broken lava country that blocked the main axis of advance to Damascus.

The General Staff's recommendations, which were conveyed by Moshe Dayan to Golda Meir, were to advance across the ceasefire line to achieve a penetration 20km (12½ miles) in depth and form a defensive enclave, bringing Damascus within the reach of long-range artillery. It was hoped in this way to inflict a crushing defeat on the Syrians while not provoking Soviet intervention. Golda Meir gave her assent. Confirmatory orders were then sent to Hofi and detailed planning began immediately.

It was Hofi's intention to give the Syrians no time to recover. In turn this meant attacking with forces that had little or no time either to reorganize after hard and exhausting fighting or to absorb reinforcements of men and equipment. In Eitan's 36th Armoured Division, Ben Gal's 7th Armoured Brigade had been reconstituted and reinforced with fresh troops from reserve battalions and had also absorbed the remnants of the 188th Barak Brigade, which had fought itself to a standstill and was now commanded by the redoubtable Lieutenant Colonel Ben Hannan.

Hofi planned to attack in echelon from the northernmost sector in the Golan. The left flank of the attacking forces would rest on the slopes of Mount Hermon that were impassable to armour. The axis of advance was on the shortest route to Damascus and it was anticipated that this would influence the Syrian deployment. The Israelis also correctly anticipated that the northern sector was less heavily defended by the Syrians. Eitan's reconstituted division was to lead off on the axis Majdal Shams–Mazrat Beit Jan in the foothills of Mount Hermon. From this wooded high ground, Eitan could direct artillery and tank fire to the south in support of Laner's armoured division as it pushed forward, abreast of Eitan, along the main Kuneitra–Damascus highway two hours later.

H-Hour was fixed for 1100hrs 11 October, to allow time for reorganization and the issuing of orders and also to avoid the tank gunners being blinded by the sun. South of Kuneitra, Peled's armoured division was to consolidate along two-thirds of the frontline and to reinforce Laner with the 9th Reserve Armoured Brigade. The Israeli plan was based on economy of effort in the centre and south in order to achieve a concentration of force in the north so as

The Yom Kippur War was the first major clash in the history of naval warfare when both sides were armed with ship-to-ship missiles. At the outbreak of war the Israeli Navy was at battle stations and quickly gained the initiative against the Syrians. At the battle of Latakia, one Reshef and four Saar class missile boats, using sophisticated electronic countermeasures, foiled the Soviet Styx anti-ship missiles of the Syrian Osa-Class boats while the Israeli Gabriel missiles destroyed five Syrian vessels and forced the rest of the Syrian Navy back into port for the remainder of the war. This was despite the fact that the Styx missile had twice the range of the Gabriel.

to menace Damascus and force the Syrians to give battle. Eitan's division on the left would make the main effort, but once a breakthrough had been achieved, Laner would exploit it, either by passing through Eitan or by pushing for a separate breakthrough along the road to Damascus.

On the other side of the hill, the Syrian High Command was now exhibiting signs of mounting alarm. The badly mauled Syrian Army was now facing a reinvigorated enemy about to strike into its territory. The IAF was now unlocking the secret of the Syrian SAMs and inflicting heavy tactical and strategic damage on the Syrian infrastructure that in turn was hindering a concerted drive by the Soviets to re-supply their allies. The bulk of the Syrian Army was now concentrated on the approaches to Damascus while Arab allies – Moroccan, Saudi, Iraqi and Jordanian – were being assigned the role of delaying the Israeli drive.

Assad appealed to Sadat for help. But this plea was undermined by the fact that a few days earlier, when Syrian forces were poised on the western edge of the Golan escarpment, Assad had attempted to secure a ceasefire through the offices of the Soviet Union. His aim had been to forestall precisely the kind of Israeli counterattack with which he was now threatened and retain control of the Golan Heights. At first Sadat, having achieved his strategic aim of a lodgement on the eastern bank of the Suez Canal, was unwilling to move, but the mounting pressure on Syria forced him to act. The armoured offensive in the Sinai, launched on 14 October, was the Egyptian response to the Syrian plight. However, it was to prove the undoing of the Egyptians. Venturing beyond its SAM umbrella, the Egyptian armour was shot to pieces and the initiative in the Sinai passed to the Israelis.

On the night of 10 October, after the command orders group, Ben Gal assembled his commanders. The events of the last four days lent his words an added layer of meaning. He told his officers that the break-in to Syria would enable them to avenge the death of their comrades who had fallen in the desperate defence of Israel. For the attack on the following day, Ben Gal deployed four tank battalions, which he allocated evenly to the Mazrat Beit Jan and Tel Shams objectives. Under cover of artillery and air strikes, the 7th Armoured Brigade broke through the Syrian minefields and anti-tank ditches on both its axes and plunged into a well-prepared defence in depth in a landscape of rocky, wooded ridges on the lower slopes of Mount Hermon.

Two brigades held this sector – one Syrian and the other Moroccan – supported by some 75 tanks. Built under Soviet supervision after the 1967 war, the Syrian defensive zone was up to 15km (9 miles) deep with closely integrated concrete bunkers linked by trenches. The zone was anchored on the right to Mount Hermon, and on the left to the impassable basalt rock Leja.

The northernmost Israeli spearhead was the 77th OZ Battalion of the 7th Armoured Brigade together with Task Force Amos, named after its commander, Lieutenant Colonel Amos Katz. The two battalions struck northeast beside the foothills of Mount Hermon towards Hader and Mazrat Beit Jan. Advancing a few kilometres to the south were the remnants of the Barak Brigade including Ben Hannan's force and the 74th Battalion, thrusting east through Jubat el Hashab towards the commanding heights of Tel Shams. The Moroccan brigade with its integral tank battalion was facing the 77th Battalion, while to its south were the disorganized remnants of the Syrian 7th Infantry Division. By late afternoon, the northern axis of the 7th Armoured Brigade controlled the Hader crossroads. On the morning of 12 October it beat off a counterattack and, resuming its advance, took Mazrat Beit Jan after a six-hour battle. The southern wing of Eitan's advance also made steady progress and the vital Maatz crossroads were taken on Friday morning. At this point, Ben Gal

ordered Ben Hannan to take Tel Shams, a rocky outcrop that overlooked the road to Damascus. However, he did not inform Eitan of this decision. This proved to be a costly mistake, prompted by a conviction that the Syrians were on the point of collapse and also by the IDF's lingering reliance on the use of armour alone. Since 1967, the IDF had reduced the organic infantry and artillery elements of its armoured formations. This erosion of the infantry strength led to the attack on Tel Shams being made by tanks alone.

With two companies providing supporting fire, Ben Hannan led a force – some 20 tanks strong – along a path that ran through the rocky perimeter of the Syrian position to take it from the rear. Initially Ben Hannan achieved surprise: the Syrian armour at the base of the position was overwhelmed at close range and eight of Ben Hannan's tanks broke through. Tel Shams was now under Israeli artillery fire and Ben Hannan ordered two of his tanks, covered by the remaining two, to claw their way to the summit. Now they came under Syrian anti-tank fire that knocked out four of Ben Hannan's tanks and sent the two survivors scrambling down the Tel. Ben Hannan himself was blown out of his turret and seriously injured. After darkness had fallen, he was rescued by a group of Israeli paratroops commanded by Captain Jonathon 'Yoni' Netanyahu, later to lead the famous Entebbe raid. Tel

Belching clouds of diesel exhaust, Sho'ts manoeuvre into formation as the Israelis mount a counterattack against Syrian positions. The major Israeli counter-offensive into Syria began on 11 October, just five days after the start of the war. In the vanguard of the attack were the combined remnants of the 7th and 188th Barak Brigades that had borne the brunt of the Syrian offensive.

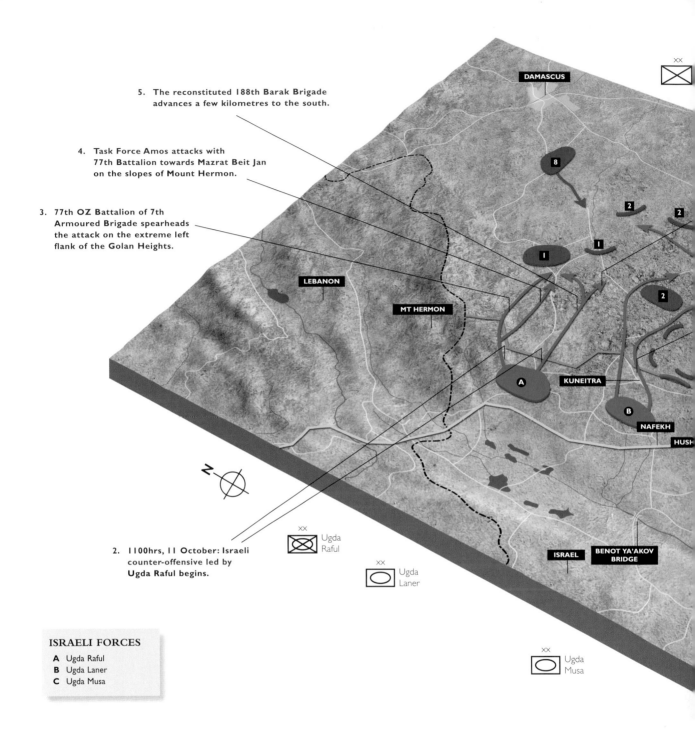

5. The reconstituted 188th Barak Brigade advances a few kilometres to the south.

4. Task Force Amos attacks with 77th Battalion towards Mazrat Beit Jan on the slopes of Mount Hermon.

3. 77th **OZ** Battalion of 7th Armoured Brigade spearheads the attack on the extreme left flank of the Golan Heights.

DAMASCUS

LEBANON

MT HERMON

KUNEITRA

NAFEKH

HUSH

ISRAEL

BENOT YA'AKOV BRIDGE

2. 1100hrs, 11 October: Israeli counter-offensive led by **Ugda Raful** begins.

Ugda Raful

Ugda Laner

Ugda Musa

ISRAELI FORCES

A Ugda Raful
B Ugda Laner
C Ugda Musa

THE ISRAELI COUNTER-OFFENSIVE INTO SYRIA

11–13 October 1973, viewed from the southwest, showing the Israeli counter-offensive on the northern Golan Heights along the Damascus road.

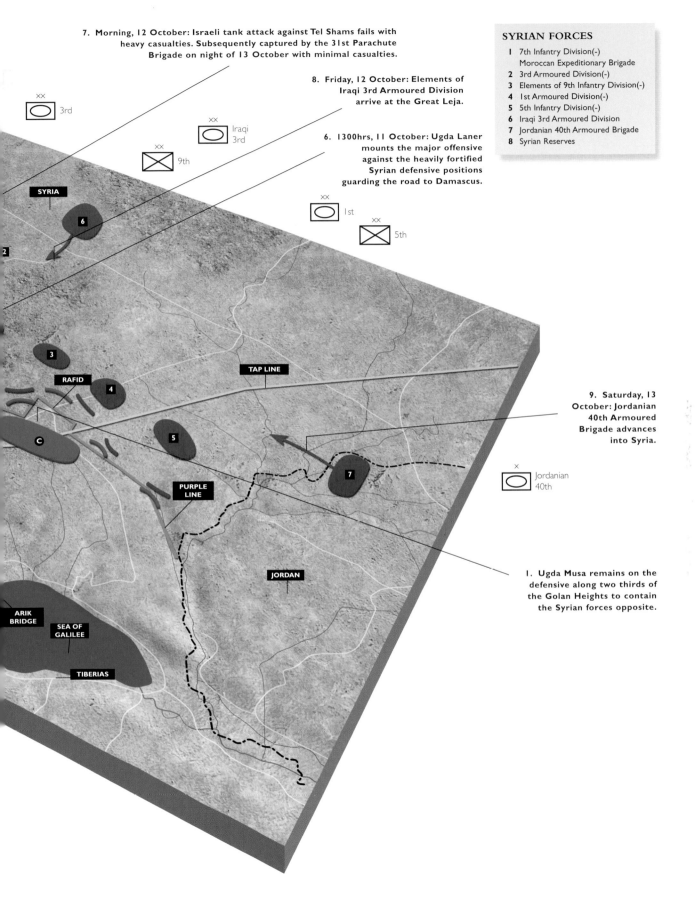

7. Morning, 12 October: Israeli tank attack against Tel Shams fails with heavy casualties. Subsequently captured by the 31st Parachute Brigade on night of 13 October with minimal casualties.

8. Friday, 12 October: Elements of Iraqi 3rd Armoured Division arrive at the Great Leja.

6. 1300hrs, 11 October: Ugda Laner mounts the major offensive against the heavily fortified Syrian defensive positions guarding the road to Damascus.

9. Saturday, 13 October: Jordanian 40th Armoured Brigade advances into Syria.

1. Ugda Musa remains on the defensive along two thirds of the Golan Heights to contain the Syrian forces opposite.

SYRIAN FORCES

1 7th Infantry Division(-)
  Moroccan Expeditionary Brigade
2 3rd Armoured Division(-)
3 Elements of 9th Infantry Division(-)
4 1st Armoured Division(-)
5 5th Infantry Division(-)
6 Iraqi 3rd Armoured Division
7 Jordanian 40th Armoured Brigade
8 Syrian Reserves

xx
3rd

xx
Iraqi
3rd

xx
9th

SYRIA

6

2

xx
1st

xx
5th

3

RAFID

4

C

5

TAP LINE

**PURPLE
LINE**

7

x
Jordanian
40th

JORDAN

**ARIK
BRIDGE**

**SEA OF
GALILEE**

TIBERIAS

A Sho't advances at speed towards the frontline. The Sho't or Upgraded Centurion can be identified from the front by the revised US-style headlight clusters and the fire extinguisher pull-handle above the spare track links. The Sho't proved to be the outstanding tank of the Yom Kippur War and fundamental to the Israeli victory over Syria.

Shams was to remain in Syrian hands until the night of 13 October, when the 31st Parachute Brigade captured it with minimal casualties.

To the south, Laner's division, comprising the 17th and 679th Reserve Armoured Brigades and the 9th Reserve Armoured Brigade, transferred from Peled's command, began its attack at 1300hrs on 11 October. Once again over-reliance on the use of unsupported armour in the thrust down the road to Damascus led to trouble when the Israelis encountered a well-coordinated Syrian defence. At the Khan Arnaba crossroads, the 17th Reserve Armoured Brigade, led by Colonel Ran Sarig, came under heavy artillery and Sagger ATGW fire. Tanks at the rear of the column ran into minefields when they left the road. The 17th Reserve Armoured Brigade was reduced to just five tanks.

Laner ordered the 9th Reserve Armoured Brigade south through Jaba, intending to bypass the crossroads, but that night Syrian infantry counterattacked through the lava beds, cutting off the Israeli units at Khan Arnaba. An attempt to drive them off with armour resulted in more losses and underlined the vulnerability of unsupported tanks to determined attack by infantry armed with

RPG-7s. The situation was retrieved by an attached paratroop battalion, which mopped up the Syrians and evacuated the Israeli wounded. The paratroopers were shocked by the exhausted condition of the surviving tank crews, begging them to rest and taking over the job of refuelling and re-arming their vehicles.

On the morning of 12 October, Laner decided to bypass Khan Arnaba with a wide outflanking movement to the south through Nasej towards Knaker that would avoid the Leja lava country blocking his path. His aim was to take Sasa on the Damascus road from the south and to establish a line within 30km (18½ miles) of the city to bring the Syrian capital within range of the IDF's heavy artillery. That afternoon, while the 679th Reserve Armoured Brigade replenished, the 17th and 9th Reserve Armoured Brigades joined forces to drive east, watched by Laner from his forward headquarters at Tel Shaar, which provided sweeping views of the Syrian plain. It seemed as if the Syrians were broken and now unable to offer further resistance west of Damascus.

While observing his troops advance, Laner noticed huge dust clouds some 10km (6 miles) to his south. A major armoured formation was deploying for action. Laner's first reaction was that the dust had been raised by some of Peled's formations, but Hofi informed him that Peled was still in position. Hofi had

As dusk falls, Shermans and Centurions of the 9th Reserve Armoured Brigade advance up the Gamla Rise to engage Syrian tanks approaching the edge of the escarpment overlooking Israel proper. The prompt deployment of Israeli tank reserves in single companies rather than complete battalions or larger formations was crucial in stemming the Syrian onslaught. (© Christian Simonpietri/Sygma/Corbis)

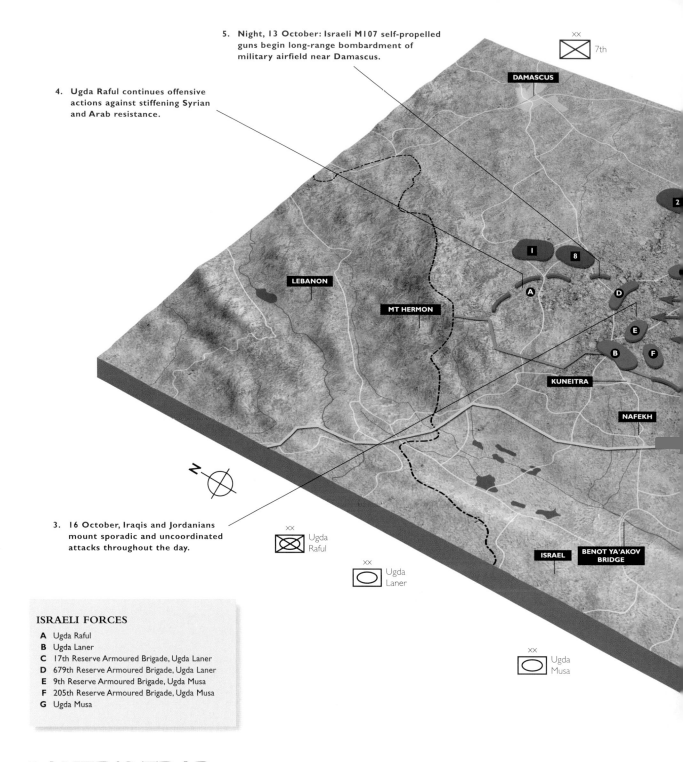

5. **Night, 13 October:** Israeli M107 self-propelled guns begin long-range bombardment of military airfield near Damascus.

4. **Ugda Raful** continues offensive actions against stiffening Syrian and Arab resistance.

3. **16 October,** Iraqis and Jordanians mount sporadic and uncoordinated attacks throughout the day.

DAMASCUS

LEBANON

MT HERMON

KUNEITRA

NAFEKH

ISRAEL

BENOT YA'AKOV BRIDGE

Ugda Raful

Ugda Laner

Ugda Musa

ISRAELI FORCES

A Ugda Raful
B Ugda Laner
C 17th Reserve Armoured Brigade, Ugda Laner
D 679th Reserve Armoured Brigade, Ugda Laner
E 9th Reserve Armoured Brigade, Ugda Musa
F 205th Reserve Armoured Brigade, Ugda Musa
G Ugda Musa

LANER'S TRAP

13–17 October 1973, viewed from the southwest. Attacks by Iraqi 3rd Armoured Division and Jordanian 40th Armoured Brigade are beaten off with heavy losses by Ugda Laner. Meanwhile, Israeli long-range artillery begins to bombard the suburbs of Damascus.

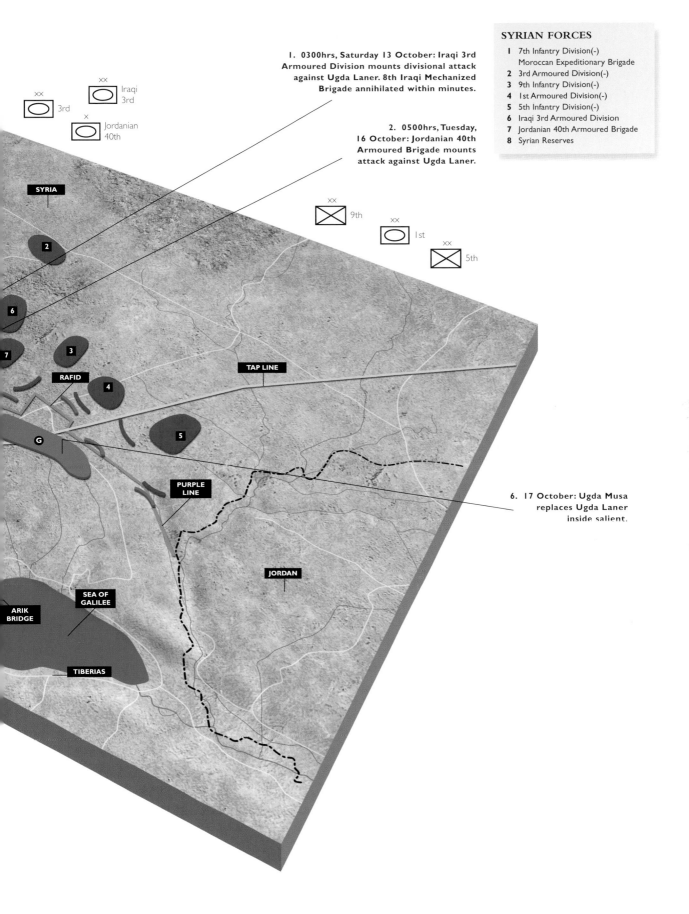

SYRIAN FORCES

1 7th Infantry Division(-)
   Moroccan Expeditionary Brigade
2 3rd Armoured Division(-)
3 9th Infantry Division(-)
4 1st Armoured Division(-)
5 5th Infantry Division(-)
6 Iraqi 3rd Armoured Division
7 Jordanian 40th Armoured Brigade
8 Syrian Reserves

1. 0300hrs, Saturday 13 October: Iraqi 3rd Armoured Division mounts divisional attack against Ugda Laner. 8th Iraqi Mechanized Brigade annihilated within minutes.

2. 0500hrs, Tuesday, 16 October: Jordanian 40th Armoured Brigade mounts attack against Ugda Laner.

3rd

Iraqi 3rd

Jordanian 40th

9th

1st

5th

SYRIA

2

6

7

3

RAFID

4

TAP LINE

5

G

PURPLE LINE

6. 17 October: Ugda Musa replaces Ugda Laner inside salient.

JORDAN

SEA OF GALILEE

ARIK BRIDGE

TIBERIAS

transferred another of Peled's units, the 205th Reserve Armoured Brigade, to Laner's command, but this was due to arrive from a completely different direction. In fact, the approaching armour was that of Iraq's 3rd Armoured Division, two armoured brigades and a mechanized brigade with a combined total of some 180 tanks. Laner ordered the 679th Reserve Armoured Brigade, refuelling near Nasej, to deploy to the south. The 205th Reserve Armoured Brigade, assigned from Peled's division, was deployed between Tel Maschara and Tel el Mal. The 17th and 9th Reserve Armoured Brigades were to return from Knaker and take up positions facing south.

The Iraqis had blundered into an armoured battle for which they were in no way prepared. Their arrival was certainly fortuitous but they were incapable of exploiting the opportunity. Laner anticipated that the Iraqis would attack at dusk, but after a probing attack, in which they lost 17 tanks, the Iraqis then halted, awaiting the arrival of the division's second armoured brigade. Early on the morning of 13 October the Iraqis advanced northward into the area between Maschara and Nasej.

Laner had deployed his four brigades in an 'open box' formation, the northern side of which was formed by the 9th and 679th Reserve Armoured Brigades deployed east of Jaba at the foot of Tel Shaar; the east side of the box was provided by the 17th Reserve Armoured Brigade in a line running north–south through Nasej; the west side of the box was formed by the 205th Reserve Armoured Brigade, deployed along the Maschara–Jaba Road.

The Iraqis remained unaware of the trap into which they were blundering. As they approached the foot of Tel Shaar they were about to run straight into 200 tanks and about 50 artillery pieces. The Israelis waited until first light, when the Iraqis had approached to within 275m (300yds) before the Super Sherman tanks of 19th Brigade opened fire. The effect of the concentric fire of four armoured brigades was devastating. The Iraqi 8th Mechanized Brigade was destroyed in a matter of minutes. Eighty Iraqi tanks were knocked out and the remainder fled in disorder. Not one Israeli tank was hit. The brief and disastrous Iraqi intervention, however, had an effect on the overall picture. It enabled the Syrians to move a brigade north to block the approach to Damascus, which they would not have been able to do had not the hapless Iraqi armoured formations briefly occupied a major part of the front. The principal role in the defence of Damascus was assigned to the Syrian 3rd Armoured Division, which remained relatively fresh and battleworthy when given the task of holding the second Syrian defence zone around Sasa, which lay about midway between Kuneitra and the Syrian capital.

After administering a drubbing to the Iraqis, Eitan was ordered by Hofi to take in more ground to his right, leaving Laner free to monitor developments in the south. Eitan now had units of the Golani 1st Infantry Brigade at his disposal

and these, in concert with paratroops, conducted tactical defence during the hours of darkness for the rest of the war. Some of the Western equipment they captured, including AML armoured cars, indicated that Saudi Arabian troops had entered the line. Meanwhile, Laner had identified the Syrian assembly area as a point 40km (25 miles) east of Rafid, known as the Great Leja. Accordingly, on 13 October he pushed out the 9th Reserve Armoured Brigade to capture two hills, Tel Antar and Tel Alakieh, which gave dominating views of the Great Leja.

Also exerting a belated influence over the course of events was King Hussein of Jordan. Hussein had decided to enter the war on 9 October. With his General

Israeli fitters replace the front idler wheel of a damaged Sho't in the field. Working around the clock, the repair teams of the Israeli Armoured and Ordnance Corps played a vital part in restoring battle-damaged equipment to operational use. Their tireless efforts were fundamental to the eventual Israeli victory.

Staff, he had studied four options. The first was to launch a full-scale offensive across the River Jordan into Jordan's former territories on the West Bank while Israel was fighting on two fronts against Egypt and Syria; the second was to distract a portion of the IDF by making an essentially defensive demonstration east of the Jordan; the third option was to commit a limited Jordanian force to the battle in Syria, where it could fight under the Syrian SAM umbrella and air force; the last option was to sit tight and do nothing.

King Hussein was operating under a number of constraints, however, not least the weakness of the Jordanian Air Force and the absence of a modern air defence system. Nor did the Jordanian Army possess any anti-tank guided missiles and although one of the best-trained and motivated armies in the Arab world, it had little in the way of reserves and fielded mainly obsolescent equipment.

Moreover, by 9 October, Jordanian intelligence was telling Hussein that the Syrian offensive had failed, a development that ruled out his first option. But the political realities in the Arab world did not allow Hussein the luxury of inaction. He calculated that the Israelis would understand his position and would not take any reprisals if, while he remained inactive on the River Jordan front, he dispatched a contingent of Jordanian troops to fight in Syria. In this fashion he could combine a watered-down element of the second option – a demonstration on the Jordan – with the third, the despatch of a limited contingent to Syria. Hussein sent a retired Chief of Staff, Lieutenant General Amer Khammash, to Cairo to inform President Sadat of his decision.

On 13 October, the Jordanian 40th Armoured Brigade entered Syria. It comprised some 4,000 men, fielding 150 Centurion tanks and was commanded by Colonel Haled Hajhouj al Majali. That same day the 40th Armoured Brigade proceeded on the Damascus road through Deraa and then northwest to the frontline. That night, Israeli M107 175mm self-propelled artillery began to fire on the military airfield at Damascus, the start of an intermittent bombardment that would last for several days. It was augmented by IAF raids against Syrian air bases and industrial plants. During one of these raids two large Soviet heavy-lift aircraft were destroyed at Damascus' civil airport.

On 14 October, the Jordanian 40th Armoured Brigade entered the frontline just north of El Hara, between the Iraqi 3rd Armoured Division and the 9th Syrian Infantry Division on the south face of the Israeli salient. Promoted to brigadier that day, Majali was placed under the command of Brigadier General Lafta, commanding the Iraqi 3rd Armoured Division on the eastern sector of the Arab line. On 15 October, Lafta's division was ordered to mount a major counterattack the next day west of Kfar Shams that was to include the Jordanians and a brigade from the Syrian 9th Infantry Division. H-hour was set for 0500hrs but the Arab preparations were interrupted by a spoiling attack launched by Laner on the afternoon of the 15th.

The final battles

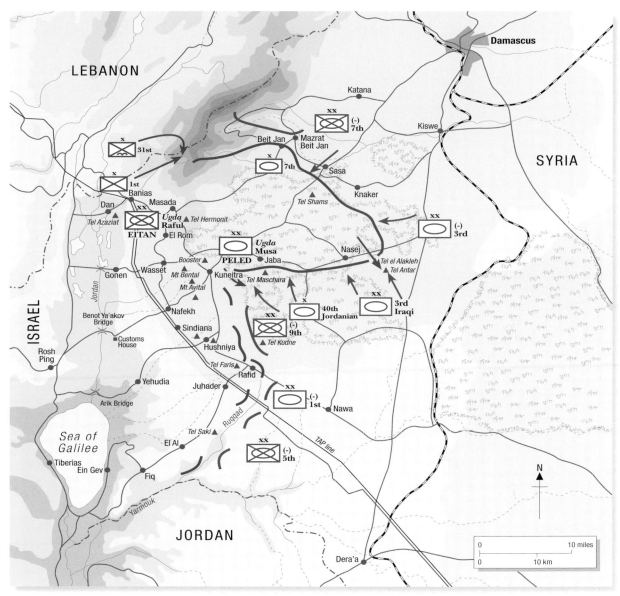

At 0500hrs on 16 October the Jordanians moved on to the attack supported by an attached Saudi contingent and a Syrian brigade. The Iraqis chose not to join them. The Jordanians advanced on Tel Maschara but were halted by accurate fire from the 17th Reserve Armoured Brigade and withdrew having lost 20 of their Centurions. The Israelis noted that the Jordanian technical and tactical performances surpassed anything seen from the Syrians or the Iraqis. Some five hours later the Iraqis attacked Tel Antar and Tel Alakieh but were driven off by the 17th Reserve Armoured Brigade. That morning, the Jordanian 40th Brigade was detached from the Iraqi 3rd Armoured and placed under the Syrian 9th Infantry Division. This produced a certain amount of bad-tempered bickering as Brigadier Majali outranked the Syrian commander of the 9th Infantry Division, Colonel Tourkmani. A general was rushed down from Damascus to act as liaison officer and smooth ruffled feathers. Over the next few days, the Iraqis and the Jordanians launched a series of ill-coordinated and abortive attacks. On several occasions these allies fired on each other's ground and air forces. The Iraqi Air Force's operations were beset by similar problems and a number of air battles were fought between the Arab allies. In the latter part of the war, the most serious offensive against Israeli positions was beaten off after a seven-hour battle with the loss of a further 60 Iraqi and 12 Jordanian tanks.

On 17 October, a lull descended on the front, enabling Peled to relieve the exhausted Laner on the eastern and southern faces of the Israeli salient. Laner's troops transferred to Peled's old positions along the 1967 ceasefire line. To the north, meanwhile, Eitan was preparing for a renewed effort to retake Mount Hermon. Simultaneously, battalions were switched to the Sinai front along with the bulk of the IAF. The IDF was to make no further advances on the ground.

This transfer of Israeli troops to the Sinai convinced the Syrians that they had a chance to regain the initiative. There were now few reserves left in Israel and the lull on the battlefield had given the Syrians the opportunity to reorganize and re-equip the formations that had been so badly battered in the earlier fighting. Now they had what they believed was a firm ring around the Israeli salient swelling inside Syria. Further allied Arab contingents had arrived and another Iraqi division was on its way to join the battle in the north, although some may have seen this as a mixed blessing.

A new offensive was planned to begin on 21 October, spearheaded by the Iraqi 3rd Armoured Division and 40th Jordanian Armoured Brigade. Once a breakthrough had been achieved, the 1st Syrian Armoured Division was to exploit northwards towards the Kuneitra–Damascus road to cut Israeli communications in front of Sasa. This plan might have looked convincing on a situation map but events on the ground were to take over.

On the afternoon of 20 October, the Iraqis announced that they were not ready and the attack was postponed until the 22nd. By now both sides were jockeying for position as the expected UN-imposed ceasefire loomed. The principal action of 21/22 October was the Israeli recapture of Mount Hermon, which had been taken by the Syrians on the opening day of the war. The Syrians held the mountain with two elite formations, one of paratroops and the other of special forces troops. Now the IDF planned to retake the position, and the Syrian OP that overlooked it, using the Golani Brigade and men of the 31st Parachute Brigade, who were to be air-dropped in to seize the Syrian positions.

OPPOSITE

The vital Israeli OP on Mount Hermon, which had been captured by Syrian commandos on the first day of the war, was finally recaptured on the final day of the war. Approaching from over Lebanese territory, Israeli Air Force CH-53 helicopters, carrying only half the usual number of troops because of the high altitude, landed on the highest point of Mount Hermon some 240m (800ft) above the captured Israeli OP. The Golani infantrymen and paratroopers of the 31st Parachute Brigade attacked supported by a fearsome air and artillery bombardment and their own mortars. The Syrian defenders resisted gallantly throughout the night of 21/22 October until the position was finally overrun. Here members of the Golani Brigade relax atop Mount Hermon after recapturing the position.

The Golanis began to climb Mount Hermon as night fell on 21 October. Two columns ascended on foot and a third travelled in halftracks accompanied by tanks and engineers. For the Golanis on foot, burdened by weapons, ammunitions and supplies, the ascent was a supreme test of stamina. The Syrians, dug in behind rocks and equipped with night sights and RPGs, put up a dogged resistance, but by 1100hrs on 22 October Mount Hermon was again in Israeli hands.

The paratroopers landed close to the Syrian OP and repulsed a heliborne counterattack, downing three Syrian helicopters. They then overran the OP and began to move down the ridge to assist the Golanis. In the attack, the Golanis lost 51 killed and 100 wounded. A young Golani summed up the action in a TV interview several days later: 'We were told that Mount Hermon is the eyes of the State of Israel and we knew we had to take it, whatever the cost.'

Ceasefire

On the evening of 22 October, the Syrians accepted a ceasefire proposed by the Security Council of the UN. Israel and Syria thereafter ceased further ground activity in the Golan Heights, although artillery fire continued from both sides for another 24 hours. On the night of 23 October, the shelling began to slow down and by midnight it had ceased altogether. Active combat operations on the Northern Front had come to a close with the Israelis having regained the ground they had lost during the war and also having taken control of a large additional portion of Mount Hermon, as well as the Sasa salient on the plain below.

It proved harder, in the aftermath of the October War, to secure an Israeli–Syrian agreement. The two nations did not sign a ceasefire agreement and for months the Syrians refused to provide the Israelis with a list of PoWs. Unlike their Egyptian allies, the Syrians declined to negotiate directly with the Israelis, or even to meet them. For their part the Israelis were willing to withdraw to the pre-October War Purple Line, but not prepared to cede part of the Golan on the terms demanded by Syria.

The result was a niggling war of attrition by the Syrians against the IDF forces in the Israeli-occupied enclave in Syria characterized by intermittent artillery bombardments and sniping. In the spring of 1974, small-scale infantry engagements erupted over the control of Mount Hermon. President Assad, an unbending negotiator, calculated that the mounting IDF casualty list would sap Israeli morale and, in time, bring them to the negotiating table.

Henry Kissinger, the US Secretary of State, shuttled tirelessly between Damascus and Jerusalem and, on 31 May 1974, the Israelis and the Syrians signed an 'Agreement on Disengagement'. Israel agreed to withdraw from the Sasa salient, the Syrian Hermon and a thin strip of territory to the west of the old Purple Line. This area, with a little no-man's-land and some Syrian territory to the east, became a 'separation of forces zone' with a maximum width of 8km (5 miles) to be held and patrolled by a 1,200-strong UN observer force. Included in the strip was the derelict town of Kuneitra. Syrian and Israeli forces were barred from this zone, although it was placed under Syrian administration. Nevertheless, this zone would prevent another surprise Syrian attack. The agreement, implemented in June 1974, also allowed for an exchange of PoWs.

The war cost Syria some 3,100 dead and 6,000 wounded. The Iraqis lost 278 killed and 898 wounded while the Jordanian figures for killed and wounded were, respectively 23 and 77. Israel's losses on the Golan front were some 772 killed, 453 wounded and 65 prisoners, including pilots. In the fighting the Syrians had lost 1,150 tanks, Iraq some 200 and Jordan about 50.

In preparing for the offensive, the Syrians had devoted considerable effort to the training of their army. In turn, their soldiers were confident in their military leadership, a new phenomenon in their history. This did not prove sufficient,

however, when they were confronted with Israelis fighting for national survival. Both the 7th and 188th Armoured Brigades fought with extraordinary resolution until they were virtually destroyed. Behind them was the cool leadership of Eitan and the crucial decision by Bar-Lev and Elazar to give priority to the Northern Front.

Like their Egyptian allies, the Syrians were sufficiently realistic when planning the offensive to select limited and achievable objectives. By restricting their advance to the edge of the Golan escarpment, the Syrians acknowledged the vulnerability of their ground forces once they had left the protective umbrella of the SAMs. After his initial success on the TAP line road, which placed the Syrian 1st Armoured Division within reach of Galilee, General Tlas failed to bring up any of his SAM-6 batteries and squandered the opportunity by committing his reserve tank division against strong opposition in the northern sector of the battlefield.

Indeed, although the Syrians achieved a strategic surprise on 6 October – the result of well-managed deception, Israeli intelligence failings and complacent assumptions by the IDF's high command – they failed to create a sufficient

Sho't Upgraded Centurion tanks withdraw from the Tel Shams area on 18 June 1974 in accordance with the terms of the ceasefire agreement brokered by the Security Council of the United Nations. (United Nations)

concentration of force for their opening attack. In contrast, the Israelis concentrated two of their three armoured divisions on a narrow front on the higher ground in the northern sector for their advance across the Ceasefire Line on 11 October.

Once they had recovered from the initial shock of the Syrian offensive, the Israelis achieved a satisfactory balance of forces. Their over-confident use of unsupported armour during the break-in phase of their operations, particularly during the assault on Tel Shams on 11 October, proved costly, however. Nevertheless, their armoured troops always had the edge on their Syrian enemy thanks to greater flexibility in tactics and command structures. The decision to commit reserve units by companies as soon as they had mobilized was crucial in turning the tide on the Golan, although it initially hampered the coherent tactical direction of the battle.

In the Syrian Army, co-operation between all arms was satisfactory. However, the same cannot be said for liaison between the Syrians and their Arab allies. Significantly, after the 1973 war, the Israelis incorporated mechanized infantry into its armoured corps and officers from both arms were cross-trained to deepen understanding of all-arms co-operation.

Sho't tanks withdraw through the ruins of Kuneitra on 25 June 1974, following the ceasefire agreement signed by the Israelis and Syrians on 31 May. (United Nations)

Co-operation between the Israeli Army and the IAF survived the initial battering that the latter received at the hands of Syrian SAMs and ZSU Shilkas. The sacrifices made by the IAF in the first two days of the war played an important part in the holding of the Golan until reinforcements arrived. The Yom Kippur War demonstrated the colossal expenditure of ammunition and missiles characteristic of modern high-intensity warfare. Neither the Israelis nor the Syrians could have sustained the battle without massive airlifts from their superpower allies.

THE END OF THE WAR

In the final count, a purely military victory in 1973 had gone to Israel. Recovering from initial and mainly self-inflicted setbacks, and benefiting from a military leadership which, whatever its faults, combined intellectual and hard-driving qualities in equal measure, the Israelis were able to cross the Canal and ultimately to threaten most of the Egyptian Third Army's combat formations with annihilation had not superpower pressure on their respective clients hastened a ceasefire. To the north, the Second Egyptian Army maintained open supply lines and intact rear echelons, but its armoured, mechanized and anti-aircraft forces had been so grievously battered by the Israelis that it was in no shape to respond to a renewal of hostilities. The Israelis had prevailed in spite of ferocious internal arguments over the correct strategy for recovery (many but not all centred around the imposing but infuriating figure of Ariel Sharon), but their flexible system of command had ultimately coped with pressures that proved too intense for the more rigid Egyptian military and political leadership.

In the Golan Heights, the brilliant defensive battle fought by the 7th and Barak Armoured Brigades remains one of the most extraordinary feats of arms of the 20th century. It allowed the reservists to conduct a chaotic yet ultimately successful mobilization despite the lack of many vital stores and the inability of units to obtain them. For instance, one reserve armoured brigade was delayed for nine hours in its deployment because there were insufficient fork-lift trucks to distribute the tank ammunition from the storage bunkers. Israeli overconfidence and the military intelligence assessment that war would not break out for several years had allowed the war reserve stores to become much depleted and often unfit for battle due to poor maintenance – the Israeli notion of 'yihyehbeseder' or 'everything will be all right on the day' was a dangerous fallacy. This was compounded by inefficient administrative procedures and a sense of panic engendered by the overwhelming Arab offensives mounted simultaneously on two fronts. But to paraphrase Napoleon Bonaparte: 'In war, morale is to matériel by a factor of three to one', and it was the superior morale and motivation of the average Israeli citizen/soldier that proved decisive in the end, with victory in both the Golan and Sinai campaigns.

But victory in war is not just measured by territory gained or tanks destroyed. The early successes of the Arab armies staggered the Israeli people and smashed the myth of IDF invincibility; and the scale of their casualties was beyond comprehension. The price of the war in blood and matériel was too awful to contemplate – the financial costs were equivalent to the entire Israeli GNP for one year; the sacrifice of the dead and the suffering of the wounded incalculable. The certainties in the Israeli cause fostered since the foundation of the nation and a Jewish homeland in 1948 and the military victories thereafter were irrevocably lost after the war.

UN disengagement forces taking up new positions in Kuneitra, Syria, as it is evacuated by Israeli troops in June 1974 in the first Israeli withdrawal from occupied Syrian lands in more than seven years. (© Bettmann/Corbis)

In April 1974, in an interim report, the Israeli Agranat Commission reached its principal conclusions on the course of the 1973 war. It charged IDF intelligence with major shortcomings in its assessment of Arab intentions and capabilities. It was to recommend a complete re-organization of Israel's intelligence services and the dismissal of General Zeira. Also censured was the Chief of the General Staff,

The IDF is sparing with gallantry medals and the highest honours are most often awarded posthumously. From the War of Independence in 1948 to the end of the Yom Kippur War, there have been only 41 recipients of the Medal of Valour, Israel's highest gallantry award, with 21 being awarded posthumously. Ten have gone to infantrymen and 13 to members of the armoured corps. Eleven were awarded during the October War. One recipient was Lieutenant Zwi 'Zwicka' Greengold for his remarkable actions along the TAP line road in the battles of the opening night of the war, when he fought continuously for 36 hours despite being severely wounded.

Major General David Elazar, who was blamed for an incorrect assessment of the intelligence he had received and for failing to prepare the army adequately for war. The Commission further recommended that the GOC Southern Command, General Shmuel Gonen, be suspended and not considered for any future high command. Singled out for particularly harsh criticism were the counterattacks along the Suez Canal during 6–8 October. The Agranat Commission, combined with political pressure, was to claim the heads of Zeira, Elazar and Gonen and also end the political careers of Golda Meir and Moshe Dayan.

The findings of the Agranat Commission did little to assuage the anger felt by Israelis, and that anger was reflected in the ballot box when the Labour Party, which had held office for almost 30 years, was voted out of office. Politically, from a country that prided itself on achieving consensus democratically, Israel split into numerous mutually distrustful factions. Respect for authority was lost after the war and has never been fully regained, with the parties of neither the Left nor Right providing a coherent voice for the Israeli people either at home or abroad. With the supreme confidence, nay arrogance, of the pre-Yom Kippur War Israeli, Prime Minister Golda Meir declared in 1972: 'There is no such thing as a Palestinian problem.' Now there is little else. The war of 1973 was a defining moment in the history of the Middle East. To the Israelis, the Yom Kippur War was a disaster from which they have never fully recovered. The image of an invincible IDF and the concept of a regional superpower were dispelled, with Israel evermore dependent on the United States for military, diplomatic and economic support in the face of a hostile world.

ABOVE

An Israeli mourner holds his head in grief at a Jewish military cemetery, after the conclusion of the Yom Kippur War. The number of casualties in such a short war was shocking to the Israeli people. (© David Rubinger/Corbis)

Ironically, in both Syria and Egypt the 'Tashreen' War was perceived as a notable military success and a vindication of the Arab soldier on the battlefield. To most Egyptians, Sadat had gained a famous victory in the October War. The Egyptian armed forces could now hold their heads high in the knowledge that the crossing of the Canal had been an operation of great skill and courage. The war also led to substantial political gains. Although a military defeat, the war did break the political log jam and thus succeeded in this wider strategic aim by securing Egypt first an interim agreement on Israeli withdrawal from the Sinai and finally a peace treaty that returned the entire area of the peninsula in April 1982. Sadat did not live to see the culmination of his vision. While reviewing a military parade commemorating the Egyptian crossing of the Canal in 1981, President Sadat was assassinated by a group of Muslim fundamentalists. Yet another threat to peace in the Middle East had emerged with a vengeance.

OPPOSITE, BOTTOM
The principal gallantry awards of the IDF are shown here with, from left to right, the Ot Hamofet with a blue ribbon awarded for distinguished and outstanding service in action. With its red ribbon, the Ot Haoz is Israel's second highest award for courage on the field of battle. Finally, the Ot Hagvura is Israel's highest award for supreme bravery on the field of battle. It equates to Britain's Victoria Cross or America's Medal of Honor. Unusually, its ribbon is yellow, a colour not normally associated with valour; but to the Jews it commemorates those who were forced to wear the yellow Star of David during the Middle Ages and under the yoke of the Nazi regime.

THE BATTLEFIELD TODAY

The Sinai

The Sinai Peninsula has been the scene of conflict throughout the 20th century from the Great War until 1989 when Taba, the last Israeli-occupied town, was returned to the Egyptians. The Sinai remains the home of several tribes of Bedu and now enjoys a thriving tourist industry along the Red Sea. From 1967 to 1974, the towns along the length of the Suez Canal were on the frontline between the Egyptians and the Israelis. For years they lay empty of their civilian populations and all were virtually destroyed during the Yom Kippur War. Thanks to Arab oil money, they have been rebuilt and are now thriving centres of commerce. Nevertheless, the Sinai Desert is still littered with the rusting hulks of AFVs from the conflicts of 1956 onwards.

At the entrance of the canal on the Mediterranean Sea is Port Said. A military museum is located on Sharia 23rd July near the Corniche, which is open daily. Although it covers several centuries of Egyptian military history, the 1973 storming of the Bar-Lev Line takes pride of place with a room devoted to the Yom Kippur War.

Midway down the Suez Canal is the town of Ismailia. Situated 120km (74 miles) east of the capital Cairo, Ismailia was originally established to house the 25,000 labourers who dug the Canal in the 19th century. It is possible to hire a water taxi to cross the Suez Canal and view some of the passages blasted through the 25m (80ft) high sand embankments of the Bar-Lev Line. Seven kilometres (4 ⅓ miles) to the south of the town is a ferry crossing point with a sculpture on the east bank depicting a fixed bayonet that is a memorial to those that fell storming the Bar-Lev Line on 6 October 1973. To the north of Ismailia there are other ferry crossing points with one for cars and another for trucks and military transport.

The road to the interior of the Sinai Peninsula passes the only remaining Israeli strongpoint on the Bar-Lev Line. Codenamed 'Ismailia East', it has been preserved by the Egyptians as a memorial to the October War but, as it is located within the operational area of the Egyptian Second Army, it is in a restricted military zone and not open to the public.

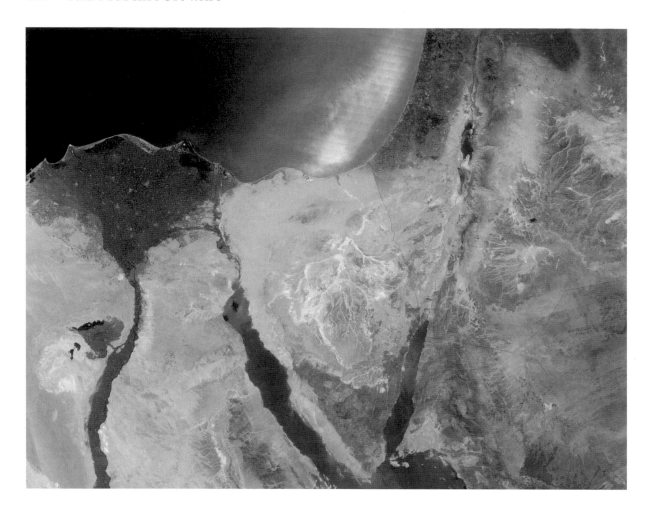

This satellite photograph clearly shows the Sinai Peninsula and the Suez Canal which saw Egypt's surprise attack on 6 October, and Israel's counterattack into Africa. (NASA, The Visible Earth, http://visibleearth.nasa.gov)

Suez City at the end of the Canal is 90km (56 miles) south of Ismailia. There is little in the city of interest to the military student except for four captured Israeli tanks displayed on the causeway to Port Tawiq (Tewfik).

The Golan Heights

The Golan looks deceptively peaceful as you approach from the Israeli side; its steep escarpment dominates the reclaimed marshland and the low rolling hills of Galilee. At first sight it is a place of rugged beauty. Waterfalls and forests lend it a deceptively pastoral air.

Look closer. See the basalt boulders that litter the terrain. The rocks are half-hidden in the undergrowth and provide an awkward footing. It is easy to twist or break an ankle … or lose a tank track. Rocks are not the only danger; the Heights are dotted with minefields of various vintages and origins. Soil creep means the minefields are difficult to mark. It is reckless to the point of madness to move from the roads and tracks that have been cleared.

These signs of war are subtle. When I first went up on the Golan, the 1973 war had finished a couple of days previously and signs of battle were much more obvious. With a handful of other kibbutz volunteers, I hitched up to the heights in an ancient American halftrack. Western war tourists, we hid from bored military police to make the journey.

Remnants of battle were all around. Not far into our journey we passed three seemingly intact T-62s alongside Route 91, which wriggled up the escarpment all the way from Galilee to the outskirts of Kuneitra, the former Syrian garrison town. The friendly reservists manning the halftrack said these tanks were nicknamed 'the monsters'. They are long gone. As we swung northwards past the farming co-operative of Ein Zivan, we saw other remnants of conflict. A couple of Arab stone houses badly damaged by gunfire, next to them, three burnt-out Syrian BTR-152 wheeled APCs. Nearby was an Israeli jeep, riddled with shrapnel, and surrounded by field dressings, scraps of bloodstained bandage and an infusion bottle. It was a sobering moment.

A memorial to the 7th Armoured Brigade stands beside Route 87 with a simple text reading 'Memorial to the 7th Brigade – In Fire They Will Come'. The memorial includes a Centurion tank bearing the inscription Sa'ar or Storm – Camp Sa'ar was one of the armoured encampments near Nafekh during the Yom Kippur War. Sa'ar was also the name given to the 74th Battalion of the 188th Barak Brigade. Curiously, this Centurion is a Dutch model with a Meteor petrol engine – not the type used by the 7th Armoured Brigade during the October War. (Marsh Gelbart)

A lonely Sho't stands as a memorial on one of the firing ramps on the Booster position overlooking the Valley of Tears. This is a later version of the Sho't with attachment points for 'Blazer' reactive armour and redesigned exhaust outlets. Curiously it carries the markings of the 679th Reserve Armoured Brigade whose tanks did not occupy the Booster feature. (Marsh Gelbart)

Kuneitra was a revelation, fought over by two armies in 1967 and 1973, it had been largely flattened. Reputedly Israeli bulldozers inflicted further damage before the town was returned to Syria. There was little left to destroy. Kuneitra was as far as we got. We tried to go further, to see the site of the 7th Brigade's epic stand, but were turned back by the military.

That was then, what of now? Is there anything left to see? There is not a simple answer to this question. There are memorials and battle sites to visit, but the most dramatic are from the 1967 war. Many of the features that were so heavily contested in 1973 are closed military areas. There is currently a ceasefire between Syria and Israel, not peace.

So what is it like to visit the Heights today and what is there to see of interest for the military enthusiast? Several years ago I took the same road, Route 91, that my friends and I took almost 30 years ago. The trip starts by the River Jordan, at Benot Ya'akov bridge (The Bridge of the Daughters of Jacob). The Jordan itself, the border before 1967, is little more than a muddy stream. The bridge is in fact one of two battered Bailey bridges, the second hidden behind foliage, constructed in October 1973 to allow a greater volume of military traffic to cross.

The Golan escarpment looms above you, some 500m (1,640ft) or so in height. Even as you start the journey upwards, reminders of war are still to be seen. A kilometre east of the bridge is a heavily battered cluster of buildings. Known as the Customs Houses, they used to be the frontier posts between the British Mandate of Palestine and French-controlled Syria. The bullet holes which riddle the buildings date back to 1967 when the Israelis stormed the Heights. In 1973, Syrian reconnaissance elements had reached to a few hundred metres east of the Upper Customs House before being pushed back. Just to the north of the Customs Houses is a set of deep Syrian bunkers captured in 1967 and left as a memorial. The bunkers survived heavy air attack; Israeli infantry had to clear them one by one. At the site of a preserved bunker, a look-out point known as Mitzpeh Gadot gives a wonderful view of the Galilee and Hula valley below. It is a clear reminder of the advantages of holding the high ground in any military conflict.

If you continue along Route 91 about another 4km (2½ miles) east from the Customs Houses there is a track to the left. Drive past an Israeli army camp and you will find the ruined Syrian village of Awinet. Shortly beyond Awinet, in a

The upper Customs House on the old border between Syria and Palestine was the most westerly point reached by Syrian reconnaissance elements during the October War. (Marsh Gelbart)

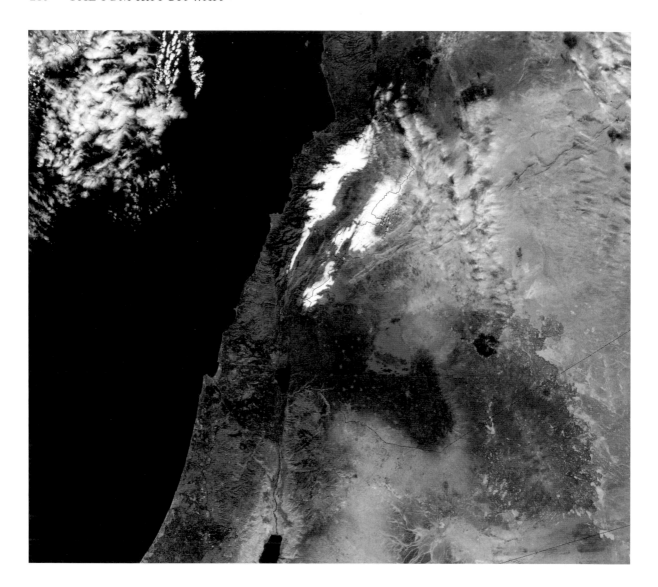

Modern satellite photograph of the Sea of Galilee and the Golan Heights, and the surrounding area. The snow on Mount Hermon and the rest of the Anti-Lebanon Mountain range is clearly visible. (NASA, The Visible Earth, http://visibleearth.nasa.gov)

wooded area, is an abandoned Syrian Army base. This is sometimes used by the IDF for FIBUA (Fighting in Built-up Areas) training. Like so much of the Golan it is a closed military area. However, the natural beauty spots of Gilboa and Dvora waterfalls are open to the public. Turn back and head east along Route 91 to Ha'shiryon (Armour) junction and you reach Nafekh. Nafekh was Israel's HQ on the Golan. The HQ was overrun by the Syrians during the 1973 war, but they were not able to consolidate their hold before it was recaptured. Drive slowly past Nafekh and you will usually see clusters of Merkava tanks hidden amongst sparse woodland. Some 6km (4 miles) beyond Nafekh is the large settlement of Ein Zivan. Turn northwards at Ein Zivan's road junction, take Route 98, and you will be heading towards a series of hills that dominate the surrounding plateaux. These hills, known locally as Tels, are the remains of extinct volcanoes. It was from around these hills – Booster, Avital, Bental and Hermonit – that the Israeli 7th Armoured Brigade broke the back of the Syrian offensive in 1973. All are still closed military areas, bristling with antennae. However, the northernmost Tel, Hermonit, is partly open to the public. There is a memorial to the 7th Brigade at Hermonit. A T-62 tank scarred by shell hits sits peacefully in a small grove of trees. Within view, but with no public access, are a number of firing ramps from which tanks can cover the rising valley below. This place was once a killing ground on a vast scale. It is part of Emek Bekaa, the Valley of Tears, in which so many Syrian tanks and their crews met their end in October 1973.

Kuneitra is back in Syrian hands and, of course, cannot be visited from the Israeli side of the border. Continue north along Route 98 to the junction with Route 99. Just before the junction is a track, marked 978. This leads to Mount Odem, and its look-out point. Mount Odem is the site of a large, sometimes occupied, bunker. If open, Mount Odem allows a great view of the surrounding area. If the track is closed, as it is when the bunker is occupied, don't even think of attempting the journey. Return to Route 98 as it spirals upwards to the vast bulk of Mount Hermon. In 1973 the snow-capped peaks of Hermon were fought over by Syrian and Israeli infantry, commandos and paratroopers. He who controls Hermon is in command of much of the plateau below. The Israeli electronic listening station on Hermon is still there; you can look from a distance, perhaps from the ski runs that are found nearby. You cannot approach the station; it is one of the most sensitive and heavily guarded places in the Middle East.

If at Ein Zivan junction you turn south rather than north, you will travel through the area where Syrian armour broke through the Barak Brigade's defences. The terrain is still rugged but less hilly. Travel southwest towards the crocodile farm and hot springs of Hamat Geder. Before you cross the old border, there is a half-hidden memorial to the Barak Brigade. Faded wreaths of flowers are to be found alongside an upturned turret of a T-62, left as a reminder to the 7th Brigade's sacrifice.

The Golan Heights is contested ground. Currently it is quiet but it has been the focal point of fierce fighting. If you are going to visit, remember, it can be dangerous. Keep to cleared paths. Take a guided tour if you can. Never try to get into a closed military area. You may not live to regret your mistake. Road routes and numbers can change over time. What was open a few years ago may be closed now. Use your common sense, there is much to see, but travel carefully.

Note: Neither the author nor the publishers of this book will be held liable for anyone visiting the battlefield and behaving in a way prejudicial to their own safety.

BIBLIOGRAPHY

The works of Chaim Herzog – *The War of Atonement: The Inside Story of the Yom Kippur War, 1973* (Weidenfeld and Nicholson 1975) and *The Arab-Israeli Wars: War and Peace in the Middle East* (Arms and Armour Press 1982) – are reliable sources from the Israeli point of view and must be seen as the semi-official histories of the war. In both books, Israeli unit designations and IDF personnel names have been altered or abbreviated for security reasons. The reader is therefore referred to the works of Samuel M. Katz (see below). For the political background to the Yom Kippur War and indeed all 20th-century Arab-Israeli wars, Benny Morris has written an unsurpassed account in *Righteous Victims: A History of the Zionist–Arab Conflict 1881–1999* (John Murray 2000). *The Yom Kippur War* by The Insight Team of The Sunday Times (Sunday Times 1974/Andre Deutsch 1975) was written immediately after the conflict but nevertheless gives an evocative contemporary coverage of the conflict with many interesting quotes from Israeli soldiers before the official version of the war was dictated by the IDF.

Of all the books written about the October War during the 1970s, Colonel Trevor Dupuy's *Elusive Victory: The Arab-Israeli Wars 1947–1974* (Macdonald and Jane's 1978) must be considered the most comprehensive and impartial account of the campaigns. Its value lies in the fact that Dupuy was able to interview combatants of all the warring nations soon after the conflict to give the most balanced account of the campaign from the Arab perspective and the statistics he quotes are generally held to be the most accurate. However, its unit designations and names of personnel of the IDF are not correct, being subject to Israeli security consideration at the time of publication.

There are several excellent accounts of the ground fighting in the Sinai campaign including *Israeli Tank Battles: Yom Kippur to Lebanon* by Samuel M. Katz (Arms and Armour Press 1988). As a former member of the IDF, Sam Katz has undertaken considerable research into the campaign, and the unit designations of Israeli formations that he lists are used in this volume as being the most reliable to date. His exciting history of the 7th Armoured Brigade, *Fire and Steel* (Pocket Books 1996) is a must for anyone interested in the Israeli Armoured Corps. The book *Chariots of the Desert: The Story of the Israeli Armoured Corps* by Lieutenant Colonel David Eshel is essential reading for any student of this campaign as Colonel Eshel, formerly of the Israeli Armoured Corps, was an eyewitness during the fierce battles on the Golan in the October War. Colonel Eshel also produced a series of monographs during the early 1980s on all aspects of the Arab-Israeli wars. The actual campaigns were recounted in a series called 'Born in Battle' and weapon systems in 'War Data' and 'Military Enthusiast'. For the discerning reader, they

The memorial to Chativa 679 – the 679th Reserve Armoured Brigade – commanded by Colonel Uri Orr of Ugda Laner. The Hebrew inscription reads 'We will remember and not forget'. (Marsh Gelbart)

contain a wealth of facts and photographs that deserve close scrutiny for their comprehensive coverage of the IDF and its history.

For an account of the tensions among the top commanders in Southern Command, *On the Banks of the Suez* by Major General Avraham 'Bren' Adan makes fascinating reading. From the other side of the hill, there are regrettably very few reliable accounts in English by the Arab combatants. *The Crossing of the Suez* by Lieutenant General Saad el Shazly (American Mideast Research 1980) is by far the most comprehensive. The description of the planning and execution of Operation *Badr* is essential reading for all students of this campaign. Similarly, *The Ramadan War, 1973* by Hassan el Badri, Taha el Magdoub and Mohammed Dia el Din Zohdy (T. N. Dupuy Associates Inc 1979) is a good account of the planning and execution of the crossing of the Suez Canal. Thereafter the book deteriorates into mere rhetoric but careful reading can unearth many statistical gems and the perceptions from the Arab perspective.

For a vivid first-hand account of the campaign on the Golan Heights, the reader is strongly advised to consult Avigdor Kahalani's remarkable book *The Heights of Courage: A Tank Leader's War on the Golan* (Praeger 1992). Awarded Israel's highest gallantry decoration, the Medal of Valour, for his leadership and courage during the war, one can only read such a book with humility and wonder at the fortitude of the soldier under the most awful duress in high-intensity warfare. There is also an excellent account of the Golan campaign in the same author's autobiography *A Warrior's Way* (Steimatzky 1999).

INDEX

Figures in **bold** refer to illustrations